Stephen Maybery was born in Porthcawl South Wales. He has worked all over the world from Siberia to the Caribbean.

The highlight of his career is a Civil Engineer was the time he spent in Baghdad building Saddam's bunkers. Equally thrilling was the period when he lived totally alone on an uninhabited island in the Indian Ocean.

Stephen's singular take on politics and politicians can be experienced on www.romannovel.blogspot.com

He now lives in the Whitechapel district of London, his meagre fame eclipsed by the area's most famous resident, Jack the Ripper.

MY PRIME MINISTERS AND I

Stephen Maybery

Dedication.

This book is dedicated to R.J. Turner, Bayswater Bob, a friend when one was needed.

CHAPTER I.

It was one of those days, God knows we each of us get them from time to time, when absobloodylutely nothing goes right and sods law swings into action with a vengeance, the heavens do not open, nor is the glory of God declared to all and sundry. In short it was the sort of day that causes a body to opine that if this be an example of the Deity's sense of humour, then the old bastard should keep it to himself and leave he rest of us to get on with our lives as best we can.

There was nothing whatsoever to distinguish this particular day from any other. To no one's particular surprise, the sun had risen as per the popular expectation, and by eight of the clock the streets of London town were already snarled up by traffic, but this day was different, although there was nobody in the land who could have testified to the fact. If Queen Elizabeth II had reigned in her wilder impulses and confined her breakfast reading on that morning to the Sporting Life, then the history of these islands would have been very different, but she had not. For some unfathomable reason the Queen had ordered a copy of the Daily Truth

The Daily Truth was noted for several things, journalistic integrity not being amongst them, not for nothing had the rag been dubbed a skid mark on the underwear of British journalism. Why on this, or any other day, H.M would have chosen to read the damn rag was beyond the comprehension of mortal man, but she had done so, with consequences that could never have been guessed at this side of the Pearly Gates.

The Queen's mood was not of the best at that particular moment, nor had it been for some time past. The Jubilee had been and gone, a monument to the organizational abilities of the Government, in short the entire jamboree had gone off like a dispso's dick in a brothel, that is they were perfectly aware of what it was that was required of it but were physically incapable of rising to the occasion. The truth of the matter was that they had no interest in making the celebrations a success. The entire Government was against the monarchy and did not take too much trouble to disguise the fact, all that stood between them and declaring a republic was a vague feeling in their intellectual bones, that the great British public, God rot the fascist bastards, might not go along with the scheme, which of course they would not. The public in their wisdom, considered it was bad enough to have to have to pay for the politicians in the first place, without having to bow and scrape to the sons of bitches, which is what would happen if they took over from royalty.

None of this had brought into play a sweetening of the royal mood over the past year, and even if the jubilee celebrations had been better organized, there were other factors which would have curdled the milk in the royal cornflakes. The press in general and the Daily Truth in particular, continued to snipe at every royal peccadillo, real or imagined, and the B.B.C, po faced and sanctimonious as only that organization can be, made it a condition of promotion that the monarch be belittled by its employees at every opportunity. No wonder Her Majesty was a tad pissed off.

Prince Phillip entered the breakfast room just as that morning's edition of the Truth went in to orbit over the table, missing the corgis, before scoring a bull's eye on one of Queen Victoria's less than distinguished daubs. This rather flatulent projectile was closely followed in its defiance of gravity by the tea pot. Fortunately this example of the potter's art was not one of the more valuable items from the royal collection. The teapot missed the painting but fragmented on making contact with a credenza parked next to the fireplace.

"Offended by the cartoon were we?" enquired the royal consort, not even trying to avoid the appearance of being facetious.

"I've had it," spat out his better half, while at the same time bringing a silver teaspoon down on a boiled egg with a force sufficient to make the offering inedible in the form originally intended. "I've bloody well had it."

"So has the teapot. You'd better ring for another one. I'm gasping. Oh, and do try not to chuck the next one up against the bloody wall, we're not made of money y'know, despite what the Truth says."

"I don't want that damn rag mentioned in my presence again." Her Majesty had commanded. However not even Her Majesty could expect to be obeyed implicitly at eight fifteen in the morning by a spouse of fifty plus years duration, dressed in nothing more prepossessing than a Marks and Sparks dressing gown which had seen better days.

"All right, All right. Keep your crown on." He plonked himself down at the table, snatching as he did so a slice of toast of impossible daintiness.

"If we are fated to start this day with a first class bitching session, can I ask, for the umpteenth bloody time, why in the name of almighty God and the choir of queens why we can't have toast served in respectable sized slices and not these pansy shaped bits that would embarrass a man to be seen holding in his fist?"

"The chefs think their professional standing would be damaged if they did not tart everything up for the royal table. I'm reliably informed by someone who knows about these things that I have never seen a natural looking spud on my plate in my entire life. Perhaps he was right, how the hell am I to know?"

"I still can't see why we find it so impossible to get a decent piece of toast on the plate. But that doesn't answer why you were reading the Truth. As far as I know you have never glanced at it in your entire life. Why now?"

"Something a little bird told me."

"Judging by your reaction it was not so much as a little bird as a shite hawk." Even at this early hour, the Prince had not forgotten to put his habitual delicacy of phrase in with his teeth.

"Come on, let's have it I don't want to have to read the damn rag myself."

"It was another of those ruddy pieces claiming to know what I am thinking before I have even had chance to think the thoughts myself."

"So. What's the problem? That is hardly pioneering a new avenue in journalism."

"Arabella Clackmannon, she's the bloody problem. The cow." Most folk, securely swathed in the incontinence pads of naivety would be terribly shocked at majesty using so intemperate a phrase; however, Prince Phillip, after fifty odd years with his trouble and strife recognized she was being frightfully restrained, which in itself was a danger signal to be accorded due respect.

"Might one enquire who exactly is this Arabella whatsit?"

"Clackmannon, Lady Arabella to be exact. The bitch."

"I'm still no wiser, but for the sake of the succession if not your blood pressure, start at the beginning and explain all, in words of Anglo Saxon simplicity. And where's that bloody tea?" H.M. picked up the phone and made a crisp enquiry that had the recipient of the call fearing for his pension, while all the time thanking whatever gods there may be, that the chopping off of heads had gone out of fashion for the time being.

"Arabella Clackmannon is a distant cousin of mine."

"Well I've never heard of her, let alone met the woman."

"She's very distant. On Mummy's side."

"Oh. One of that lot, no wonder. I wouldn't put anything past that crew, but how come I've never met her?"

"Well, as I said she is very distant, almost an antipodean in genealogical terms, you'd literally have to dig to find the connection, and when you got there, there would not be much to examine. I last met her about sixty-five years ago, Margo and I were in the Brownies, she was brought to the palace to meet us for some reason. We neither of us liked her and she was never invited again. That was that, I never saw nor heard her again until I read that bloody rag this morning."

"I still do not see why you bothered with it. The woman can hardly have said anything that has not appeared in Woman's Own over the years, which is where she probably got hold of her info."

"Sir Ralph thought I should see it, he'd been tipped off by a friend in the Truth's office."

"Sir Ralph!" The Prince looked as if he had been stabbed in the backside with a hypodermic charged with divine revelation, his questions had just been answered. "That flaming great pansy. Probably the wrong time of the month." The Queen winced visibly, the lady could not by any stretch of the imagination be described as politically correct, but she did wish her spouse would be a little

more understanding of the help, they were getting harder and harder both to find and to keep these days, especially with the wages she paid, which owed a lot to the age of Dickens, and buggerall to the current cost of living.
"Just shrug it off like you always do. It's not worth the aggravation."
"I know, but this time it has well and truly got to me. Believe it or not I have just about had a belly full, no, not about, I definitely have, right up to the eyeballs and beyond."
"But why, what's so significant about this nobody, why does a few columns of journalistic drivel derived from her get you so riled up?"
"Straws and camels backs I suppose. This is it Phillip, I have had enough, the last ten years have been snipe snipe snipe, the press, the T.V., the damn politicians smiling in my face while all the time sharpening the knives they so delight in shoving in my back, and now this silly bloody nobody hell-bent on using my name and status to grab herself a few headlines. Enough God damn it." Practically foaming at the mouth, H.M. broke into a steam of imprecations the intensity and originality of which surprised her husband, who realized that one or two of the phrases, had not been learned at his knee. He admired his wife's originality but could not help but wonder who she had been keeping company with to pick up such language, the sound of Princess Anne outside in the garden, cussing about the weather in general and the rain in particular, for causing the dye to run in the new cardi she had only bought the day before from an Oxfam

shop, gave him an inkling as to the origin of the latest additions to his wife's vocabulary.

Prince Phillip allowed his wife to continue with her rant until the fresh tea arrived. He poured them both a cup before retrieving the littered corpse of that morning's edition of the Daily Truth. It did not take the Prince long to find the article which had caused the bats to flutter in the royal belfry. He read the article swiftly, with a ferocious contempt born of much practice, he could see why his wife had been so offended, no-one with any intelligence whatsoever could possibly believe such copper bottomed crap, but, as most of the population were not possessed of great riches in the brain department, (for which politicians were supremely grateful come election time), the Truth's bilious diatribe would be believed by all too many people.

Lady Arabella Clackmannon, the fons et origo of the Truth's most recent offering on the altar of literary journalism, could, with much charity be described as eccentric, but if one was to indulge in a little unfashionable honesty and call a spade a bloody shovel, then the woman would unquestionably have to be described as barking mad, a condition of the mind exacerbated by a persistence in her affairs of a state of fiduciary incontinence. In short the woman was flat broke. Such a mode of life had shadowed her through most of her journey through this vale of tears, what little money there had been in the family, she had managed to blow within a short time of inheriting it. From that time on she had had to rely on her shaky connection with the Royal

Family as a means of drumming up credit, an activity she had turned into a cottage industry, her efforts would have won the Queens Award for Fantasy if there had been such a distinction. Loyal friends (She had one, who sadly had passed away fifteen years before the time of writing), averred it was this poverty that had led to her wilder exploits, such as her leaving the Church of England, after the failure of her campaign to persuade the Archbishop of Canterbury to substitute gin for the communion wine.

Whenever cash was in exceptionally short supply, Lady "A" had milked the American market, her selling point being intimate revelations by a member of the Royal family. Knowing no better, the Yanks had swallowed this hook line and sinker. The trashier American scandal sheets were eager to take her offerings for ludicrous sums of money. Unfortunately for Lady "A", her talent did not match up to her imagination, basically, she had one story to tell and only one version of it, and even the yanks were only prepared to continue to print the nonsense so many times. After a few years that particular well had run dry and so had her supply of booze. Lady Arabella was a raving dipsomaniac, her party trick was to go into the Champion, a gay pub on the Bayswater Road, get herself well and truly tanked up, then stagger out onto her royal cousin's main drag and make an offer to all comers to show them her fanny for the price of a pint of Fosters. In light of her age and physiognomy, this was not a wildly successful activity.

Such was the tenor of her life, when on a day when news of a substantive calibre could not be found for love or bribery, the features editor of the Truth contacted Arabella with the offer of a contribution to her private benevolent fund for the propagation of interest in Gordon's gin. The old girl grabbed it by the optics, she spent three days holed up in a hotel next to Euston Station spilling the beans to the Truth, a more mold drenched platter of re-fried pulses it cannot be imagined, but the paper bought them and happily dished the mess up to the great British public.

Not to be outdone by his wife, Prince Phillip tossed the Truth across the room on completing his perusal of the offending article. His action triggered off another diatribe by the queen against the paper and its Australian proprietor, Bondi Paterson, known the length of Fleet Street as the obnoxious ocker.

"Really Lil, do take a grip of yourself." Pleaded the Prince, more in hope than anticipation.

"Don't call me Lil," stormed the Queen. "It's so common and it makes me sound like the fucking cleaner".

"No. We couldn't have you sounding common now, could we?" Perhaps it was as well his wife failed to see the irony behind his words. "So they printed a load of ridiculous nonsense by a silly old cow who should have been drowned at birth. It's happened before darling. It'll happen again, every time the sods want to raise their circulation figures, why get yourself all het up about it?"

"As I said, it's like some of my Foreign Secretaries, the last straw. We are going to have a conference at Windsor on Friday night. Just you, me and the children, no others. No excuses."

"But aren't they a bit scattered at the moment? Ed in America, Charles in Saudi having a love in with Allah for the Foreign Office."

"I don't give a damn where they are, I'm having the lot of them fished back for the weekend. Sir Ralph can dream up some suitable lies for their hosts". The regal will having expressed itself, swept out of the room to attend to it's daily round of constitutional duties before settling down to watch the three thirty at Epsom.

CHAPTER II.

If one is prepared to say fuck Christian charity, the state will provide, and call a spade a manually operated earth-disturbing implement, then one could undoubtedly be classified as the sort of pillock who thinks that our glorious leaders in Parliament know what is best for us and should be left undisturbed to get on with things. Fortunately, for the health and sanity of the nation, the vast majority of the populace while being certifiably thick, possess a certain modicum of native cunning and common sense that would impel them to demur from the aforementioned prejudice, and would accept the following definition of a politician as a being intellectually sterilized but unfit for public consumption, that is, a politician is nothing but the apotheosis of ego chasing after very little talent and losing the race. The current Prime Minister of the United Kingdom fitted that particular bill like a Japanese sumo wrestler would a corset built for an anorexic.

The Queen and her spouse were not the only inhabitants of the stratosphere to be found reading the Truth that morning, the chief citizens of Downing Street were having a good sniff at the knickers of British Journalism, and like their counterparts across the park, they had been tipped the wink, and not by any old snout either, they had been told what to look for by no less a personage than Bondi Patterson himself, the proprietor not only of the Daily Truth, but of far too great a chunk of the British media to be considered healthy. The man had started off as an Australian, tinkered with becoming a Canadian but ended up an American. In spite of these lush meanderings through the byways of various nationalities, the man remained true to himself, periodic changes of passport had altered him not. To those who knew and understood the extent of his talents, he was the true blue ocker, to those who did not work for him and were confident they would never have to, the fellow would always be the Windarra wanker. The relationship between the Prime minister and Bondi could most graphically be described as one of mutual masturbation behind the parliamentary bike shed.

Bondi had provided generous funding for the Prime Minister's party, but more importantly he had instructed his editors to proclaim that there was no need for our dear Lord to undertake a second coming now that Alfred Sawse was leading the Labour Party, and who would, on winning the election, lead the nation to the promised land, the electorate, daft bastards that they were, swallowed that line with an eagerness vouchsafed only to the truly gullible, Sawse was returned with a landslide majority and the Truth promptly kissed the man's arse by dubbing him Alfred the great, but those who knew the fellow did not take long to assess his performance, to them he became H.P., all sauce and no bottle.

A large section of his party regarded the Prime Minister with that special concentration of loathing they reserved for middle class Tories who joined the socialists to assuage the rampant guilt they felt for having inherited their prosperity, the sort who instinctively tried to turn the red flag into the official banner of Volvo land. Alfred Sawse was the perfect identikit for the type. Now to be blunt, to be very blunt in fact, our Alf was not overloaded with brains, indeed, there were some of an uncharitable bent who opined that it was as well for the continuance of his marriage that he had more between his legs than he did between his ears. Dim as he was, Alf acknowledged the loathing a significant section of his party felt for him, and you know what? He did not give a fig, for he could not stand them either. To Alf, the party was a means to an end. Prime Minister Sawse was not lacking in political nouse however, it was the one field in which he could be said to excel; he might despise the parliamentary shock troops, but he realized the distressing necessity of keeping them on side and trimmed his sails accordingly.

Much of what Sawse and his trendy pals were up to was disliked by the country at large as well as his party. He bought the acquiescence of the party by pandering to some of their more obdurate social prejudices, the most prominent of which was their hatred of the Monarchy. As for the country at large, personified by the electorate, they did not count between elections, why should they? We're a democracy for Christ's sake!

Bondi never started a day without sprinkling a generous portion of anti British prejudice on his cornflakes, he had a chip on each shoulder the size of the pyramid of Mycerinus. The fact that the British establishment so supinely allowed him to trash them in his publications only served to increase his contempt for them. He was actively encouraged in this indulgence by Prime Minister Sawse. In that morning's offering in the Truth, Bondi had excelled himself, as he had recently remarked to the editor of the rag.

"Shit all over the bloody Poms and all the bastards do is turn around and give you another tax break".

The Prime Minister's wife, Wincarnis, lifted a slice of organic whole meal toast smeared with low fat spread to her lips, and took a delicate nibble, just like she had seen duchesses do in the films. Her eyes gave an admiring glance at her nails, freshly painted by the manicurist that morning, they were as red as her politics and just as hard. Wincarnis headed up her own accountancy firm, earning upwards of half a million a year, a slight anomaly as the dame never shirked the opportunity to denounce the rich and privileged. The only area of life in which she could be said to endure poverty was in humour. In that field the woman was totally bankrupt.

"Alfred!" she snapped with all the charm she was capable of. "Stop that giggling. How can you be so frivolous when there are people starving in Bactria?"

The Prime Minister who had never heard of Bactria, or anywhere else east of Clacton and relied on the Foreign Secretary to tell him where he was when on one of his numerous overseas trips to save humanity, looked warily across the table at his spouse, unaware of what he had done to offend but certain that he would receive a bollocking for doing it. He gazed warily at his wife. She was wearing her favourite sweater, he wished she would not, as it made her tits look like a pair of balloons which had been hanging around for too long after Christmas. Not that there had ever been balloons in their house, Wincarnis did not approve of balloons. In an attempt to turn away the wrath that deigned not to hide its face, he tried to titivate her scruples with a rendition of that mornings anti royal splurge in the truth.

"Darling." Oops! He knew that had been a mistake before the expression had left his mouth. Wincarnis did not approve of being referred to as darling, much too middle class. Her mouth assumed an aspect that in sweetness and compassion was an exact facsimile of a horse's twat. "Listen to this love," he babbled trying to retrieve his blunder. "It's a piece in the truth giving the Buck House mob a right going over. I asked Bondi to do a hatchet job on them for me. You'll approve of this all right."

"Of course I'll approve of it, I vetted it last night before it went to press you damn fool." The Prime minister of England looked crestfallen. He had so wanted to impress his missus, yet as so often was the case, he failed miserably, and she had taken his lollipop off him as punishment. "Don't bother faxing your thanks to Bondi. I've already done that for you."

Crestfallen, Alfred positioned himself in front of the nearest mirror to practice his smile, he was very good at smiling. It was his one indisputable talent, there may have been serious doubts as to the validity of the others, but put the man in front of a camera and he would smile with an intensity of insincerity which would do justice to a Church of England Bishop declaring his belief in Christianity. He whispered dolcelatte at his reflection in the glass, inordinately pleased with the result, he decided he would use that one when he next played the Co-op hall in Accrington. Contemplation of his visage had sufficiently restored his confidence in himself to enable him to re-engage with his wife.

"You must admit though, the Truth really gave it to them. I bet the corgis got a kicking when they read that."

"Assuming that is that they read the Truth, with their intellectual capacity they probably think looking at the pictures in Tattler constitutes keeping abreast of the news." Wincarnis was no lover of royalty. She had two overriding ambitions for her husband's administration, to ban fox hunting, and to so undermine the monarchy that it would not survive the decade, thus making way for president Sawse and the first family; Wincarnis considered they were half way to establishing the desired outcome, so assured was she of her impending status, she had gone so far as to insist on being addressed as first lady.

"They can't last much longer," declared Alfred with as much pomposity as he could muster at short notice. "We've got them on the run. A few more scandals then it's curtains for the Windsors." There was a palpable increase in Alfred's confidence, he knew he would always be on safe ground with Wincarnis when he indulged in a bit of royalty bashing, one of the few recreational habits she actually approved of.

"Absolutely. If Bondi can keep the pressure up with some more articles of this morning's caliber, then I don't see why we can't give them their marching orders shortly after the next election." Wincarnis actually made the effort to smile at her spouse. She was perfectly aware the spineless twit had not the guts for such a fight, but that did not really matter as long as she wore the balls in the family, and he was scared witless by her.

"Of course we will. We'll have to go carefully with the electorate though. Don't forget the trouble we had in trying to dampen their enthusiasm for the Jubilee, some of the persistent devils even went ahead with street parties despite the health and safety regs we put in their way. Pig headedness I call it, bloody pig headedness."

"Language."

"Sorry dear." He slipped up there in his desperation to impress. Wincarnis did not approve of swearing, she was a strict Seventh Day Adventist. "Won't do it again," he gulped, displaying his contrition like a medieval cod piece. "But we will have to keep the voters sweet."

"Nonsense" snapped Wincarnis, having had a basinful of charm for one morning. "Democracy is far too important an institution to allow the electorate to get in it's way, they're far too right wing, which is why we have to think for them. God knows where we'd be if ever they were permitted to have their own way. No. We'll offer them a few new hospitals before the next election. That'll shut them up. It is truly miraculous the amount of votes attached to a roll of bandages." Alfred beamed at his beloved, she was always happiest when she was being prime ministerial. If he could keep her in this mood she might let him nip over to the Chairman for a half of Guinness to night.

"Oh joy. Oh rapture" cogitated Alfred unto himself as he sauntered back to the mirror better to contemplate himself and the anticipated delights of the black stuff.

"Stop preening yourself Alfred!" Wincarnis did not approve of vanity, well in others she did not, she made allowances for her own personal peccadilloes in that particular field.

"Shite! There goes me Guinness," he muttered to himself.

"What are you looking so shifty about? You are not thinking of going off to that pub again are you? Because if you are you can put that notion out of your head here and now. You had a drink ten days ago and you are not having another one. Heavens above Alfred, if you're not careful, you'll be turning into an alcoholic, just like Uncle Sid."

"Yes dear." Not the most inspired response, but the dear leader's bonce was not home to the more original of cerebral instruments, and that was the best he could come up with at such short notice.

"Sit down. We've one or two things to sort out." His heart sank with all the certitude of the Bismarck going down. One or two things to sort out, was code for him having his gonads turned into steak tartare. Alfred did as he was bid, he even ventured a dutiful smile to the only man in the family. Quite a coquettish smile actually, it was perfectly safe for him to flirt with Wincarnis at this hour of the day, for she did not approve of sex during daylight. He did so appreciate those long summer days when the nights were so brief and the hours of darkness shorter than the time it took to say foreplay.

"What's to sort out?" his tone emollient.

"Your Diary. That's what."

"Eh! MacMurdo does all that. I don't even know what's in it."

"Then it's time you started to take an interest. Mac must be slipping. I'll have to have a word with him."

"I still don't understand." The man was genuinely perplexed. Hardly surprising really, with his wife running the Government and his personal assistant, MacMurdo Dunlossie running the Prime Minister, how was the fellow to know what was going on.

"He's got you visiting Birmingham."

"So?"

"You can't do Brummie. For goodness sake Alfred. Wake up." The longed to be implemented Euro finally dropped, Alfred finally understood what it was his wife had been rabbiting on about, accents. When speaking in public, the Prime Minster tailored his accent according to his audience, he would allude to some vague connection to the area he happened to be in, then spoke in the appropriate local dialect, thereby pretending to be indigenous to the working classes. The ploy usually worked although a few wires now and again became crossed, like the time in Cardiff when he alluded to a mythical auntie Blodwyn and a childhood spent in the Rhondda Valley, then went on to speak in a scouse accent for an hour and a half.

"Oh."

"Exactly. Well not to worry. I've told Mac to send you to Leeds instead, you're safe enough in Ee Bah Gum land."

"Oo yes, and they have lovely pork pies up there."

"Don't you dare."

"Why not?" She'd turned the tap off his Guinness, surely she would not deny him a pork pie?

"Eating pork might offend the Muslim community." Alfred groaned a reaction Wincarnis construed as rebellion and as such to be nipped in the bud. "Don't be difficult. It could also be misinterpreted as a racial affront, and we can't have that can we?" There was a direct challenge in the interrogative, as if she sensed spousal independence might rear its impertinent head. Wincarnis need not have worried, she had Alfred too well trained for him to even consider kicking against the traces at this late stage in life.

"You're right of course dear." This was an extremely reluctant admission, perhaps Ikey Solomon could sneak a few pies to him. In addition to being Alfred's constituency agent, Ikey had the distinction of being the only kosher pork butcher on the Mile End Road.

"And no sneaking off to Ikey behind my back." Give the woman her due, she was nothing if not thorough.

"As if I would." Alf managed to infuse his protestation with that special concentration of offended outrage peculiar to politicians regardless of their ability to read, write, and do sums.

"Yes. Well we'll leave it at that. Now there's a school run and you're late for it."

"But I can't." squealed the Prime Minister. "I'm meeting the Prime Minister of Tonga."

"No you're not. You look ridiculous in a sarong. You are going to take the kids to school and I am going to meet the Prime Minister of Tonga. There's that lovely little Dorothy Lamour number I've been dying to try out."

"But Win..."

"But nothing! Now don't dawdle, you've got the children to see to and I've got a country to run as well as a business, which I might remind you keeps you in the virgin pressed olive oil you're used to." Meekly, Alfred Sawse M.P., P.C., P.M., shuffled off to perform his allotted tasks on this most normal of days, only it was not a normal day. This was the first day of the last week before the World changed forever, only he did not know that, neither did anyone else actually, not even Wincarnis.

CHAPTER III.

Jesus, would it not be grand to go completely over the top with an indulgence in literary hyperbole, by writing a work of the variety which inspires the panjandrums of the Soho Cosa Nostra into grabbing the nomination forms for the Booker Prize. The sort of tripe that everyone who is anyone in the arts, praises to the skies, but never reads beyond the first paragraph. That, unfortunately, is not an option open to me in the production of this little tome of wisdom. There is no point in getting all airy fairy when dealing with the subject of politics and politicians. Contemplation of neither of these topics merits a judicious application of the richness and niceties the English language is on occasion capable of. If one is standing in the mire of Parliamentary skullduggery, and the effluent is tickling the lower extremities of ones unmentionables, then frankly, it is better by far to confront the situation head on by honestly stating with no further equivocation, that one is up to ones balls in the crap, such verisimilitude will not win literary prizes, but it will alert the reader as to what to expect.

Therefore, in deference to the above dicta, Windsor Castle was not, on this particular day, a silvered stone necklace, it's radiance whispering to all who cared to observe, it's hallowed antiquity under the beneficent balm of an English summer sun. Oh Lordy no. Let's get real folks, the joint was a dirty looking pile giving the appearance of a council estate built around the corporation gasometer, and what's more this was not an idyllic summer's day, it was an English summer's day. In short, the sky was blocked out by coal coloured clouds, it was cold, it happened to be blowing a gale, and, surprise of surprises, the rain was coming down in stair rods, and had been doing so without the benefit of divine intervention for the past two weeks. The consequences of the prolonged exposure to this aspect of what the geographers describe so humorously as our temperate northern climate were predictable, Britannia was not cool, it was bloody freezing and the entire population was fed up with the situation, which was exactly how the fates found Queen Elizabeth this not so fine day.

Her Majesty, in the form of our Sovereign Lady had calmed down a little since her perusal of the Daily Truth earlier in the week, which is to say she was no longer chucking the china about the room, her return to equilibrium was still a far from accomplished fact. The only beings who felt it safe to approach H.M were the corgis. The remainder of humanity, her staff, family and friends continued to give her as wide a berth as possible, her consort had even gone so far as to discover an urgent need to go on a tour of Uzbekistan with the Moriston Orpheus Choir despite the fact that he could not abide Welsh community singing and the opportunities for him to insult people were limited, as the Welsh refused to speak any English and the Uzbeks did not know how to. So out of sorts was Her Majesty that she had broken with all precedent and strictures of duty and cancelled her weekly audience with the Prime Minister, whose secretary had failed to inform him of the cancellation. Not that this made any difference to the situation for he had had no intention of keeping the well established appointment as Wincarnis had insisted he accompany her to the bingo that night. Macmurdo Dunlossie was terribly keen for the Prime Minister to be seen at events like the bingo as he felt it gave working class cred to the Dear Leader.

Her Majesty was accustomed to being obeyed, and apart from the politicians of all parties, most people had no difficulty in indulging the lady in her preferences. Therefore when she ordered that all of her family be present at Windsor on this Friday it had not crossed the minds of any of those summoned to disobey. Although there were one or two who may have been inclined to disport themselves elsewhere on that ordained date, they did not do so, even if they felt brave enough to weather the inevitable bollocking, they were acutely cognoscente of H.M.'s control of the purse strings and her willingness to pull them tight shut should the need or inclination arise. Lucre vincit omnia.

Dutifully, as ordered by their matriarch, the senior members of the House of Windsor assembled in the red drawing room of the castle, the decor of which could not fail to cheer the soul, taking one's mind off the abysmal weather outside, except that some of this lot were not at that moment amenable to a spot of cheering, having been forcibly dragged back from more amenable climes and pastimes. However the boss had spoken and after that there was nothing left to be done other than obey.

Dinner had preceded the regal confab, a nightmare of a meal that lacked only Béla Lugosi playing the part of the butler to complete that tableaux vivant of gothic hilarity. The repast could be said to have started with a bang, quite literally so, as Andrews, the head footman, while dishing up the mulligatawny, had made his contribution to the ambience of the occasion by way of an almighty fart that damn near rattled the china. What little conversation that had managed to survive so cataclysmic a statement on royal domesticity was rapidly killed off shortly afterwards by Ben, the least disciplined of that unruly pack of canine delinquents the Queen quaintly insisted referring to as household pets. Having been fed a bottle of milk stout by a page of the backstairs with a whimsical sense of humour, Ben mistook a leg of the sideboard for a Scots Pine and piddled all over it, then he bit Prince Charles on the calf because the Prince refused to share his bread roll with him.

In the best of British traditions, the entire assemblage pretended nothing had happened, except that is for Prince Charles, who made a perfectly reasonable comment on the Corgis imperfect understanding of what constituted house training. The Prince followed up this intrepid foray into forbidden territory with a statement as to what he would do to the ruddy mutt if were it his. The Queen, to whom criticism of her beloved pooches was tantamount to having St. George replaced as patron saint of England by Oliver Cromwell, promptly laid into her eldest, telling him if he was incapable of saying anything worth listening to then he should go back to Highgrove and talk to his beloved weeds.

And with that little salvo, concord and amity went out the window, never to return that evening. From that point onwards, through the boiled mutton to the spotted dick and custard, silence bestowed its blessings on those assembled, except for the servants, who continued as per usual to bitch and moan at full throttle, hoping by their tantrums to nudge their employer into paying them a living wage, if only to shut them up. Fat chance.

In the red drawing room coffee was served, after which the servants retired from the presence.

"Christ. Bloody Nescaff again," spluttered Princess Anne. "Why in God's name can't we have some decent coffee in this place?"

"Coffee costs money," chorused her siblings in unison, a predictable refrain learned at their mother's knee. A determination to be revenged for the indigestion they were already beginning to experience had given the Queen's offspring the courage to lob this mild challenge to her legendary generosity at the feet of their formidable ma.

"Now don't start you lot," growled Prince Phillip. "Your mother's been very upset this last week."

His wife nodded her agreement, while at the same time thinking it had been a mistake to have permitted her children a glass each of parsnip wine with their dinner. If this was the effect alcohol was having on them, then it was back to Ribena from now on. Such a nice colour Ribena, looked just like claret when it was in the glass, and a fraction of the price.

"You've no idea what she has been going through."

"Neither have you."

"That's right Anne, you tell him," cried a gleeful Prince Edward. "He buggered off to God knows where to listen to a few choruses of Bread of Heaven," the Prince found his enthusiasm for troublemaking expertly castrated in the form of a thump in the ribs administered by his furious better half.

"Shut up yer clot," hissed Edward's countess. "We need a sub this month."

"Oh yes," groaned the abruptly chastened Edward, recalling the state of his finances, then broke out in a sweat on remembrance of what that mornings post had brought, cancellation of his one remaining credit card and a returned cheque, the one he had used to pay for a bottle of vodka at the offie round the corner from Buck House.

"She'll go ape if she finds out what you've been spending money on, then we won't get a penny out of her," Edward nodded in painful comprehension of his wife's logic, and resolved to keep his trap shut for the remainder of the evening.

"What was that dear?" enquired the Queen sweetly while at the same time spearing the countess with that special look she reserved for daughters-in-law, a species of the human condition she felt ought not to be encouraged to take any steps which might result in them avoiding extinction.

"Nothing ma," responded Sophie with equal sweetness. "Just reminding Ed to take his Rennies, he's feeling a bit out of sorts."

"Feeling the pinch more likely," countered Princess Anne, who was spoiling for a fight now that the effects of the parsnip wine were beginning to kick in. "How much are you hoping to tap ma for this time?"

"I am not," yelled Edward, furious at being rumbled before he'd had the chance to produce a creditable sob story for his understanding mater, which was half the problem, she understood only too well. He'd have the devil's own job in trying to chisel some brass out of the old girl this time round. The last thing he needed was Anne queering his pitch. "I'm not, I'm not," repeated the Prince, infuriated to the point of petulance.

"Oh yes you are," pantomimed everyone in the room. Including Andrews, the head footman, who had passed out behind the sofa and had just come 'round.

"Clear out Andrews," bawled Prince Phillip. "This is family."

"Yes sir."

"And don't answer back. Just bugger off." The prince took a slightly closer look at the servant. "You're pissed again aren't you? Yer short arsed Welsh git." The hapless retainer would have scarpered in a record breaking demonstration of velocity had he been able, unfortunately, he was encountering a crucial lack of coordination between the cranial cavity and his bodily extremities, compelling him to make his exit on all fours with Princes William and Harry in the background volubly setting the odds on him reaching the door before passing out again.

"The old sod's discovered where you've hidden the keys to the wine cellar gran," opined Harry, who had also found out where his grandmother had secreted the passports to that particular Valhalla, but was rather more discrete with his discovery than the somewhat egregious footman. "You'll have to change the locks again. I'll help you gran."

"There's a good boy Harry. I'll give you the money tomorrow morning then you can nip down to B.&Q., then we'll change the locks before lunch." Harry beamed at his doting grandmother, his smile cuddling a tincture of disdain for his aunt and uncles. It was easy as pie to handle the old girl if you knew how.

"This is all very well," announced Princess Anne. "But can I be the only one wondering why some of us have been dragged half way around the World to face a plate of jaw breaking mutton and a glass of parsnip wine?"

She looked across at her mother, the very silence demanding an answer. She was not intimidated by the Queen to the extent her brothers were, but then the family had always specialized in producing women who excelled at ruling the World and men who were fit only to run from it.

The Queen dipped into her diamante evening bag and fished out a packet of rizlas, methodically she rolled herself a fag.

"Now belt up you lot and listen to what your mother has to say," ordered Prince Phillip, trying to give the impression he knew what was about to enfold, which he most certainly was not. The entire clan assembled turned to look at their matriarch, offering her a collective smile, hoping they were not in for a going over followed by a dictat to tighten their belts yet again just because some caviar guzzling newspaper proprietor thought they were spending too much. The Queen took a satisfying drag at her cigarette before getting down to the nitty-gritty of the reason for the family pow-wow.

"You all know what has been going on here over the past week," said H.M., savoring that indulgent foray into the bleeding obvious.

"Yes," replied her tribe in a beautifully modulated descant that did not quite disguise their impatience, and which in Prince Charles case could not suffocate his distaste for his mother's choice of weed, wishing that if she had to smoke then she could at least inhale something a little classier than a roll-up. He pondered the possibility of giving her ten Woodbines as a present next Christmas.

"Well it's the last straw," continued the Queen. "I've had a bellyful of those morally constipated posers who call themselves opinion formers and I am not taking any more. No. I'm bloody well not. It's time to make a stand."

"But ma," intervened Princess Anne, eager to demonstrate she had polished her common sense along with the brass that morning. "This has been going on for donkey's years. It's all so bloody predictable we could, any one of us, sit down here and now and write the script for the next episode of 'Sensational Royal Revelations!"

"I'll produce it," volunteered Prince Edward with unseemly enthusiasm." His wife gave him a clip across the ear.

"I told you to shut up," hissed the furious countess, her sibilants sprouting offshoots of venom as she saw their much needed sub about to go down with all hands on deck.

"Don't interrupt," commanded H.M. The family subsided into quiescent anticipation of what might be heading in their direction. "As I said, I have had enough," she enunciated the words with a regal deliberation. "Fifty one years of snipe snipe snipe, and all I'm expected to do in response is smile and wave back, 'Oh thank you Mr. Patterson, so kind of you to crap all over me, and don't keep me waiting so long for the next dump." Even Princess Anne winced at her mother's crude alliteration.

"Well" continued the Queen. "I'm like the camel, there's a hell of a lot of straw that's been loaded on to me and the latest addition has broken my bloody back."

"But I still don't see what we can do about it," persevered Princess Anne. "We've put up with it for so long it's like living with piles, irritating but nevertheless a fact of life."

"You can do nothing Anne but I sure as hell can, and what is more I damn well will. This time the empire is striking back. Ed dear, pour me a drop of mother's ruin, I'm in the mood for it." The Queen sipped her gin while the family helpfully suggested what it was she could or should do, none of the proffered solutions coming anywhere near her intentions.

"More gin gran?" asked Harry, hoping to be offered one himself.

"No thank you dear, but as a special treat you can have one." The rest of the family glared at Harry, why should he get a slug of gin when all they got was a glass of parsnip wine?

"Now, you've all said what I should do, so I am now going to tell you what I actually will do. I am going to abdicate."

Silence in its most pristine manifestation followed this statement. H.M. noticed the look on Prince Charles face, which said all too clearly he could not wait to order the Archbishop of Canterbury to set to with the Mansion polish on the Coronation Chair. "Don't plan on booking the Abbey just yet Charles. I have plans for each and every one of you, and this is what you are going to do.

The Queen spoke for a full fifteen minutes, there was no attempt to interrupt her, they were all too appalled to say anything. When she had finished, with great dignity she rose and left the room with no further ado, taking the gin bottle with her, no sense in leaving temptation sitting around for them.

CHAPTER IV.

Percival Tcherkoff was a man of immense consequence, as he never tired nor failed to impress upon all whom he encountered, irrespective of the number of times he met them, lest any should fall into forgetfulness and think him common and lower middle class. As a Fleet Street editor, Perce never lost a chance to expound to his readership on the depth and quality of his poshness. The man could not so much as write an article on buggery in Timbuktu without somehow bringing his mother's butler into the narrative. Did his mother have a butler? Well, not quite, but her father certainly did.

Perce's anecdotal diarrhea on the subject of his family's overwhelming poshery was a mite selective. Yes, his dearly beloved mater, as he unfailingly referred to the old dame in print, was indeed everything he made her out to be, well, more or less, we will not split hairs at this stage of the narrative. What Percival routinely failed to bring to the attention of his audience was the fact that his mother, at the tender age of thirty eight and ten months, had climbed down a ladder from her bedroom window, in the early hours of a February morning, where her father kept her locked in at night to stop her molesting the male servants, to elope with a fish and tater hawker from Birkenhead. To misquote the Bard, Ivan Tcherkoff was but a bastard shoot, the outcome of a bit of slap and tickle which had gotten out of hand behind the Odeon in Chester one Saturday night between a deserting Russian sailor and one of the town trollops. Ivan was Percival's pa, only he never got mentioned in print, no siree bobcat, common as bollocks Ivan was consigned to oblivion, even though he was alive and well and still frying fish in Birkenhead on a nightly basis.

Now it may give the impression, these brief jottings on his character, that Perce Tcherkoff was a pompous pain in the arse, a charge against which the man could have no creditable defense, and all of Fleet Street knew it, not for nothing was he known to his staff at The Daily Telegraph as jerking Perce. Along the length and breadth of the street of shame, he was a laughing stock, in private of course, Fleet Street only stuck pins in the rest of the population, its own citizens were sacred territory, never to be trespassed against. To those who had never met him, lord god-aweful and mighty Tcherkoff was a pillar of society. Unfortunately for him, he was not a Lord, not even a Sir, he affected to despise titles, and by so doing fooled most people, but not quite all, Buckingham Palace certainly knew their man.

It was a Monday evening, the paper had been put to bed, or at least, was being put there by Percival's deputy. Perce was not at Canary Wharf, he was in his Westminster flat, settling down for an evening of Glenmorangie and the Magic Flute, he did not really like opera, and did not in the least understand what was going on, but he felt that listening to songs being sung in a foreign language was a upper class recreation, so he indulged himself. It was while thus engaged in suffering for his cultural pretensions, that Perce's agony was relieved by the intervention of the telephone, gratefully he punched the cancel button to silence the Queen of the Night and picked up the receiver.

Perce went to immense trouble to disguise his social origins, the corsets of pretence held the common inner man securely in check, a state of affairs able to withstand most seismic shocks, most but not all. When the party on the other end of the receiver announced himself as Sir Ralph Settles, the Queen's private secretary, Perce's self control slipped a little. Perhaps it was the Scotch, maybe the Mozart, but nevertheless, all the old boy could come out with was a supremely inelegant.

"Horse shit."

"Oh no Sir Percy. Oops! Slip of the tongue there," lisped Sir Ralph in sibilants of Castilian affectation. Do please promise me you won't repeat that in company. Well not until tomorrow at least." Perce managed a few splutterings which indicated no discernable affinity to the English language but failed utterly to impede the flow of Sir Ralph's dialogue. "Now, I do know you have never met me, although how we could have missed each other is beyond me." No it wasn't, Sir Ralph, despite his mistress's instructions to butter up the Fleet Street mob, whose egos were second only to those rampaging around Westminster had made it a point to avoid being bored to the last canapé by posh Perce. "However Sir Percy. Oh drat! There I go again, do forgive me. As I was saying, as far as you're concerned, this could be anyone on the other end of the line, therefore I think it would be best for you to ring me back here at the palace." Sir Ralph read out the number of the Buck House switchboard together with his extension number. "If you could do that straight away, dear Mr. Tcherkoff, then we can continue with this conversation, for which I would be most grateful to you, not to mention H.M. Bye now." The line went dead.

The first thing Percy did on replacing the receiver was to pour himself another drink, he then phoned the Telegraph office and ordered one of the subs to provide him with the number of Buckingham Palace, telling the sub that it was none of his effing business why he wanted the number.

"Just do as I fucking tell you yer prick." So agitated had Perce become that he had even forgotten to couch his crudities in his habitual upper class accent and Birkenhead seeped out between his bridgework. The sub would have a field day down at the pub with this one, but if he wanted to continue in life as a wage earner he had better get that info to the boss P.D.Q.

Perce checked the number against the one he had been given, they tallied, he dialed the number. At first he thought there had been a mistake, as he could make no headway with the switchboard operator. Persuaded, after shelling out oceans of cash to a P.R. firm that being go ahead, modern and democratic meant that nobody should be able to understand a word one said, the Palace had staffed it's switchboard with a complement of Geordies whose impenetrable accents fooled everyone into thinking they were speaking to the under manager of the Sunderland Co-Op. He was about to work off his frustration on the operator, when to his huge relief, Sir Ralph came on the line.

"Thank you so much for calling, we do so appreciate your sacrificing your time to help us." Perce did not know who the "we" referred to anymore than he was aware he was sacrificing his time, but he had no intention of arguing the toss with someone who might be able to take the dust covers off the knighting stool for him.

"My pleasure Sir Ralph," his voice had gotten even posher in the brief interlude since they last spoken, a fact that had not gone unnoticed by the Queen's chief goffer, who silently congratulated himself on scoring a bull's-eye first time.

"We really do need a little help over here, and we genuinely feel you are the only one who could bring home the gravadlax so to speak." Perce noted the phraseology, he'd be using that one over lunch with Conrad at the Garrack the following day.

"I know my duty Sir Ralph."

"Which is why we came to you my darling chap," purred the courtier, admiring his suave duplicity as his words trilled into the handset.

"You have only to ask and it is done."

"Oh, how British that is in its simplicity. Why don't you come over here to-morrow morning?"

"Absolutely delighted," warbled Perce as he dived into the spirit of things and only just managed to avoid blurting out "Oo ta."

"Excellent. How about ten thirty to-morrow morning, I don't think we need make it any earlier do you? Oh, and better make it formal dress, as I may not be the only individual you might encounter."

"Of course, I do so understand." You bet the old blighter did." A nudge might be as good as a wink to a blind man but that was not a nudge, it was a friggin great thump in the ribs.

"We'll have a glass of sherry first," concluded Sir Ralph. "Then we can talk things over quietly. As I said, ten thirty, I don't think we need make things any earlier. I abhore this trend towards these early morning get-togethers. So Trans-Atlantic, so uncompromisingly plebian don't you think?"

"I do so agree Sir Ralph," gushed Perce unctuously, determined to establish his anti plebian credentials with the uncompromisingly patrician Sir Ralph. "It would be disastrous if we were to start following in the footsteps of the great unwashed wouldn't it?" The prat was entirely unaware that in English society the only people who washed were the middle classes, the nobs and the slobs couldn't abide the concept of soap and water together with its possible application to the human form.

"Until to-morrow Mr Tcherkoff. Goodbye," deftly Sir Ralph concluded the conversation before Perce could start in on the "We aristocrats must stick together" line, followed by an invitation to lunch or worse. There was only so much the gallant cove was prepared to suffer for his Monarch, and getting all pallsy wallsy with the likes of Perce Tcherkoff was not on the index of acceptable martyrdoms.

2.

Eight thirty in the morning following his conversation with the Queen's secretary, Perce was just across the road from the Palace at Canada gate, breakfasting on hot dogs and fried onions purchased from a vendor who dispensed Balkan hospitality in broken English along with his provender at prices only a tourist would be daft enough to contemplate paying, he threw the salmonella poisoning in for free.

Perce would have been the first to agree that he was a little premature for his appointment, but he did not want to risk the chance of being late for what he was convinced would be his one opportunity to play footsie under the table with true destiny, therefore, done up to the nines in full formal fig, he spent the best part of an hour and a half parading along the perimeters of green Park while stuffing himself with a reckless quantity of hot dogs and fried onions.

At ten of the clock he positioned himself directly outside the palace gates, staring intently at the entrance, so rapt was his gaze that the guardsman on duty thought Perce was trying to proposition him and called a police officer. By the time Perce had convinced the constable he was not attempting to undermine the virtue of the nineteen-year-old guardsman, it was ten forty five before he was able to present himself at the Privy Purse door. When at last he was ushered into Sir Ralph's office, the grand old man of Fleet Street was drenched in sweat and unrealized by him had lost totally his control over his accent.

"I don't know how to apologize for being so late Sir Ralph. Deplorable of me, quite deplorable."

"Nothing to worry about my dear fellow, the police rang through with an explanation. These things happen you know." Sir Ralph speared Perce with a 'looked that screamed of understanding and tolerance and not a little fellow feeling come to think of it. Percy's overwrought complexion achieved a rickety balance somewhere between puce and a rich magenta. He tried for an explanation but all he could achieve was a concentration of spluttering, which to the casual listener could have been Serbo-Croat for all the sense it made. "Let's have that Sherry I promised you shall we?" continued Sir Ralph, while managing to imply this happened to all the Queen's guests and that he was not to worry if the missus found out. He moved over to a sideboard, partly to dispense the wine, principally to avoid passing out as a consequence of being brutally assaulted by the onion punctuated breath of his guest. "I have a particularly fine Manzanilla for you to try."

"Oh! My favourite." The lying git. Perce liked his sherry dark brown and tasting like treacle, but he knew the upper classes liked their wines to be as near to lemon juice as possible. He accepted the crystal sherry glass and stuck out his pinkie at an impossible angle while taking a sip at the liquid he considered would be more at home in a specimen jar. "This is delightful Sir Ralph, you must give me the name of your shipper," the private secretary smiled, he was not fooled for one minute, Percy Tcherkoff had been investigated to a degree that the Palace even knew his favoured brand of lavatory paper.

"Let's sit down shall we?" Sir Ralph indicated a well worn green leather Chesterfield, taking care to position himself out of range of his guest's dragon breath. "I have invited you here for a particular purpose. Although I don't need to tell you that as you've probably worked that out for yourself."

"Er, yes." A self-satisfied smirk indicated his ego was once more cantering out of control.

"An announcement is to be made and you have been selected to make it. I have assured Her Majesty you are the ideal candidate for the task."

"Oh. Sir Ralph! I am overwhelmed. The dear Queen can put her trust in me without qualification." Sir Ralph inwardly winced at the "Dear Queen" bit, but what else could one expect of such a specimen?

"Very reassuring. Her Majesty is going to abdicate, and you, my good little chappie are going to tell the World. What do you say to that?"

"Fucking hell." Was what Perce said to that, before dropping his glass on the Axminster. In the shock of the revelation he'd failed to notice his accent had once more done a bunk "Me?"

"You. A Faberge quality scoop isn't it? Apart from advance notice of the second coming you won't get a better one for the rest of your career. Well, not quite anyway."

"What does the Prime Minister say? More to the point, what does his old woman, Win the Macclesfield mouth have to say, has the cow been over to measure up for the curtains yet?"

"What a piquant description of the lady, the Macclesfield mouth. Prince Phillip will love that one."

"That's what she's known as along the Street. Nobody's ever seen a photo of the dame where her mouth is not open so wide that you can see last week's breakfast."

"This gets better and better. But, in answer to your question, the Prime Minister does not know, and will not know until you tell him on the front page of the Telegraph."

"Christ in clogs and a jock-strap. Wait 'till I tell Conrad, the old sod will double me wages after this."

"The noble lord will have to learn of the news along with the rest of the population I'm afraid, but don't worry, we'll smooth things out with him for you. I'm sure he'd love to be an hereditary, don't you?"

"Aye. That he would an' all," Percy's syntax had gone galloping off into the wild blue yonder in search of his accent. "Alfred Sawse'll be in a bit of a spin so to say."

"He'll be that all right, for once he is going to get a dose of his own physic, the man has made a bit of a career of making policy announcements and such like via the press and his tame TV. Pundits, well now he's going to know what it feels like to be on the receiving end. This will definitely put him off his nut cutlets."

"No. That's his missus, it's she what don't approve of eating meat. Come to think of it there ain't much what she do approve of, but he sneaks off down the Mile end Road to Ikey Solomon's for a plate of pork chops with apple sauce. And what's more the poor sap thinks she doesn't know about it, but she does, take it from me she does."

"You are wonderfully informed. Now, shall we go through to Her Majesty? This way."

Sir Ralph swept Percy into the presence of majesty. So overawed was Percy, that for the first time in his existence, having nothing to say worth listening to, he had the sense to keep his trap shut.

"Mr. Percy Tcherkoff your Majesty," announced the secretary. Sir Ralph gave the customary bob of the head, so would Perce have done if he had not gone completely to pieces and curtsied instead.

"So pleased you are able to help us Mr. Tcherkoff, Sir Ralph sings your praises highly. Very highly."

By now, Perce had completely lost the plot, thousands of pounds worth of grammar and elocution lessons departed to dance with the fairies at the bottom of the garden.

"Hi ham most 'appy to 'elp your Majesty." Before the import of what he had just let slip had a chance to ravish his self esteem, the memory of his curtsey boomeranged back on him. Percy thought to make good the faux pas with a bow of music hall flamboyance, just as his nose came within six inches of the floor, the interaction between the onions and the second glass of Sherry came into play, with the result that he let rip with an epic fart of Chaucerian resonance, which no one in the room could pretend not to have been introduced to, and as the Queen had left the Corgis elsewhere, they could not have been blamed in order to save Percy's face.

However it would take more than a fart dropped at an inopportune moment to knock Elizabeth II off her stride. The Queen gave a brief nod to her equerry, who placed a gilt stool with handlebars before her. Sir Ralph indicated to Percy to kneel on the stool. Quite overcome by this coronation of all his social ambitions, he dropped to his knees, missing the dubbing stool by a good six inches. The shock to his system as his knees thudded into the carpet triggered another emission of cataclysmic proportions, forcing through his lips an agonized "Bugger." All his life he had dreamed of a moment such as this and now such a moment had come, all he could do was to make a right pig's ear of it and sound as common as an anal reverberation in a cow shed.

The Queen lightly tapped Percy on each shoulder with a sword, gave him two fingers to shake, muttered a few inconsequentials then stepped back a pace. This was the signal for the private secretary to ease the freshly minted Sir Percy up from his knees and to usher him out through the door, an operation he achieved with practiced smoothness, but not before Sir Percy had managed to drop another Knightly ripper, which, for all his precipitate social elevation, smelled no better than his previous offerings.

"There Sir Percy, that was not so bad was it? Another glass of Sherry I think." He handed a brimming glass to the new knight, who due to the pressure of nerves, downed it in one.

"Ee. Our Mabel'll be right chuffed about this, that she will an' all." His posh accent was still on safari and had yet to return to home base. "Now then, let's get down to the nitty gritty Sir Ralph. When do you want this notice published?"

"To-morrows edition."

"Good as done. The Q need have no fear, all will be exactly as she wants."

"None of us has any doubts about that Sir Percy." His emphasis on the Sir Percy had the required effect, the man was putty in the Palace's paws. Sir Ralph handed the latest recruit to the ranks of chivalry two typed A four pages. "Now these must be kept utterly, utterly, secret. Her Majesty places her entire trust in you." Percy read the pages with concentrated care, when he had finished he was too stunned to offer any comment."

"Well?" asked Sir Ralph.

"You are not serious. You can't be."

"Oh but we are Sir Percy. Still the Queen's man?"

"More than ever, I've waited years to put one on Alfred Sawse, the sniveling little pipsqueak. But God help us all."

"He might at that." Sir Ralph smiled triumphantly in Percy's direction but not necessarily at him, gave his guest a light, almost royal shake of the hand. The door opened, suggesting someone was either listening at the keyhole or the entire proceedings were being videoed.

Within ten minutes, Sir Percy Tcherkoff was off the palace precincts and on his way to the Garrick for lunch with his proprietor. By the time he was marching up the steps of the club, he was so relaxed and confident that even his posh accent had returned to him, not that he was aware it had ever taken leave of absence.

CHAPTER V.

At this point in time, a phrase beloved of intellectually spayed politicians, Number Ten Downing Street was an oasis of calm and well being. Nothing untoward disturbed the draughts which intruded through the sash windows, nor impeded the flow of hot air generated by the exercising of puny minds which took the place of air conditioning in the building. To cut a long story off at the knees, the occupants of what had become to be known amongst the cognoscenti and bum kissers of Whitehall as the Residence, were pig ignorant of the events which swayed and ignited the interest of the outside World, a state of affairs which had not come about via the application of the laws of random chance but due to the edicts of Wincarnis Sawse.

The first lady, as she liked to be known as, had, in her feminist zeal, insisted that all the Downing Street telephonists be given maternity leave. In fact none of them had been recently pregnant. Two were approaching sixty and Virgo in both the gynaecological as well as the astrological sense, and the fact that one had a bulge in the area of the crotch which hinted that such an individual giving birth to an offspring would have had the same impact on the medical profession as the immaculate conception, was neither here nor there. Wincarnis had decreed that all telephonists be given maternity leave and that was that. The denizens of Number Ten, could of course, have been kept au courant of current affaires via the medium of television or radio, but, and here we go again folks, Wincarnis did not approve of the telly or the wireless.

Macmurdo Dunlossie was having his second cup of tea of the morning, using the tea bag used for the first infusion. Wincarnis did not approve of extravagance by anyone other than herself, and if anyone in Downing Street wanted to be sure of still having a job a week hence, then it was advisable to stick to Wincarnis's rules like a certain substance is known to adhere to blankets. Macmurdo had been granted no exemption from the rules, he might be the Prime Ministers most valuable political hit man, his crutch and stalwart in government, but he still had to obey the first lady, as did the P.M and everyone else. Macmurdo hated her guts.

Wincarnis was not alone in being a recipient of Macmurdo's dyspeptic loathing, there was one other he hated almost as much as Wincarnis, not quite as much, but as sure in hell as damn it. The object of these somewhat negative vibrations was Condo Maites, so close was Condo to the first lady and her consort that he was almost an ex-parte member of the Sawse family, not that he would have applauded that description. While Condo thought the Prime Minister a bit of a dish and the principal tool in his advancement up the greasy pole, he could not abide the man's wife. Ambition being the most efficient known antidote to sincerity, and Condo was nothing if not ambitious, Wincarnis had only to enter a room for his peepers to switch on like fairy lights. Of course, in reality he could not stand the bitch, although they angled in each others waters for compliments, and obliged one another with the occasional catch, the reality was slightly different. In Condo's book, fish should be sampled solely on a Friday, and then only if one were a Catholic and in straightened circumstances. There you have it, the dramatis personae of Number ten, at least the ones who counted, on the morning the political world changed forever.

Alice Gunthorpe seethed with righteous indignation, she had been seething during the journey from Whitechapel Road, and by the time she had clocked on at Downing Street, was on the point of boiling over. The building was no stranger to indignation or moral outrage, the difference in Alice's case was that it was the real thing and not posturing for the cameras. Clutching a tightly rolled up edition of the Telegraph, to what would have been her bosom had nature not been a mite niggardly in that department, Alice stormed into Macmurdo's office which had formerly been the cabinet room.

Macmurdo Dunlossie had just finished his tea when Alice poked him in the chest with her newspaper, causing him to regurgitate the liquid down his front which had been fresh on the week before.

"For Christ's you crazy old bat! I'll have you fired for that. Get the fuck out of here you pox riddled old shit." Unimpressed by his Gorbels subtlety, Alice compounded her offence by giving him a clout across the chops. "You're dead woman, you're fucking dead. You'll never work again in this town. And I'll make damn sure you don't get any dole money either."

"God will strike you down Macmurdo Dunlossie. God will punish you, you and that disloyal master of yours upstairs, and that sanctimonious trollop he's married to. God will smite you hip and thigh for what you have done to the poor Queen." Having been short changed insofar as chivalry was concerned, Macmurdo was about to silence the Lord's avenger with a right hook to the jaw, when she threw the paper in his lap then turned and fled the room while demanding the Almighty visit fire and brimstone on the heads of the ungodly.

Macmurdo picked up the paper and reacted much as Count Dracula would have done on being handed a string of garlic and a crucifix, he had actually touched a copy of the Daily Telegraph. If Macmurdo agreed with Wincarnis on anything, it was her forbidding anyone in the Government to read the Telegraph, the paper had been banned from the sacred precincts of Downing Street, to be seen reading the offending publication was to guarantee exile to the real world where one would be compelled to work for a living. Macmurdo was frantically trying to figure out how to get rid of the evidence before some sneaky sod caught sight of it in his possession and shopped him to Wincarnis, who would have taken the opportunity to slit his throat with all the enthusiasm of a halal butcher stocking up for Eid-ul-Fitr, when he chanced to glance at the headlines. 'ABDICATION.'

"Never!" he squawked, "It's a bloody piss take." He rummaged amongst the detritus on his desk for that morning's Guardian, found it, and compared the two papers. The Guardian carried not a dickie bird about any abdication. He took another look at the Telegraph, "Abdication," in six-inch capitals. As he turned the pages he discovered there was not another topic covered in that days edition.

"It can't be right, it friggin well can't be."

"Ah, but I think it can sweet cheeks."

"What the fuck are you doing here? Piss off you bloody fairy." Condo Maites, Macmurdo's arch rival for the affections of the leader, stood in the doorway to the cabinet room.

"I see you've been overdosing on the charm liniment again. I've just bumped into one of out skivvies. Seems Wincarnis can get fitted out for the ermine sooner than she thought." He sauntered over to Macmurdo' s desk, perching himself on its edge, not for artistic effect but because he knew that would get up his protagonists nose like nothing else.

"It's all a load of bollocks, I'm telling you. Percy Tcherkoff has finally gone off his fucking chump."

"According to Alice Gunthorpe, the morning TV's talking abdication, abdication, abdication."

"We'll soon see about that."

"How? We don't have any telly or radio in the building." Wincarnis did not approve of TV. Or radio.

"That fucking woman."

"For once I agree with you."

"Well how the hell are we going to find out what's going on?" pleaded Macmurdo. "We can't even use the piddling telephone cos the exchange isn't managed because every menopausal virgin in the joint has been told she's up the duff ".

"Tut tut. That's sexist. What you should have said is - "

"I don't give a stuff what I should have said, I want to know what the fuck is going on."

"I'll go and ring the B.B.C., they might fool the rest of the World but they won't try it on with me."

"And how do you go about that with no phones?" asked Macmurdo in the tone of voice habitually used by social workers when confronted by the terminally retarded.

"I shall use one of the phones down the road actually." He smiled delicately at his opponent before heading off down Whitehall for a public phone booth. He returned fifteen minutes later.

"Well?"

"It's world wide news. We are about the only ones on the planet who don't know that Elizabeth the second has hung up her tiara."

"Then why haven't the Guardian got it? Useless public school wankers."

"The Palace gave an exclusive to Tcherkoff. He's now doing the rounds of the television studios, by the way, he's now Sir Percy Tcherkoff."

"They can't do it. They can't fucking do it," raged Macmurdo. "For Christ's sake, we'd already planned the abdication."

"Don't tell me," lisped Condo. "Tell Wincarnis."

"Oh Jesus. She will go through the roof," said Macmurdo, emphasizing each word with the sonorous deliberation of a medieval peasant announcing the onset of the bubonic plague. "Where is the sanctimonious cow?"

"Azerbaijan. Representing the leader at the international congress for lesbian and gay hospital porters."

"Let's hope they've got telly out there, then she'll have worked off some steam before coming back."

"You can hope, but I doubt it. Poor cow, she did so want to be the Madam Roland of British politics, with a different ending of course." Condo's allusion to French History went way over Macmurdo's head as he had received the benefits of an insurance education, fully comprehensive and absolutely useless when needed.

"There's nothing for it," declared Macmurdo. "I'll have to go and tell the leader."

"No, you damn well won't. I'm his closest confidant in government. I'll tell him."

"I'm his director of Interpersonal Situations."

"If you are trying to underline the fact that you are his spin doctor, then all I can say is that the poor man would be better off with a ruddy tree surgeon."

"Is that so Mr. Condo-bloody-Maites. Well, better a fucking tree surgeon than the people's poof ."

"You can't say that to me," shrieked Condo. "It's homophobic. I'll tell Wincarnis when she gets back."

"When she gets back, old Port and lemon is going to have other things on her mind. Now, I'm upstairs to tell the boss," pursued by Condo, he raced off in the direction of the private quarters.

2.

Alfred Sawse was busily employed ironing the underwear, a task he was not very good at in actual fact, but Wincarnis did not approve of men who did not do their stint as house husbands and therefore Alfred had been allocated the tasks of ironing, hovering, dusting and bed making. All other domestic chores were undertaken by the hired help, a geriatric old besom who Wincarnis had ordered off on maternity leave. He was just finishing off Wincarnis' vests when Macmurdo and Condo came bursting in to the flat, fighting would perhaps be a more apt description as there was a pronounced physical tussle to see who could be first through the door.

"I'm telling him first."

"Fuck off yer middle-aged turd burglar."

"That's outrageous! Tell him Alfie, he's not to talk to me like that. Make him apologize."

"Great news boys. The Queen's abdicated." The P.M. beamed at his minions, giving them a pyrotechnic display of his one and only talent.

"Who told you?" they chorused in a harmony reminiscent of a drag act impersonating the Dolly Sisters.

"Somebody called Alice Gunthorpe. She's a cleaner I think, said it was all over the Telegraph. By the way, what's the Telegraph doing on the premises? You know Wincarnis said nobody is to read it."

"Don't worry," Macmurdo assured the Government's second in command. "Nobody, absolutely nobody reads the rag."

"Then how did a copy of it get into the building? Wincarnis definitely won't approve of this." The prospect of incurring his wife's displeasure had nudged the abdication to the periphery of his understanding of events, which could not cope with more than one situation at a time, even under the most propitious of circumstances.

"Don't panic," soothed Macmurdo. "I told you no one reads it, that copy was the cleaners."

"Oh, that's alright then, they don't count thank God," said Condo, seeing the chance to slip in his two pennyworth. "Now, to get back to the abdication,"

"Yes. Isn't it wonderful news? Wincarnis will be over the moon."

"In a pigs ear she will." Macmurdo was not noted for his subtlety, probably because he did not possess any. "She'll start chucking the china about the minutes she gets to hear of it."

"What do you mean? This is what she has always wanted."

"Not quite. You tell him Maites."

"The King is dead, long live the king. That's the constitution. The very minute the Queen signed the instrument of abdication, Charles became king. What Wincarnis wanted was to abolish the whole kit and caboodle, not replace one Sovereign with another. So, your better half will be livid," explained Condo in the tone one would normally employ when explaining to a half wit the inexpedience of refraining from reciting the Lord's Prayer while swimming under water.

"But we're half way there," pleaded the prime minister. "One down..."

"And fucking hundreds to go," interrupted Macmurdo with no consideration for the accepted niceties of discourse between master and servant. "It has to be either all or nothing."

"I hate to agree with Mac, Alfie, but this time he is right. Nothing will change, the succession will go on and on."

"As I said," emphasized Macmurdo. "Wincarnis will be frothing at the mouth like a preacher at a revival meeting."

"In fact," continued Macmurdo. "The situation is worse from our point of view than if things had stayed the same."

"He's right for once. That Charles has been getting a bit too popular for my liking. It's unconstitutional, the people will support him, the sentimental bastards."

The Prime Minister slumped down on the sofa, the better cogitate on the complications of life. He was not worried about what course he should take under the circumstances, as Mac and Condo would tell him what to do until

Wincarnis got back from Azerbaijan. He was brought back to the realities of life by the smell of singeing, he had forgotten to turn the iron off and his wife's new peach coloured satin corset was going up in smoke.

"Oh shit! She's only worn that once. What am I going to do?" wailed the leader of the country. Condo felt it was time he rescued the situation.

"Now don't go getting your Janet Raegers in a twist. You finish the ironing then get on with the hovering. While you are doing that, Mac and I will decide what to do." Condo was reluctant to include Macmurdo in the decision making process but thought it prudent to suspend hostilities. "Then when you've finished up here, we'll take you round to the Chairman for a pint of the black stuff and a pork pie." The Prime Minister brightened up considerably.

"Will you really boys?"

"Yes we will," added Macmurdo, determined not to give any ground to Condo. "And as Wincarnis is not back for another couple of days, you can get absolutely bollocking legless."

"Great. You're not telling me fibs now are you?"

"Us tell you fibs!" declared Condo with a concern for veracity which would have curled the pages of a family Bible.

"That's right," added Macmurdo with all the indignation he was able to muster at such short notice. "Whoever heard of anyone in this administration tell porkies?"

With that the Castor and Pollux of Downing Street left their master to the burden of his domestic chores.

3.

Within an hour of Macmurdo and Condo leaving the P.M. to his domestic necessities, a ceremony as old as the monarchy was enacted at the Friary Court of St. James's Palace, where the titles and dignities of king Charles were read out before an audience of six jet-lagged American tourists and a Polish sailor gnawing on a hamburger. The television companies had not been informed of the event lest they blab to the B.B.C., but there was a reporter and a photographer from the Telegraph to record the ceremony.

The man from the Telegraph was not too well versed in the subtle nuances of the constitution, indeed, the man could not have told the difference between Bagehot and Bailey's Irish Cream, therefore he was ill equipped to grasp the salient points of the proceedings, they passed completely over his head. Charles was not proclaimed head of the Commonwealth or of anywhere of the overseas territories maintaining allegiance to the British Crown. Queen Elizabeth II had abdicated as queen of The United Kingdom of Great Britain and Northern Ireland, but not of any else, she remained Queen of Australia, Canada etc., a minor detail that had flown unimpeded over the heads of all in Downing Street.

CHAPTER VI.

Condo and Macmurdo held to a rigid moral code, they never lied to their glorious leader if they had first assured him they would not do so over a particular issue. Therefore, having promised him an alcoholic binge, they would never have dreamed of reneging on their commitment, so, it was at precisely thirty minutes down the line after the noon hour, that they set off down the underground tunnel to the foreign office, from whence they exited into Birdcage walk. A few brisk, anticipatory strides saw them along the perimeter of the park, up the Cockpit Steps and though the heavenly portals of The Chairmen.

Discretely disporting himself on a corner bench in the panelled downstairs bar, Alfred noisily slurped on a pint of Guinness.

"Should have given the tosser a straw, then he could have blown bubbles," mused Condo to himself. "He's getting as common as that bloody wife of his." He placed a plate before the Prime Minister. "Here you are Alfie babes, all your favourites." He gave his master the sort of smile that would have given a bad name to sycophancy had it not been the established religion in Downing Street.

"Ooh," squealed Alfred with testosterone drenched enthusiasm. "All my favourites, pork pie, Cheddar, crisps and pickled onions."

"More to come leader," announced Macmurdo, who dumped three packets of pork scratchings next to the P.M.'s trencher.

"Oh boys, you do spoil me, we ought to have an abdication more often if this is what I get for it." His companions gave him a look that gave only the vaguest of hints that he should open his mouth only to eat crap and not to speak it. What have you decided we're going to do? We do have a policy on the abdication now don't we?"

"Sort of Alfie." Condo looked to Macmurdo for back up, none was forthcoming, Mac delivered only glad tidings to his master, the brimstone and treacle he left to others, Condo whenever possible.

"Atta boy Condo. Tell it as it is," urged Macmurdo, much as the headsman might have encouraged Anne Boleyn to look on the bright side as she would no longer have to worry about her lumbago.

"There's good news and bad news," continued Condo.

"What's the good news?" asked the Prime Minister.

"The opposition do not know whether to laugh or cry."

"That's not new that's reiterating the flaming obvious."

"You'll have to do better than that," chirruped Macmurdo, ever ready with the stiletto to the back. Come on give us the bad news."

"Well," continued Condo, hopeful that on this occasion the messenger would not be shot. "The bad news is that Charles is quite popular at the moment, in fact he is too damned popular for our purposes. In short our plans for a republic have been knocked to one side for the foreseeable future."

"Wincarnis won't like this one little bit. She's sick of yawning through State occasions and having to forget to curtsy. What am I going to say when she gets back?" wailed the Prime Minister, wishing his wife would take a dose of the medicine she had forced down the throat of others and take maternity leave, preferably in Azerbaijan. Macmurdo set another pint in front of his master, broke out into what he fondly thought of as a smile, but in reality had all the charm and allure of a horse's clitoris.

"It just so happens, Alf me old lad that I have come up with something that might just turn things around for us." Condo gave his colleague a genocidal look, this was something they had not discussed earlier, he suspected, all too rightly, that he was about to be made to look like the Marx Brothers crammed into a prophylactic.

"Come on Mac. What have you got for us then?" So excited was the Prime Minister that he spilled half his pint into his crutch, thereby giving the impression he did not earn enough to be able to afford incontinence pads. Condo stomped off to get a replacement.

"It's like this," purred Macmurdo as Condo returned with the P.M.'s pint, he had deliberately waited to launch his strategy, wanting Condo to be exposed to the maximum humiliation possible. "We play the money and privilege card," Mac sat back in his chair, savouring his triumph. Of course, Alf had no idea what it was Macmurdo was driving at, but Condo did.

"Smart bastard aren't you." This, neither in tone nor inference was a complementary statement. Condo was absolutely livid at being bested once more by the devious Mac, who only a few short hours previously had declared to Condo that the Government had been thoroughly trumped by Buck House and there was nothing they could do about it.

"What do you mean Mac?" pleaded the Prime Minister, anxious not to be left in the dark and feeling peeved that it was so necessary to employ clever people if one wished to continue to win elections.

"Simple Alf. Simple. If you can rely on one thing in politics, it's that band of twenty-four carat envy that's a mile wide and runs through the British electorate. They can't stand anyone having something better than they have."

"Tell me," murmured Condo wistfully. "All I wanted was the key to my own front door. The way they reacted you'd think I'd done a bunk with the keys to the Bank of England."

"Not now Condo," added the Prime Minister. "Go on Mac."

"Well, it's like this. All we have to do is bang on about the wealth of the Royals then leave it to Joe Public to grow a chip on his shoulders."

"Do they really have that much money?" asked the Prime minister.

"Who cares," chipped in Condo anxious to make up for lost ground. "We've enough tame journos and pals at the beeb who'll broadcast anything we feed them and not ask awkward questions like is this true old bean."

"Oh good," enthused Alfred. "Win will be pleased."

"We'll get them on grace and favours as well. All those royal relations living in palaces at taxpayers expense... we'll turn the heat up on that one, that'll really get the voters going."

"Great. Absolutely great. You are Macmurdo and on you I shall build my government," declared the P.M. getting a sudden attack of God, like someone who has spent too long in the tropics is prone to go down with a bout of malaria. "By the way Mac." The Prime Minister looked pleadingly at his lieutenant. "Dickie Otter, over at the Foreign Office wants an official residence for his brother-in-law, any chance?"

"No problem Alf. He can have the flat over Admiralty Arch."

"Wonderful Mac. You really are good to me, did I ever tell you that before?"

"Too many fucking times," thought Condo, wishing he had the guts to put his thoughts into words.

The Prime Minister was allowed three more pints, after which he was well away and loath to depart the premises. He could only be induced to leave on being offered a bribe by his two henchmen, if he would agree to return to Number Ten and sober up. Then the following night, his last of freedom before the return of the gorgon, then Mac and Condo would take him to dinner at the Aspidistra. That did the trick, the Asp, as it was known to the cognoscenti, was one of those ludicrous eateries which made the average punter wait three months for a table. Celebrities, or at least those who had appeared twice on the telly over the last ten years, were admitted at a moments notice. The celebs loved the place, they could eat mediocre food while being gawped at and admired by mediocre people. What more could have been asked for?

With distinct merriment, the doughty trio retraced their steps to Downing Street and the joys of governance, but fate has a nasty habit of castrating the aspirations of the undeserving of this world with an abruptness that owes absolutely nothing to Christian charity. As they staggered out of the tunnel with the Prime Minister half way through the twelfth verse of Eskimo Nell, who should be waiting for them but the Macclesfield Mouth herself, large as life and twice as sanctimonious.

"Oh shit," screamed Alfred in terror, then promptly pissed himself.

"You're drunk Alfred Sawse." Wincarnis had a talent for the egregiously obvious that was unparalleled.

"No I int" squeaked her spouse in a creditable imitation of a Vatican castrato.

"He didn't mean to Win," ingratiated Condo. "It was the shock of events. You'll never guess what has happened."

"I don't have to. Bondi Patterson texted me, which is more than you three thought to do." At least two of them had entertained no ambition to hasten her return to interfering in the processes of government, which they both thought of as their sole preserve and prerogative.

"Mac has a great plan for the future," offered Alfred, his eagerness dampened by the piddle trickling down his leg to form a puddle around his shoes which should have been polished but weren't.

"Go and clean your self up Alfred, and where is my new corset? I can't find it anywhere." The Prime Minister skedaddled before he could be coerced into disclosing the fate of the aforementioned garment, leaving his two Horatii to hold the bridge against the onslaught of marital attentions. Condo was first into the breach.

"Look on the bright side. With the Queen now gone, at least things are starting to move in our direction. It's only a matter of time before we foreclose on Charles. Mac and I have quite a good game plan to deal with the scenario."

"Why is it I get the impression neither of you two beauties has grasped the true nature of the situation?"

"Steady on Win," blustered Macmurdo. "The Queen's gone, that's a start."

"But she has not gone anywhere you gormless clots."

"Now Win," explained Condo, rather as one would highlight to the cerebrally challenged, the mechanics of counting from one to two. "She has abdicated. Abdicated."

"Yes, as Queen of this country you fools. Not of anywhere else. Lord knows what trouble she can cause for us from Canada or Australia. The Aussies would love to use her to stick the boot in. Am I getting through to you two now?"

The answer of course was that she had. Wincarnis left them in order to pursue the case of the lost corset while Mac and Condo hurried off to find someone to sack. Somebody had to be blamed for their not realising the true import of the abdication and they were united in their resolve that it sure as hell was not going to be one of them.

2.

Life in Number Ten continued along its accustomed pattern, that is, everyone associated with the building continued with practiced diligence to pretend they knew what they were doing when, naturally, they did not. The civil servants, who certainly had a few solutions to hand, naturally kept such wisdom to themselves, to do otherwise would be to jeopardise their pensions, therefore they continued to say yes to everything while privately marvelling at the gullibility of the electorate who had placed such a shower in office in the first place.

The day after her return from Azerbaijan, Wincarnis convened a cabinet meeting, as Macmurdo had commandeered the cabinet room at Number Ten for his office, that august body had taken to meeting in the canteen of what had been the Ministry Of Ag And Fish before that department had been abolished. As the urban sophisticates of London logically pointed out, what did the nation need with agriculture when everyone knew that food came from Tesco's. The Cabinet had huffed and puffed and generally argy-bargied to no visible outcome. They were utterly baffled, the press was hostile, blaming them for the abdication, and, what was worse, there was an unalloyed enthusiasm for the new king, which the Cabinet felt to be most disloyal of the voters. The Prime Minister suggested that as the Telegraph had obviously been given inside information, then perhaps that publication should be allowed to rape the front door letterbox of Number Ten. That particular offering was slapped down hard, fast and brutally by Wincarnis, who was having none of that nonsense thank you very much.

Seeing that the Prime Minister had no stomach for any more proposals, and the rest of the cabinet appreciated it was not their place to contribute, Condo stepped in to revive the enthusiasm of those assembled by pointing out that the sensible option would be to recall all the telephonists and secretaries etc. now on maternity leave, which would if nothing else improve the chances of those in government of knowing what was going on in the World. This sensible addition to what passed as discussion in these circles, was put down by Wincarnis with the same ruthless lack of subtly she routinely employed in silencing her spouse. Apparently, principles came first and principles decreed all females should have maternity leave.

That was how events stood, when, like the resurrection, all hell broke loose on the third day and Downing Street was filled with doubting Thomases. Once again, it was Alice Gunthorpe who lit the blue torch paper. Alice burst into the private flat at Number Ten brandishing that mornings Daily Telegraph much as would Boadicea would have flourished a gelding knife while in search of a legionnaire's testicles. Wincarnis was outraged as only the socialist intelligentsia could be, when confronted by the servants stepping out of line she would have given the cleaning woman a thorough dressing down, only Alice got in first.

"Whore of Babylon. Whited sepulchre. You two are an abomination in the sight of the Lord. It's all your fault." She screeched at Wincarnis. "And yours." Here she turned her attention to Alfred. "She's your wife, you should control her. Any man would, but you are not a man, she neutered you years ago." The Prime Minister thought a little pacification might not go amiss, but was given no opportunity to put his theory into practice, Alice had foolishly paused for breath and Wincarnis had stepped in.

"That's enough woman. You're fired, and don't think of going to a tribunal because we're the Government and we can't be sued. Now get out."

"I'm going you slack mouthed trollop. I would not stay under this roof another minute." Before stalking out of the room, she flung the paper at Wincarnis feet. "Read that, yer lah-di-dah cow." The Prime Minister retrieved the paper from under his spouse's feet, intent on disposing of the sacrilegious artefact before his wife realised what it was that had so nearly come into contact with her. Alice had the satisfaction of hearing pronounced moaning as she descended the stairs which led to the ministerial quarters. Alfred handed the paper to his wife, the headline consisted of one word. ABDICATION.

The rest of the paper was dedicated to the abdication of King Charles III. The paper carried detailed stories from the usual "Palace sources", saying that the King, feeling he was being undermined by the Government, felt he could not continue in office under those circumstances. This was not strictly true, the Government had not undermined the King, but that was only because they had not yet got their act together and started to, but the ammunition had been stockpiled ready for firing all right. For once Wincarnis was gob smacked, the dame could not say one word, she had the political nouse to realise that the great British public might start getting a wee bit restive.

The public was not restless, it was damned angry, it sensed that someone was playing ducks and drakes with their constitution. Having observed the Government assiduously infer, by word and by deed what it thought of the Monarchy, and what the fate of that institution should be in the civilized, rationalised Utopia it was determined to construct out of what had been a green and pleasant land, the people were no doubt whatsoever, where the blame for these unfolding events should be placed.

The Cabinet had scurried over to the canteen at Ag and Fish for an emergency session. Those who had not the prescience to use the tunnels, had been un-nerved by the crowds which seethed along Whitehall looking for government ministers on which to vent their displeasure in the antique manner, i.e., with a pelting of eggs and tomatoes, topped off with a ducking in the nearest available expanse of water. It would have been a brave politician who would have dared throw a punch at one of that lot, they were out for blood on this occasion.

As the cabinet waited for Wincarnis to arrive, they were further unsettled by a strange noise. This turned out to be the crowds, estimated at a million plus, who had surrounded Buckingham Palace and had taken to belting out the National Anthem and Rule Britannia with obvious enthusiasm and an imperfect appreciation of musicality.

Fear of the mob had one beneficial side effect on the Cabinet. While they were all republicans, Wincarnis had encouraged them to be more articulate about this collective enthusiasm than they would otherwise have considered prudent. With the crowds baying for their blood, they, like the folk on the streets of the capital, knew exactly where the blame was going to be laid to rest. The jollifications kicked off the moment Wincarnis took her seat. The opening salvo was provided by the Deputy Prime Minister, a specimen who managed to make a complete fist of everything he attempted, including reading his name from a printed sheet.

"What's that fucking bitch doing here?" he bellowed. Condo and Mac exchanged smirks, before the meeting, Mac had primed the fool with a few shots of Jack Daniels. "Get back to your knitting woman, this is men's work." The politically correct indoctrination mandatory for all Cabinet Ministers had obviously not penetrated the epidermis of this individual.

"Bert!" Exclaimed the Prime Minister, rising to the defence of his wife, not because he thought she needed defending, he did not, but he was more frightened of her than he was of the crowds outside, they at least had no chance of getting at him. "That's totally out of order." Bert cared not one whit for his leader's displeasure, he was one of the few around that table who had actually worked his passage through the ranks of life. He was as common as muck and disproportionately proud of the fact, to the Prime Minister the man was the token peasant who had to be endured for the sake of party unity.

"And what's that wanker doing here?" He croaked, jabbing his finger in the direction of Macmurdo. "Another bastard who's never had the guts to face the voters. Alfie's bully boy." Condo smiled contentedly, he'd had a quiet word with Bert before Mac had had the chance to get to him.

"Right," snapped Wincarnis. "You've had your fun, now pipe down and listen to what you are going to do."

"You're not telling us damn all any more," yelled the Foreign Secretary from somewhere down wind of Wincarnis, a man who had not spoken for so long folk actually wondered if he knew how to.

"Shut up the lot of you" Wincarnis took one of her Doc Martins off and banged the table with it. "Some of you are forgetting who is the boss around here."

"Oh no we're not," chorused the assembled nobodies, their performance resembling a mass audition for the part of Widow Twankey. Chameleon like the Prime Minister's face adapted to the circumstances of the occasion and went a shade not dissimilar to a Ruabon brick.

The Cabinet meeting continued for some time, the incipient rebellion eventually collapsed into self pity and was rounded off by a weeping and a wailing and a gnashing of teeth, at least by those who had remembered to put them in there was.

Later that day the real cabinet met in Macmurdo's office, it consisted of Mac himself, Condo and Wincarnis. They had not quite figured out how to handle the situation, but an agreement had been accommodated along several salient points. The Earth shattering decision had been taken to add the Daily Telegraph to the index of permitted reading matter at Downing Street, although this privilege had been restricted to Mac, Condo and Wincarnis. Condo tried to have the maternity leave cancelled - principles were all very well, but at the end of the day, survival took precedence. Unfortunately Wincarnis could not be budged on this one. Finally, the most heretical move of all, Sir Percy Tcherkoff's name was to be added to the official invitation list. The old fool obviously had inside sources of information at the palace and these needed to be tapped.

So ended the second abdication of the week. William V had been proclaimed king, the people adored him, and Wincarnis who had been seriously religious all her life, came close to a falling out with the Almighty.

CHAPTER VII.

Wincarnis Sawse stood by the doors to the pillared drawing room at Ten Downing Street gritting her teeth in anger. She felt the substance of her power seeping away from her, and unable to put a finger on the how or the why, it merely served to increase her irritation with the hand fate had determined to deal her. That any of this could be ascribed to her own meddling would have been inconceivable to her, though not to her husbands chief advisors, who had long despaired of her regularly manicured fingers being superglued to the levers of power.

For Wincarnis, it was bad enough going about the place feeling like Caesar on the Ides of March, without having to entertain the man she hated most in the universe, and Lord knows that was a list so long it trailed from the tangible present to the edges of obscurity. Old Perce Tcherkoff, Knight of the Bath, and God bear witness to the fact he was hardly ever out of one, fearing the merest whiff of body odour would cause folk to think him common, had been duly appended to the invitation list and was expected to arrive any moment, probably before the caterers, who operated under the name of Revolutionary Grub. Whether the grub was revolutionary, no body quite knew as the company had never managed to turn up on time for any of their bookings, but as the outfit was owned by one of Wincarnis's brothers they continued to get lots of Government contracts. If all that was not enough to drive a Seventh Day Adventist teetotaller to moonshine, then the continuing mystery as to what had happened to her peach satin corset had still not been solved, she had been too busy with affairs of state to take the matter up with her husband so far, but she had certainly not forgotten the matter, and he knew it.

"Anyone arrived yet?" Asked the P.M. of his spouse, a redundant enquiry as the room was empty. People tended to turn up late and leave early at Prime Ministerial soirees, even supporters and true believers in the cause found the boredom of these events an insufferable burden, not that they blamed Alfred, they knew him to be of a convivial disposition under the skin and were alert as to where onus for the dreariness of these all too frequent dos fell.

Slowly and with reluctance the guests trickled in, shaking hands with the presidential couple as they passed through the doors. On the advice of Condo, Wincarnis had employed a fashionable minimalist decorator, who had painted the walls canary yellow and removed every stick of furniture. Over the Mantelpiece, a notice proclaimed "Rejoice o ye of cheerful heart." Well at least someone in the joint had a sense of humour even if the tenant in chief did not.

Normally, Percy would have been early for such a do, practically arriving with the milk, but his elevation to knighthood had made him even grander than he was before, as one of his less reverent journalists had commented "The bastard won't even have a piss these days unless there is someone to hold his dick for him." A consequence of this haute grandeur was that he was late for everything, feeling it to be incumbent on himself to keep the lesser mortals waiting. Percy was one of the last to be greeted by a smile from Wincarnis that would have put the wind up Count Dracula. Wincarnis managed a frigid "Good evening," her husband could not even manage that, he was too busy smiling.

Percy looked around the room. It was deserted and he was mortified. He thought he had not been late enough. A waiter grabbed him by the lapel.

"In 'ere mate," hissed the man, dragging Perce into an adjoining room. The grub had not arrived from Revolutionary Catering, but Condo had taken the precaution, based on passed experience, of ordering from an alternative supplier. The waiter plied Percy with refreshment, a glass of alcohol free Chardonnay for one hand and a tofu burger for the other one. Percy could not look anything other than disgusted with the muck he was expected to consume. "Don't worry about this crap," continued the waiter. "None of 'em like the stuff, you just nip down the stairs and out the window, you'll find them all around the corner in front of the whips office."

Percy took the proffered advice and soon found himself in a different world where about two hundred people were crammed onto a small patch of lawn indulging in all sorts of activities such as smoking, knocking back gin by the bucketful and guzzling bacon butties. There was even entertainment in the form of the Chief whip belting out dirty ditties while thumping away on a battered old Joanna. Of course, this was all far beneath the dignity of the great editor, but what the hell, anything was better than that funeral parlour upstairs.

Macmurdo sauntered over to Percy, his nostrils flaring in excitement like a dog encountering a lamppost.

"Nice to see you here Sir Percy, and congrats on your K. I can't think why it took you so long to get one."

"Because your lot blocked it, you four eyed, buck toothed son of a bitch," thought the newly minted knight. What he actually replied with was an enigmatic smile, for Percy knew exactly why he had been invited and why Macmurdo was keen to extend the hand of camaraderie to him, he might spend an overly large proportion of his allotted span trying to fool the populace that he was posher than God, but he was first and foremost a Grub Street hack of the old school. No insincerity was too great a sacrifice to make in the pursuit of a good story. "Neither can I Mac. Life's a bastard isn't it? Talking of bastards, I notice the caterers didn't turn up again," Macmurdo winced, his bosses missus had an endless supply of siblings and they were always popping up from some corner of the globe or other. Unfortunately none of them was legit, they were all on the wrong side of the blanket, a sore point with Wincarnis, who had banned the use of the word bastard. This was an action which nevertheless could not alter the fact that her family tree was littered with them.

"One of the first lady's little foibles," said Mac, "a little too smoothly to qualify for a certificate of sincerity"

"Do I detect a whiff of mutiny in the ranks of the righteous believers Mac?"

"Now you know better than to ask a question like that Sir Percy" Replied Macmurdo, his evasion supplying the answer. "I see the Telegraph's circulation is going through the roof of late. Bondi won't like that."

"There's a lot Bondi won't like that's coming his way," replied Percy.

"What aren't you telling me Perce old son," said Mac, with an unaccustomed mateyness which Percy felt bordered on Lèse majesté. "You got a private line to Buck House then?"

"As if," smiled Percy.

"Nice drop of gin this," Macmurdo took the hint and busied himself with topping up Percy's rations. Macmurdo spent another half an hour keeping his guest in gin before the great man declared it time for him to go.

"There's a story I'm working on at the moment" said Percy, giving Macmurdo a conspiratorial wink which conveyed a lot while actually saying nothing.

"I'll see you out." Macmurdo escorted his guest back to the drawing room where he made his farewells accompanied by a declaration as to how much he had enjoyed the event and looked forward to being invited again. As a reward for his observance of good manners he was treated to a diatribe from Wincarnis on the evils of the right wing press topped off with a summary on the subject of her missing corset, which amused Percy as much as it embarrassed Macmurdo and the Prime Minister. Mac hustled the great editor into the street before Wincarnis could get her second wind and return to a savaging of the right wing press and those who wrote for it.

"I'm always here if you need to talk anything over Perce, anytime, night or day."

"I thought the switchboard was down."

"Not any more. You are going to see changes around here, take it from me."

"I know you are Mac, take it from me." With this parting shot, Sir Percy marched off down Whitehall leaving Macmurdo Dunlossie a worried man. Something was brewing, Percy knew what it was, and he, Macmurdo, did not, a situation he was distinctly uncomfortable with.

2.

Macmurdo was right to be concerned. Every instinct he possessed told him there was something being carried on the wind which boded ill for his master. He could not put his finger on it, nor did he dare say anything to the Prime Minister, who was distinctly jumpy at the moment, and it was not in anyone's interest to make him any jumpier, as he would only go running to Wincarnis and God knows what the silly cow would do. "Sleep on it," he decreed to himself. "Whatever's coming can't be any worse than the last few days. Oh! The innocence of babes and spin-doctors."

Macmurdo had an uneasy night, thoughts of Shakespearean melodrama flitting between his ears along the lines of "a leak, a leak, my pension for a leak." He arose early and walked from his official residence in the old Admiralty building to his office at Number Ten. The poor man was disturbed by the smirks on the faces of the few security men and cleaners on duty at that time of the morning. He wanted to ask what was so amusing, but felt he was too important to have to descend to communing with such underlings, besides he was nervous as to the response he might receive.

The Telegraph was spread out on his desk awaiting his arrival. Some office wit had used a tube of anti diarrhoea tablets as a paperweight. Macmurdo took one look at the headlines then fainted clean away. ABDICATION. Such was the shock, Macmurdo was out for all of twenty minutes. Finally he came around, his return to consciousness prompted by Wincarnis kicking him in the ribs. The Prime Minister was crouched under the table sobbing his eyes out while Condo stood in the doorway looking as if he had lost a fiver and found a Soho rent boy.

"It's not my fault," wailed Macmurdo.

"Nor mine," blubbed the Prime Minister from under the table.

"It's nobody's fault is it," drawled Wincarnis, practicing her sarcasm in case she had to give a television interview. "And you can wipe that grin off your face Condo, you're in this right up to your false eyelashes." Condo managed to look suitably contrite, no point in antagonising the old cow when he might be able to swing things around to his advantage. "Nobody is to blame," continued the Macclesfield mouth. "You're all innocent aren't you? I don't think! There was that pompous old poser Tcherkoff round here last night, practically eating us out of house and gravy train, and not one of you three had the gumption to winkle anything out of him. He was giving us the run around and enjoying every minute of it, and what did you lot do? Shook his hand and told him to drop in any time he fancied like it was open day at the bookies.

Her tirade was greeted by the silence of the petrified. In this mood she was capable of giving them all the sack, including the Prime Minister, not that the poor dab would be missed by anyone in authority. Wincarnis ordered the Telegraph to be photocopied, when this was done, she sat down with the other two members of the Government to study the publication. Happy reading for them it was not, Henry IX was now Sovereign Lord. The paper devoted itself to praising the new king while damning the Government for sedulously undermining the Royal House to the extent that none of it's senior members felt it worthwhile to take up the torch. The Telegraph speculated that at this rate it would only be a matter of time before the succession passed to some minor Balkan princeling who would leap at the chance to jump the queue of asylum seekers.

The people were none too pleased with the way things were panning out and were inclined to accept the Telegraphs version of events. Up to now, folk had contented themselves with grumbling into their beer, but with the loss of their beloved William, crowds had gathered outside the Palace calling for the king, although nobody could be quite sure which king would come out and wave to them. One enterprising spark had hijacked a number twenty-four bus on Victoria Street and taken it to Knightsbridge Barracks, where the passengers were induced to fill up the vehicle with manure. The bus was then driven to Horse Guards Parade, where people were soon lining up to chuck horse turds over the garden wall of Downing Street at fifty pence a go. One of these organic projectiles went sailing through the open window of Macmurdo's office.

"What on earth is that?" shrieked Wincarnis, fearful one of the plebs was trying to do a Sarajevo on her.

"You should know, you speak enough of it," mumbled Macmurdo, his courage starting to return, although not to the degree where he was ready to try his hand at open mutiny.

"What was that you said?" snapped Wincarnis.

"Just clearing my throat, nothing more." Mac even managed to smile as he spoke, a not inconsiderable achievement when taking into account his true feelings for his bosses wife. Both Mac and Condo had reached a tacit understanding that the woman would have to be neutralised, politically spayed, before she brought the roof down on all of them. Life as currently lived was too sweet to be sacrificed to the whims of a silly old bint who could not grasp the horizon of her own limitations.

"Well what are you going to do about all this?" Wincarnis gave them her best scowl. "Listen to that mob out there, they're singing now. I ask you, singing."

"Rule Britannia I think," said Condo pretending to be helpful while knowing full well would be infuriated by the mention of the patriotic hymn.

"Not again! it's disgusting. That song's racist. It should have been banned years ago." Wincarnis was all for banning things she did not approve of, and as there was so little in this world which did meet with her approbation, that left an awful lot of banning to be gotten through. Little wonder rule Britannia had slipped through the net. "I'm waiting" she continued. "I want solutions and if I don't get them, you two are going to be spinning in the dole queue." Macmurdo lunged at the chance to burnish his fading image.

"We'll announce a three billion increase in the health budget."

"We've already done that," snapped Wincarnis.

"Yes, but that was all of three months ago. The daft sods will have forgotten by now and think it's a new initiative. Don't forget it's promises, not payments, which win elections.

"It will take more than a few tried and tested fibs to shut that lot up," announced Condo indicating the horse turds which continued to fly through the air. We have to distract their attention. As I said the other day, get to work on the envy factor. Start banging on about the Royal's money and all those relations in Kensington Palace."

"OK," said Wincarnis. "But this time do something about it."

"I will," promised Condo. We still have enough influence in the press to get our message out, a few more knighthoods should do the trick.

"Very well," agreed Wincarnis. "Get on to it straight away. I don't want any time lost."

"One thing though Win." Condo was at his oleaginous best.

"What's that then?" she enquired resigned to having to cave in to some outrageous demand.

"We have to get communications back to standard. Those on maternity leave will have to be brought back." He smiled at Wincarnis, knowing he'd get what he wanted, and she, recognising his tactics for what they were, directed at him a look of over-riding venom, which completely negated the effects of her plastic surgery.

"Done," she snarled, determined to settle once and for all with Condo once they were safely out of the woods." Let's get to work then." Macmurdo and Condo followed her out of the room, the Prime Minister was still under the table sobbing away, so the others left him to his misery, he would only get in the way if there was serious work to be done and there was no ironing for him to occupy his time with.

3.

The best laid plans of mice and men are said to go astray with enervating regularity, which is nothing in comparison to what happens when governments lose their grip, a situation which descends with ferocious speed, taking its victims entirely unawares. This administration possessed no immunity to the laws of random come-uppance, all governments at some time in their existence must submit to these unpalatable dictates, and are judged by history on the grace with which they submit to the inevitable. Predictably the current outfit were unstintingly graceless.

For the first time, its resident stooges in the media had declined to parrot the Government's line on events. There were more exciting stories to print than one about a few obscure royals living in Kensington Palace of whom the populace at large had heard little and cared less, the Nation was on the move and that was what the press wanted to record. There were riots in the streets and Whitehall and Parliament Square had been closed off with police barricades. Things were starting to look ugly, this was more than a case of the Proles letting off steam between elections, and there was a definite change in the national mood. Up to now, politicians had been despised but tolerated, there now came about a sense that people had taken enough from the remote intellectual elite who ruled them with openly patronising contempt, and there was a reckoning in the air. The Government was frightened.

Of all who sat at the top table of the establishment, there was one who remained largely unperturbed by the history that was knitting it's future at her feet. Wincarnis, who, had she sported a bolt through the neck could have won a Frankenstein look-alike competition on any day of the last millennium may have been forced to give ground over the Telegraph and maternity leave, but there was a limit to her concessions. The refusal of the media to play ball had sent the woman into epileptic spasms of rage, she saw conspiracies everywhere and lashed out accordingly. Apart from the Deputy Prime Minister, who did not give a damn, there was nobody to stand up to her, and she neutralised Bert by striking him off the list of those entitled to attend Cabinet meetings and by moving his office to a disused dockyard in Newcastle.

It was largely due to Wincarnis that the Government announced that it would not continue to fund the Civil List. This would normally have attracted banner headlines, but the intelligence was banished to the inside pages as the Telegraph announced the abdication of king Henry. Long Live King Andrew.

By this time the public were tearing up the paving stones in the streets and the time was long gone when they would be content with lobbing a few turds over the garden wall of Number Ten. Macmurdo along with Condo was at his wits end, for all either of them knew was how to spin the news and now that tactic no longer worked they were at a loss as to how to cope with a situation developing at a pace greater intellects than theirs found difficulty in grasping.

King Andrew did not last any longer than any of his immediate predecessors, he too abdicated, to be succeeded by Queen Beatrice. By this time the commercial life of the country had, for all practical purposes come to a halt, as people were too busy rioting or looking for M.P.s to duff up, to waste time on going to work.

In all this turmoil Sir Percy Tcherkoff had never had it so good, he had become a national celebrity. The nation was privileged to be able to appreciate those traits of snobbery and pomposity the observance of which had been one of the consolation prizes of working in Fleet Street. The man was never off the box, he had become more famous than the nations favourite brand of dog food. After all it was his paper that had made all the abdication announcements, it was his paper which had the inside information. He obviously knew exactly what was going on, but true to his pact with Sir Ralph Settles, he only told what he had been instructed to tell and nothing more.

When Sir Percy was not pontificating in front of the cameras or engaged in the editing of his newspaper, he was being monopolised by a Macmurdo Dunlossie desperate to get any info that was going, and while Percy talked a lot, he actually said nothing, a fact that only became apparent long after the conversation was over and done with. Such was Macmurdo's desperation, he continued to court Sir Percy, who remarked to one of his sub editors at the Telegraph, with a crudity that owed more to his antecedents than it did to his present social eminence.

"If that Scotch fucker kisses my arse any more, I'll have more bruises on my ring than Wincarnis has on her ego at the moment." That one had done the rounds of Fleet Street within the hour, before the day was out it had reached the ears of Macmurdo, who could not have afforded to take umbrage, much as he would have like to have given Percy a smack in the chops. Mac promptly invited Percy to dine with him at the Aspidistra for some cheap grub washed down with expensive Claret.

The accession of Queen Beatrice removed what was left of a backbone from the body politic, headless torsos of chickens came readily to mind when in search of what passed as a government. So wrapped up was the administration in its survival prospects; it failed to grasp the salient outcome of King Andrew's abdication. It was left to Sir Perce, half way through his second bottle of Chateau Petrus, to point out that Queen Beatrice was a minor who could not abdicate and would require a Regent. The buck had come to rest. Macmurdo was completely stunned by this exposition, it had so impaired his vocal faculties, he could not even protest when his guest ordered a magnum of vintage Krug at a price which would have fed a family of four for a month.

CHAPTER VIII.

Her Canadian Majesty had been having quite a day of it, and it was not yet lunchtime. Most of us at some time or another in our misspent lives, have paid for our transgressions with a diamond studded outbreak of the screaming ab-dabs, brought about by nothing more innocuous than moving from one three bed roomed semi to another, along with our accumulated goods and chattels, it can therefore be imagined, the trouble undergone by Her Majesty when packing up the accretions of centuries from a string of palaces each the size of a small town in acreage. For the past week, fleet after fleet of containers were heading for Liverpool docks where ships of the Royal Canadian Navy were waiting to transfer the treasures of the house of Windsor to their new home in Canada. Sir Ralph poked his head round the door to the room where Her Majesty was directing the packing of family memorabilia.

"Ah, Ralph, have you found it yet? I'm not budging without it, been in the family since fifteen forty-seven."

"No mam, still looking, but I have found the Canadian High Commissioner."

"Well that's as much use to me as Charles old high chair, what pray do I want with that old bugger? I'm far too busy packing, tell him to clear off."

"I think you should see him mam, if only to give him instructions regarding your accommodation in Canada."

"Our accommodation Ralph. You are coming too, whether you like it or not." Sir Ralph looked a mite crestfallen, with the Queen safely on the other side of the pond, he'd formulated a plan to open a sauna and fitness centre in Brighton. All he could manage in response to the royal will, was a desultory.

"Yes mam."

"And don't sulk man, I can't abide people sulking, I won't have it." He offered up what he hoped could be misconstrued as a smile, before putting two fingers in his mouth, in order to produce a piercing whistle, which had the effect of conjuring up Her Majesty's Canadian Representative, who came charging into the room only to fall over one of the Corgis, who took umbrage at such treatment and bit Sir Ralph.

"Lovely doggie," purred the Commissioner, repositioning himself from the horizontal as fast as rheumatism would permit. The Queen was delighted, as she always was when people took the trouble to praise her pooches.

"He is, isn't he?" enthused the Queen. "Ralph, take Clarence for a walk, and make sure he goes this time." Clarence, who had no desire to go anywhere with Sir Ralph, instead attempted to transform the courtiers leg into his dinner, and chased the shrieking fellow down the passage, much to the Queen's amusement.

"That fellows no good with animals. I don't know why I keep him on." The Commissioner replied with a few suitably ingratiating phrases, but Her Majesty was not in the mood, besides, she'd heard it all before. "Yes, yes, most gratifying, but I am pressed for time and you are running out of it. Has Sir Ralph given you a copy of my plans?" She did not wait for an answer, secure in the knowledge that her wishes would be carried out to the letter. "Good. That's all then. Now off you go, oh, and be a dear, let the dog out on your way." Bemused by the abruptness of the reception he had received, the diplomat retreated in the face of disinterest, clutching a thick manila package, which Sir Ralph had previously given him.

"Not even a glass of Sherry," he grumbled on the way out. "You'd think they would have given me a glass of Sherry."

The Queen continued with her preoccupations, frustration mounting within her.

"Where the hell is it?" she fumed. "It's supposed to be in this room, it's always kept in here." She kicked the piano in a sublime outburst of irritation.

"Where's what?" Princess Anne stood behind her mother, arms akimbo, hair in curlers, the whole coiffure topped off by a head scarf done up in a turban.

"King Henry's doo-dah. I can't find it anywhere."

"Oh that. Come off it ma, you're not going to take that old thing with us are you?"

"Yes, I am. It's a priceless relic."

"If it's priceless that's only because you couldn't give the damn thing away. For God's sake, who in their right mind would want that thing on their sideboard?" The object in question was an old oak and brass reliquary, which legend insisted contained Henry the Eighth's dick, pickled for posterity and handed down ever since in the Royal Family.

"I am not going anywhere without King Henry's doo-dah and that's the end of the matter."

"Well if you must know, I do know where it is. Charles gave it to the Archbishop of Canterbury, told him it was the inspiration for the Christmas Carol Ding Dong Merrily On High. I believe the old fool plans to feature it on his Christmas Card, not that he refers to it as a Christmas Card these days, might offend somebody y'know."

The Queen picked up the telephone. "Ralph. That you? Get on the phone to the Prince of Wales, tell the blighter to get himself round to Lambeth Palace. I want King Henry's doo dah back."

"Surely mam, he's ex-king Charles now, not the Prince of Wales,"

"He's whatever it is I say he is and at the moment he's mincemeat if I..." Princess Anne cut her mother's diatribe off at the pass.

"Yes, yes. If you don't get old Henry's pickled dick back."

"I would not have put it that way myself. You can be so crude at times Anne. It quite distresses me." H.M. fumbled about in her handbag. "Shit. I'm clean out of Rizlas. Oh, there you are Ralph, go down to the newsagents and get me a packet of Rizlas, here's fifty pence, and don't forget the change," said his mistress with a touch of asperity, remembering that on his last errand for her into the world of commerce, he had diddled her out of twenty pence.

"Go on Ralph," said the Princess. "I want to talk to Her Majesty in private."

"Won't do you any good," opined Sir Ralph, remembering the definition of schadenfreude. "She'll not make you Regent."

"Fuck off you revolting little squirt," hissed the Princess out of the side of her mouth.

"What's that dear?"

"Just telling dear sir Ralph to hurry along. Don't dawdle Sir Ralph, Ma's gasping for a fag, aren't you ma?"

"As your Majesty pleases," whispered the courtier, and backed out of the room, silently mouthing the word bitch at the Princess as he departed. She in turn stuck two fingers up at him, then got to work on her omnipotent mother.

"Ma. Can I be Regent for Beatrice?"

"Certainly not. That has to be a political appointment, besides you'll love Canada, they're as common as dogs bollocks out there, you'll be in your element."

"But ma, I'd be in my element as Regent. I'd be ab fab at the job. I can just see me going fourteen rounds with those bloody politicians. I'd knock seven bells of shit out of them, honest I would. Six months with me and the bastards would throw in the towel, they'd be so fed up, they'd quit and actually go out and earn a living, that's if anyone could be found who would employ them, which is debatable."

"Very debatable. We did things so much better in the old days and then when a politician had reached his sell by date we just cut off his head."

"Oh go on ma, be a sport, let me be the Regent. If you do, I promise to go out and spend fifty quid on a new wardrobe."

"That's what I'm afraid of. No my girl, it's Canada for you with your brothers and their offspring. There now, think of the fun you'll have falling out with them on a regular basis."

"But I want to be Regent."

"Well you can't, and that's an end to the matter. My mind is made up."

"You haven't even told us where in Canada it is we're supposed to be going."

"Prince Edward Island."

"Where? I've never heard of it."

"Well don't let the Canadians know that, they'd be mightily offended. Actually. It's an island in the Gulf of St. Lawrence. A nice quiet little back water."

"Oh Christ. I might have known you'd pick somewhere like that. There'll be no life there, that's obvious."

"I don't know about that but there is a mission for fallen women, that should give you something to occupy your time with." So ended the conversation. Princess Anne would have liked to continue, but recognised her chances of achieving her goals were marginally below zero and falling, so she decided to cut her losses and went off to ambush Sir Ralph when he returned from the newsagents with the Queen's fag papers. She blamed the private secretary for turning her mother against the idea of Anne for regent, so therefore she would console herself by giving the poor man a thick lip.

2.

When the Prime Minister thought things could not get any worse, and fate would have to turn a gentle face in his direction and part with a gobbet of kindness, sod's law asserted it's supremacy and the whole frigging crisis became absolutely diabolical. To cap it all, Wincarnis was still banging on about her missing corset, and last night had locked him out of the building, telling him he could not return to the shelter of his loving interpersonal relationship unit until the said artefact was found and returned. This resulted in the P.M. having to spend the night in the guard's box at the gates to the street, where it was that Macmurdo found him the following morning. Macmurdo smuggled his boss in through the kitchen window. It would be imprudent for the Prime Minister to occupy his normal office in case Wincarnis discovered him, so Macmurdo set him up in a temporary office in the china pantry, sparse but adequate to the man's needs, a desk, a chair and a jigsaw puzzle of the Newcastle gas works, which should be enough to occupy him for the next three days.

Leaving the Prime Minister to his jig saw, Mac made his way to his own office and the problems of the day, most of which, he guessed would have been caused by Wincarnis. Out of the corner of his eye, he caught sight of Condo on his way upstairs. "Probably going to butter up the old witch," he reasoned. He settled himself at his desk, ordering coffee and the papers to be sent in. The headlines in the Telegraph put him clean off his coffee. "DODGY SHARE DEALING IN DOWNING STREET." There it was in black and white, every detail. Naturally he would deny it, but these days people were having the impertinence to question his veracity, not that had not always been the case, it was just that these days a disquieting number of folk had disinterred the amount of guts necessary to call him a liar to his face.

The report the Telegraph had published was simple in its essentials, using companies registered offshore, Mac and Condo, using money borrowed from Bondi Patterson, who had thought he was lending the dosh to refurbish the party headquarters, had invested heavily in shares in the Telegraph group. Due to what the public erroneously thought were the papers stunning insights into the constitutional crisis, the papers circulation had gone through the roof and the share price lost no time in galloping after it. Macmurdo and Condo, between them had made a staggering bundle. Now here was the telly blowing the gaff, ain't life a bitch!

Mac followed his instincts and hid the offending journal under the sofa, Wincarnis still had not relaxed her rules regarding the admission of radio and T.V. to Downing Street, so there was a fighting chance it would still be a fair while before notice of the scandal was brought before the imperial couple. As rational analysis went, that one was fairly commendable, by the time Alf, or, more probably, Wincarnis started to ask questions, he would have had a chance to concoct a plausible explanation, which in the normal run of things is what would have happened, but alas, these were not normal times, and destiny was in a skittish mood, eager to widdle on the boots of the unwary.

Unbeknownst to Mac, Condo had seen Alf being smuggled in via the kitchen window. He was on his way to work, and therefore unaware of the background to the situation, but avid to get one up on his rival, he went rushing up to the private flat to enquire of Wincarnis why Macmurdo was assisting her husband through the kitchen window. He could not in his wildest dreams have anticipated her reaction, to trample on the corns of delicacy in search of an aphorism, she went ape shit. Fortunately for Macmurdo, her screams and imprecations, echoing through the house, alerted him to the fact that something was up. Cowardice being the guiding light of politics, he high tailed it next door to discuss the economic situation with the Chancellor, who could not stand him, but, by the time the guardian of the national kitty had digested whatever codswallop it was that Macmurdo was able to come up with on the spur of the moment, and told it's perpetrator to "Fuck off back to that bloody wanker next door who pinched my job," things would have simmered down.

It did not take Wincarnis long to locate her errant spouse, he was perfectly content with his jig saw, and the cook had taken pity on him with a donation of instant coffee and a plate of tofu burgers left over from last night's do, Wincarnis did not approve of waste. The Prime Minister did not see his wife until it was too late and she had crept up behind him with calculated stealth, predatory as would a cobra have been on sighting a harmless bunny taking its afternoon nap.

"Gotcha." She grabbed him by the shirt collar and yanked him to his feet, the poor man was too terrified to protest. "I told you that you don't come back in here until I get my corset back. Three hundred and fifty pounds that cost me." The cook pretended to be busy opening tins of baked beans as Wincarnis dragged her quivering spouse from his sanctuary, then up the stairs to the front door, several members of the staff looking on horrified at the spectacle, including Condo, who promptly hid behind the harmonium in the front hall as he heard Wincarnis approaching. She opened the famous door, and thrust the Prime Minister out into the street. "And don't come back without my corset," she screamed in a voice which could have been heard the other side of St. James Park.

This modern version of a Christian being savaged by a wild animal did not go unnoticed, the entire press corps was assembled in the street to hear a statement on the latest abdication, and were hanging about, as is customary on such occasions, waiting for the

Government to think up something plausible to say, instead, this time they had something worthy of their attention. The sight of the Prime Minister being slung out by his missus wiped the latest abdication from their minds and concentrated their attentions on the marital status of the first couple.

"Why'd she sling yer out Alf?"

"Do you think it anti feminist to be the dominant partner in the marriage?" That was the Guardian.

"How's your sex life Prime Minister? Are you getting enough?"

At this point, the Prime Minister finally lost the plot and fled back to the sentry box where he had spent the night. Fortunately, Macmurdo had seen what was going on, he rescued the prime minister from the sentry box and hid him in the Treasury Passage, where the domestics were allowed to park their bikes.

"What the fuck am I going to do Mac? How did she find out where I was? You did not split on me did you?"

"Course I didn't. I bet Condo's behind this."

"Oh, he wouldn't do that to me, I trust Condo, he'd never dob me in, I'm certain of that." Mac ordinarily would have argued the toss, but as events were moving so fast, his options were severely circumscribed.

"We've got to get you away from here now. There is a Cabinet meeting."

"I did not know about that."

"The Chancellor just demanded it. I had to give way, no option."

"Do you think he'll cause trouble?"

"That bastard's been causing trouble since the election, what makes you think he'd suddenly change his ways?"

"Will Wincarnis be there?"

"No. We decided to keep it to ourselves." The Prime Minister's eyes lit up, in the absence of his wife he might get to say something.

"But how will we get to the tunnel? She won't let me back in the house."

"Don't worry Alf, I've got an idea, you wait here." He patted the Prime Minister on the head. "I'll be back in a jiff, just huddle down behind them bikes." With that he bustled off to the back door. Constrained behind the barriers, the press could not see their quarry, but they could scent his fear, which they continued to encourage with a blast furnace of journalistic whimsy.

"Who wears the trousers in your house Alf?"

"Is it true that Wincarnis rules the country while you iron the knickers?"

By the time Macmurdo returned, the Prime minister would have consented to anything provided it took an oath to release him from his predicament, which was just as well considering the rescue package Macmurdo had devised. Mac dumped a large furry bundle at the Prime Minister's feet, it was the horse's costume which should have been used in the staff panto, however, Wincarnis did not approve of pantomimes and the performance had been cancelled, but not before a considerable amount of money had been spent on scenery and costumes, money which had as its source the Home Office stationary budget.

"Here you are. Get into this," said Mac, handing his dear leader the section of the disguise appertaining to the rear half of the costume. When properly attired, they set off for the Ministry of Ag and Fish. Macmurdo had intended to decamp via the Treasury Passage onto Horse Guards. Unfortunately the gates at the end were locked and some fool had neglected to replace the key in the jam jar which was kept in situ specifically for that purpose and this necessitated them having to make the conventional exit from Downing Street. Those of the fourth estate whose wits were not permanently addled by expense account whiskey and contraband fags, immediately cottoned on to what was up, jumped the barriers and set off down Whitehall in pursuit of the vaguely moth eaten dobbin.

Respect for the Prime Minister, wilting in the heat of public contempt, did not encourage the press corps to temper their questions with either mercy or good taste, concepts, it must be admitted they were not entirely cognoscent of.

"Which end are you Prime Minister?"

"Trust the Guardian not to be able to work that one out. You're the horse's arse aren't you Alf.'

"Hey Alf. Is it true you have to put a request in writing to Wincarnis if you want to get your leg over?"

The tenor of this questioning had an unsettling effect on Macmurdo, so flustered had the man become, that he swung a right turn too soon and ended up on the embankment. Pursued every inch of the way by the sweating reporters, the panto horse trotted along the embankment, up Northumberland Avenue to Trafalgar Square, before finally stumbling back onto Whitehall and the Ministry of Ag and Fish, where their colleagues awaited them in the canteen.

3.

Politicians are like professional trollops in as much as that they sincerely and forever love those who at any particular moment who are giving them what it is they want, which is primarily to win elections, a duty the Prime minister had, up to now found no difficulty in performing. But the waters of perfidy were beginning to trickle over the ankles of the parliamentary party. The electorate, ungrateful bastards that they were, took to giving unmistakable hints that they believed there was not a politician born whose moral integrity could not but be improved by the act of being strung up from the nearest lamp-post, and in consequence of this, their lords and masters in Parliament were becoming more than a little jittery. The rumblings of discontent amongst the cabinet were on the point of fermenting into open rebellion, fear putting guts into the body of the vintage.

News of the manner of Alf and Macmurdo's escape from Downing Street had preceded them. On entering the canteen, still in their disguise, a great cheer went up, and it was not one of encouragement or support. Alf and

Macmurdo struggled out of their costumes and took their places at the table.

"We don't want to waste time," rapped Macmurdo, determined to take charge for the home team before either he or they had a chance to discover whether old fashioned backbone formed any discernable feature of their physiognomy, and took it in hand to launch the storming of the Bastille, which Alfred and his cronies had come to represent to the rest of the Government.

"So, Let's get on with it before anything else happens." What he really meant was that they should conclude their business before Wincarnis discovered what they were up to and stuck her oar in.

"I'm for a republic," declared the Chancellor, to the surprise of no one. "This is an historic opportunity to remould the nation. We should stick to our principles and to hell with trying to grab a bit of cheap popularity with that rabble out there on the streets." What the man actually meant was, and this was perfectly understood by the rest of his colleagues, that the prime minister should declare the abolition of the monarchy. The resulting outrage would sweep him from office, after which he, the chancellor and his partner, Ms. Lavender Liaison, who he did not have the desire to marry nor the guts to drop, could start measuring Number ten up for new lino. Nobody around the table was going to fall for that one, they all had their particular ambitions in that department.

There was another bar to the Cabinet going for an out and out republican regime. They were all very much against pomp and privilege, that is when those states of being were enjoyed by others, they had no reservations about themselves engineering a reverse takeover of the ancien regime. They were positively enthusiastic over the prospect, the Deputy Prime Minister had even given up going on overseas fact finding missions in order that he would not miss out on any of the impending developments. The man had actually spent three days on the trot in the country, whereas in normal circumstances he only returned every few weeks for a fresh supply of underwear and condoms. The D.P.M lost no time in staking his claim to the regency.

"As D.P.M. I've an automatic right for the job, I won't have you circumcising my authority." He sat back in his chair, smugly satisfied by his skilful rendering of the English language, a skill which had persuaded the party hierarchy to ban him from speaking anywhere near a reporter or a video recorder.

"You couldn't possibly carry off the job Bert, you just haven't got what it takes," added Condo, who had his own designs on the Regency.

"I got two fings I can bring to the job that you can't," snorted Bert.

"Oh? And what are they?"

"A pair of balls and a woman on my arm." So much for the caring sharing politically correct politics.

"Alfie! You heard that. Tell him he can't talk to me like that."

"I do Condo, repeatedly," soothed the Prime Minister, but he won't listen to me."

"Then sack him."

"Do that and we'd have to sack the whole bloody lot of them," opined the home secretary with a judicious dollop of malice.

"They've all leaked stories of your love life to Fleet Street."

"That's it." screamed condo. "I'm not staying hear to be insulted."

"Nobody asked you to," chanted all those assembled in a passable imitation of a Gregorian chant.

"That's it. I'm going," sobbed Condo in rage and frustration.

"And what's more I shall resign from the Cabinet "What, again?" trilled the Home Secretary, as if he were St. Paul seeing the light for the first time. "You are a creature of habit aren't you." To the sound of crude laughs and alludings to his sex life, Condo fled the canteen.

"Don't worry," Mac reassured the Prime Minister. "He has no more intention of resigning than you have for paying for your own holidays." The Prime Minister smiled in gratitude, he hated it when Condo had to resign, he was the only one who could handle Wincarnis, and God knows she needed handling at the moment.

"Now," said the Foreign Secretary, who was not quite so working class as the others, but nonetheless worked extra hard to cover up that social deficit. "Now that bloody poof's buggered off, let's settle this once and for all. Who's getting Buck House?"

"A vote, a vote," pleaded a minor member of the gathering, his enthusiasm smothering what little intelligence he possessed.

"As one of the few people here," intoned the Foreign Secretary. "Who married his mistress because he wanted to and not because he was told to, I can bring to the office a dignity others may have difficulty in encapsulating." He launched an anticipatory parting of the lips ninety degrees short of a smile in the direction of the Prime Minister.

"Ow posh we is all of a sudden," observed Bert, having noticed his rivals slip from the straight and narrow of working class diction.

"Gentlemen, Gentlemen." This was the prime Minister trying to take charge. "Don't forget we are brothers, we must not fight amongst ourselves."

"Why not?" asked the Trade Secretary. "We always have up to now." He was a man very new to government, his colleagues looked askance at him, the poor sap had yet to realise that to that lot, honesty of expression was considered vulgar and unprofessional. This continuous thread of bickering was broken by the Party Secretary.

"I had Bondi Patterson on the blower from New York earlier, he's bloody fuming. Wants to know how his loan to the Party to fund the headquarters refurbishment ended up buying shares for Condo and you Mac."

"A temporary divertissement Mark, nothing more. It will be returned to Party funds at the closing of settlement day. Nothing to worry about."

"Nothing to worry about," raged the Party Secretary.

"You trouser half a million quid then shrug it off. Not only that, it turns out that the excuse for lifting the dosh from Bondi in the first place was that the money was needed for the staff bog. Half a million so that a few clerks can have a crap!"

"It's the new building regs," said the Prime Minister coming to the defence of his lieutenant. The Secretary gave him a look Wincarnis would have been proud of.

"What about this flaming Regency," exploded the Home Secretary. "That's what this flaming meeting was called for in the first place and it has hardly been mentioned. There's more important things on the agenda than who fiddled with a bung from Bondi Patterson." This was followed up with a copious helping of hear hears.

"Quite right," declared Condo who had returned to the meeting having restored his equilibrium with a good cry and a snort of coke. "We are going to talk about it, and in great detail too. The Prime Minister has decided to establish a steering committee to discuss the matter in depth and take soundings." The Prime Minister beamed at this refreshing news, he did so like it when he was told what it was he had decided, it made him feel terribly important.

"That is it then," ripped Macmurdo. "Meeting over, must dash. Ta ta all." He grabbed the Prime Minister by the hand and led him off to the tunnel.

"But what happens when we get to Downing Street Mac? She won't let me in."

"She won't be there Alf. I fixed it up with Ikey before we left, she'll spend the rest of the day bottling pickles for Palestinian refugees, and when she's finished with that, she'll be spending the night in a cardboard box at Walthamstow Market to highlight the plight of the homeless. Wincarnis ain't coming back till after breakfast tomorrow."

"But Mac," said the Prime Minister uncomprehendingly. "I thought we had abolished homelessness."

"Really Prime Minister," retorted Mac, momentarily lapsing into formality. "How many times must I tell you not to believe all the Government tells you? Come on, we've work to do."

4.

The Prime Minister and Macmurdo returned to Downing Street to find Condo waiting for them, indignation wreathed around his torso like seven veils, and unlike Salome he had no intention of discarding them before he had let loose an epidemic of complaints. Macmurdo excused himself, leaving the Prime Minister to suffer the caress of Condo's indignation. Mac had been gone only fifteen minutes, insufficient time for him to dry but enough to blunt the force of his sordid fusilade.

"It's not fair Alfie, they are always saying these awful things to me. There are laws to prevent it, but what's the point of passing them if people just ignore them?"

"None at all," observed the Prime Minister, "But it looks fabulous in the Guardian when we do, they love that sort of thing."

"Honestly! The way you carry on about that rag, who reads it anyway?"

"Nobody of course, but everyone round at the Beeb pretends to, they are always running about with an expense chit in one hand and a copy of the Guardo in the other."

"Ok you two, time to get down to the nitty gritty and decide who's to be Regent," said Macmurdo on returning to the room, determined to take control of the proceedings before Condo could disengage himself from the mechanics of self pity.

"Well darlings, let's face it, it's got to be me. Nobody else, present company excepted." He looked in the direction of the Prime Minister, deliberately excluding Macmurdo from his glance, "Has the class to carry it off. Could you imagine Bert in the job? Per-lease. And as for that wife of his with her sixties hair dos and three inches of slap. We would be the laughing stock of Europe. I could just see the common trollop in the Elysee, drinking her tea out of the saucer." Condo shuddered in genuine horror, as did his audience, they could imagine only too easily such a scenario, but unlike Condo they could also see what would happen if Condo's ambitions were crowned to his satisfaction.

Condo lived with the love of his life, a status enjoyed by many previous individuals, so many in fact that it was sworn to in certain circles that you could not walk the dog along Hampstead heath without passing at least three of his former one and onlys. The current candidate for Corido's undying love was known to him affectionately as Shepherds Pie on account that the lad could not exist without a great deal of mincing. The Pie was twelve years younger than Condo, with numerous artefacts hanging out of or stitched into improbable parts of his anatomy, not all of them unfortunately hidden from the gaze of mankind. Add all that to a visage which suggested he had been attended to by a trainee undertaker who had failed parts two and three of the embalming course, then you begin to get the picture. Not quite, a tad more intelligence on the matter will be forthcoming, Condo's bantam cock loved dressing up in women's clothes whenever there was a party to go to. The thought of the repercussions of Condo, with S.P. in tow all done up in a tiara and chiffon ball gown doing the rounds at the next G8 meeting in London, sent shivers down the spines of even the densest members of the Government.

The dilemma was who could possibly tell any of this to Condo? Well everyone in the cabinet was lining up to do so, Mac being first in the queue to dish out the bad tidings. The Prime Minister however would not let them do so, not that they cared one whit for his opinions, but they were still afraid enough of Wincarnis to hold back, although nobody could figure it out why a body so intrinsically miserable as she could be so passionate about gay rights.

"You've got plenty of class Condo, nobody could deny you that." The Prime Minister was sincere.

"Yes Condo, you are in a class of your own, that's for sure, everyone says so." Mac was also sincere in his comments, but his intent was not so guileless as that of the P.M.

"There you are then," said Condo, unable to see further than his vision of S.P. dressed from head to toe in Zandra Rhodes and doing the conga down the length of the Buckingham Palace ball room, "So when do I get installed as Regent? Will it be a service at the Abbey? Ooh yes." He clapped his hands in ecstasy. "S.P. will love a carriage procession."

"I'm sure he would," thought Macmurdo. "And so would Joe Soap on the Clapham omnibus, we'd be crucified at the next election." He forbore from offering an open comment.

"Well Condo, there's an awful lot to organise isn't there? Not to mention the legislation that would have to be rammed through Parliament," soothed the Prime Minister, hoping the prevarication behind his words would not be too obvious.

"And I can have one of those long velvet cloaks with lots of ermine?" Condo was truly getting carried away with the spirit of things. The Prime Minister was hoping someone would come and carry Condo away, while at the same time wondering why Macmurdo was not doing something to get him, Alfred Sawse out of the hole Condo was digging for his benefit. The phone rang.

"Yes? Oh, right Ikey. I'll put him on." Mac held the phone out to Condo. "It's Ikey for you." Condo took the hand piece.

"Hi there Ikey. What is it?" He listened carefully

"Sure I can, what, now? OK."

"What did Ikey want?" asked Macmurdo.

"Just passing on a message. Wincarnis wants me out in Whitchapel right away, I'll have to leave at once, do you mind?"

"Not at all," reassured the Prime Minister, you get along, we'll sort things out this end."

"That's it then. I'd better be off, ta ta." And off he went, humming the tune of Zadock the Priest, the anthem composed by Handel and sung at every Coronation since that of George II.

"Well," said the Prime Minister when Condo was safely out of earshot. "That was a bit of luck, Ikey phoning up."

"Luck, Alfie boy, had nothing to do with it."

"Oh Mac, you didn't did you?"

"Of course I bloody well did. Condo's been gabbing all over the place how he'd like to be Regent. I got Ikey to head him off at the pass. He'll keep both of them out of the way until we've passed the regency Bill."

"But we haven't even got a regent," spluttered the P.M.

"Yes we have."

"Who for fuck sake?" enquired Alfred, momentarily forgetting Wincarnis' strictures on the use of bad language.

"Ivra Maninand," announced Macmurdo triumphantly. "What do you say to that then?"

"Well I admit she would be all right, but what about Wincarnis? She ain't too fond of Ivra you know."

"The bill goes before the house within the next hour. It'll have passed all stages by the time they get back tomorrow morning, by then it will be too late for her to argue."

"That's not likely to stop her Mac, you should know what she's like by now."

"This will take her mind off things," Macmurdo fished a package out of his desk. "Here, open this." The P.M. did as he was bid, he gasped audibly.

"A peach satin corset." His voice filled with admiration.

"That it is Alf."

"Mac, as she won't be back until tomorrow, do you think we could nip over to the Chairmen for a jar or two?"

"Mr. Prime Minister, I think we could."

CHAPTER IX.

Ivra Maninand was gazing in the large mirror which dominated the second drawing room of her large official residence in London's Belgravia, an activity which had occupied her time since late the previous night when Macmurdo Dunlossie, three sheets to the wind, had came staggering in and announced.

"Madam," he had smiled, but that was only to emphasise the implied sarcasm of the mode of address. "The Prime Minister has made you Regent, yer promiscuous old trollop. The bill is going through the house as we speak and it will be official by two in the morning." He sighed with relief, then walked over to the corner where some sort of shrub resided in a large, ornate tub, he unzipped his flies, gave out a cracking great fart, then with a sigh of intense unregulated relief, pissed all over Ivra's prize horticultural specimen.

"I wouldn't complain Dunlossie if you had something worth looking at, but frankly I've seen better specimens in a catalogue for slug powder. I'm phoning the P.M."

"Suit yourself you old cow. I know you love me really. You've loved every man in the party at one time or another haven't you sweetie? Bye." With that he trotted off in the direction of Downing Street, where he and Alf had lain on a few bottles to go with the pork pies Ikey Solomon had sent over from Bow.

Macmurdo had scarcely left Ivra's before she was on the blower to the Prime Minister who was equally as plastered as Macmurdo had been, but he did confirm what Mac had told her. She was the new Regent, destiny had beckoned her to its bed and was about to screw her until her teeth rattled.

Ivra was a luminary of the party. She had class, not in the sense that ordinary folk would calculate that distinction, but her father had been a former Foreign Secretary, which in party terms made her an hereditary. Ivra had been born to the gravy train and had not had to submit herself to the indignity of having to get herself elected to that lucrative caravanserai. Ivra had been given a ministerial portfolio, as befitted her birthright. She had succeeded beyond the wildest expectations of those who had appointed her, in lousing up the job to a spectacular degree. Naturally, after a short time she had to be sacked, not that she was given the bum's rush in the way lesser mortals would have been manhandled out of office, no, the pill was sweetened by appointments to various boards and quangos, along with an official residence staffed by twenty servants.

The new Regent had one talent, which nobody could deny, her only talent if truth be not denied its rightful standing, and that was an almost religious dedication to running off with other women's husbands. The dame was notorious for snatching anything in trousers already spoken for. Most females felt it safe to invite Ivra round to tea only if their partners had safely been delivered to the undertakers and pumped full of embalming fluid. Wincarnis could not stand her, but then Wincarnis found it intolerable that any female should so much as shake hands with her well trained Alfred. The feelings of antipathy between the two women were mutual. Ivra looked forward to rubbing her prime antagonists' nose in the mire now that she was officially the first lady.

2.

Two days after the establishment of the regency, Queen Elizabeth departed for her new residence in Canada, taking with her, her family of ex monarchs. The Canadian government had sent a plane to R.A.F. Brize Norton. Mutiny was in the air as the Royal party boarded the aircraft, Princess Anne being in a particularly bolshie mood. If she could not be Regent, the Princess had planned to stand for parliament, a seat had recently become vacant and opinion polls indicated that she would walk it if she were to put herself forward. This was the reason Macmurdo had given the job of Regent to Ivra and not declared a republic, the same polls showed that should that happen, Princess Anne would be elected President, and no politician of either party was prepared to let that happen, fearing as they did that the princess would loose no time in putting them all out of a job and start governing the country properly. At that moment she was advertising her views on the Regent.

"That bloody old slapper has spent so much time on her back she could draw a map of the heavens from memory, she's done everything bar give out co-op stamps for it. She'd stuff the country in more ways than one." Ex King Henry gave his aunt a tap on the shoulder.

"Auntie, gran says if you don't stop effing and blinding we'll all be struck down by lightning and never get to Canada."

"Don't want to go to fucking Canada. I don't want to go to fucking anywhere. I want to stop here." The Princess would love to have worked out her frustrations by kicking one of the Corgis, but realised that would have been a tantrum too far in her mother's eyes. Sir Ralph at that moment was foolish enough to present himself within range, the princess consoled herself by giving the poor man a boot in the crutch, an action observed from the plane by Prince Phillip.

"Christ Lil." He expostulated. "You've got to stop Anne kicking Ralph in the bollocks, the poor man will have nothing left if she continues like that. Not that he knows what to do with them in the first place."

"If I've told you once I've told you a thousand times. Don't call me Lil." Snapped Her Majesty. "It's common, common, common." The Queen stuck her head around the door of the aircraft. "Anne. If you don't shut the fuck up and get on this plane, then

I'll stop your allowance, then you will have something to grizzle about. Make no mistake about it." And that was that, with a muffled expletive she was careful not to let her mother hear, the Princess boarded the aircraft.

The last to board was Prince Andrew, dragging with him the reigning Queen of Great Britain, Beatrice, who was being as obstreperous as her aunt who she consciously modelled herself on.

"I won't go I tell you. I won't." She shrieked at her despairing pater.

"Yes you friggin' well will."

"You can't make me. I'm the Queen"

"Don't let your grandmother hear you say that or you'll get a clout across the ear. And she'll give me one for letting you say it in the first place."

"I want to stay and give the Government a kick in the balls."

"Beatrice. I've told you before, you are not to use language like that, it is not nice."

"That's what auntie Anne said I should do."

"Well auntie Anne's not nice either. You'll get your name in the papers saying things like that."

"What's wrong with that? Mummy's always getting her name in the papers. Auntie Anne says she."

"Enough," bellowed the prince, fearful of hearing from his daughter what the rest of the family said about his wife. "Now get on that plane before I take my belt to you and give you a bloody good leathering, queen or no queen."

With those cultured litterings, the last of the Royal party boarded the plane. Shortly afterwards they took off for their new home in Canada, a happy and united family. Well, that's what the Telegraph reported the next day.

3.

The Regent Ivra, lost no time in laying claim to her new residence, she had phoned the palace to order a fleet of cars to convey her to Buckingham Palace, only there was no one manning the switchboard. Macmurdo had refused to allow her a car from the Government pool, which left the poor woman with no other option than to take the bus or to hoof it, and as it was coming down in stair rods, the bus it had to be. She could have taken a taxi, but thought it beneath her new dignity to carry money, which was a bit of a problem as that was the medium required before one could travel on the bus, and as the driver told her she could be the Queen of Sheba as far as he was concerned, but she was not getting on his bus without first buying a ticket, she had to walk after all. Ivra arrived at the palace with her latest husband, both soaked to the skin.

Instead of a red carpet awaiting her, Ivra found the place locked up and spent the next hour wandering around rattling doors and windows to no avail. There may have been plenty of rooms at the inn, but there was no way of getting to them. Eventually a property services locksmith arrived and managed to gain access for the Regent. By this time it was dark, leaving Ivra and Billy-Bob to wander around the vast edifice wondering how it would look if there had been any furniture. The contents were well on their way to Canada, leaving not so much as an orange box to sit on.

"Why don't we switch some lights on honey pie." whined Billy-Bob, straining to see more than six feet in front of his nose."

"Because there aren't any you damn fool. She's taken every bloody light bulb in the joint. God, I knew she was tight but this takes the Chocolate Oliver."

"What we gonna do then honey pie?"

"Christ!" thought Ivra. "I'm choosing my next husband for his brain and not his dick."

"Ah cain't see."

"Go down to the twenty four hour store on Trafalgar Square and get some light bulbs."

"But I don't have any money. You said we's royalty now and don't have to carry any."

"Use your wits Billy-Bob." Optimism was ever one of Ivra's failings. "Put them on the account."

"We have an account?"

"Of course. I'm the regent. I can have accounts wherever I go."

"Ok sweetie pie. I'm a going."

"And don't dawdle."

Billy-Bob did not dawdle but was still some time in returning. The manager of the twenty four hour store, like the bus driver, displayed a marked lack of awe at Ivra's new distinction, and Billy-Bob was told to bugger off and not come back until he had something in his wallet. Too afraid to return empty handed, he trotted off to Downing Street, where he found the prime Minister doing the last of his chores for the day, polishing up the brass door knocker and letter box. The Prime Minister was sympathetic to Billy-bob's plight, he scurried off to confer with Wincarnis, who took the matter in hand.

"Still in the dark Billy-Bob? That woman treats you like a mushroom." Wincarnis smiled as she spoke, a rare boon for the world, the replacement of her peach coloured corset had put her in an uncommonly good mood.

"Hi there Win. We got a little problem over to the Palace."

"I know. Alfred has explained it all to me. Here you are." She handed him two candles. "And tell Ivra I want them replaced to-morrow. And also tell her that just because we're neighbours now, that is no excuse to come round here borrowing all the time."

"Ah sure will honey. Bye now." Billy-Bob would have liked to return with something more tangible as proof of his efforts, but, at least he was returning with something. Wincarnis waved him off, she turned to her husband, remarking.

"Every time I see that man I realise why the confederacy lost the American Civil war."

Ivra was not best pleased with Billy-Bob's gleanings from Downing Street, they were next to useless. There was nothing for it but to return to Belgravia, and as it had started to rain again, they once more got soaked.

Things turned up for the Regent over the next couple of days. The Chancellor, eager to get one up on the Prime Minister and his wife, had given Ivra a generous allocation of funds, which enabled her to start hiring staff for the

Palace, and how she hired, you could not move for flunkies.

For Ivra, life was like winning the lottery every day. She ordered thirty stretch limos in lime and gold livery which accompanied her everywhere and caused considerable congestion to the capitals already dire traffic problem, as she swanned around the town in her motorcade for no other reason than to wave at the peasantry in regal fashion, but, as the peasantry invariably waved back with two fingered salutes, she stopped waving at them. She did not however desist from driving around the town.

The first few weeks of life in Buck House were saddled with privations. Ivra had refused to stay in Belgravia and had moved into the palace immediately, despite there being no furniture. She had planned to take the furnishings of the Belgravia house, but Wincarnis had got wind of that scheme and put the moccas on it, with the result that Ivra and Billy-Bob spent their first days of residence in the throne room. Making do with a couple of camp beds and a picnic stove.

Furnishing the Palace was obviously a priority, and as Ivra had no official tasks worth speaking of, there was no insuperable barrier to the place being rapidly filled up with the most unspeakable collection of knick-knacks, which would have appeared vulgar even at the end of a seaside pier. As for the furnishings, the less said about them the better. Ivra had positively looted the contents of London's tattiest emporia who sold Louis everything style furniture in moulded plastic to oil sheiks who thought gold leaf slapped over every available surface, proved that money could buy good taste. Buck House and it's contents became the talk of the town in no time.

Equally tacky was Ivra's choice of jeweller. Unable to afford the Bond Street boys, Wincarnis had put her foot down and made sure the Chancellor was not that generous, Ivra did a deal with one of the high street jewellery chains, the sort of shop where the windows were chock full of plastic Japanese watches and chains, the gold on which rubbed off the minute you breathed too hard over them. One or two of the national dailies had started to comment on the extravagance and hoity toity manners of the regent.

"Where will it all end?" they asked,

"The sooner the better," replied their readership.

4.

While the people's regent was busily employed in blowing the peoples brass, the Government had more serious problems on it's hands. First and foremost of these was how to divvy up the spoils between them. Wincarnis wanted Windsor Castle for herself, and announced in cabinet that she was withdrawing Alfred's conjugal privileges until she got her way. This caused the Deputy Prime Minister to remark that.

"As the poor sod had not had them for so long, that was hardly a threat."

The Foreign Secretary wanted Hampton Court, and the Lord Chancellor thought the Tower would be entirely appropriate to his station and taste in wallpaper. The Lord Chancellor also wanted to be made an earl. The Leader of the House, who thought of himself as an intellectual, considered this to be entirely appropriate for his pompous colleague, remarking that once the fellow had taken up residence in the tower, and been made an earl, of Clarence, then perhaps some kind soul would be public spirited enough to drown him in a butt of cooking Sherry. This particular sally ended in a punch up, which was becoming the standard ending for Cabinet meetings of late. Wincarnis would have abolished Cabinet meetings but for the fact that she sensed that its members might start fighting her husband if they did not have each other to take a swing at.

The Telegraph had not run out of scoops, far from it. They may have run out of abdications to announce, but there was plenty more to trumpet to the nation. As the Government fought relentlessly amongst itself for the left over perks of royalty, another bombshell buffeted them over their heads. The Telegraph announced a series of orders in council, signed by Queen Elizabeth before her abdication. The Queen had reserved for herself the powers of patronage, removing from the Prime Minister his right to bestow honours and titles. If that was not bad enough, there was worse to come, much worse. The Queen had taken back control of the Crown Estates and given all tenants of official residences six weeks to quit, this included the tenant of Number Ten. Such was the shock of this to

Wincarnis, she actually forgot to admonish her husband when he swore on hearing the news.

Wincarnis was not going to take this lying down, no way. Macmurdo was instructed to issue a statement saying the orders would be ignored as they were unconstitutional, he knew that was not true but this was no time for nit-picking. The announcement went out, and within the hour, the High Commissioners for Canada, Australia, and New Zealand were round to Downing Street like rats up a drainpipe. The diplomatic trio were received by Wincarnis, Alf, Mac, and Condo, in Mac's office. The diplomats refused to indulge themselves in the conventional subtleties of their profession. The batting was opened by the Canadian.

"The Canadian Government will not tolerate any attacks on the properties and prerogatives of her Majesty Queen Elizabeth."

"Too bloody right they won't," added the Aussie.

"Gentlemen, this is a domestic matter, and I regret to say, no concern of yours."

"Mr. Maites is right," declared Macmurdo, anxious that Condo should not commandeer the discussions.

"Not when it concerns the Queen of Canada Mr. Dunlossie. Any attack on her Majesty's rights would be seen as an attack on Canada, and we would react accordingly."

"So would we," averred the Aussie and Kiwi in unison.

"I have," continued the Canadian, enjoying every moment of the confrontation. "Discussed the matter with my two colleagues here, and there is no way we tolerate any attacks whatsoever on her Majesty." This was altogether too much for Wincarnis. Before the meeting it had been impressed upon her the importance of keeping her lip buttoned, that advice now went out of the window.

"Don't you tell me what to do you colonial upstarts, if I want the Crown Estates, then'll have them. If I want to make Lords I'll make them." The Prime Minister, Mac and Condo, cringed, sensing that nemesis was measuring them up for the box. "Now you three get out of here. Go back to your penny ante administrations and tell them to mind their own business. In fact I have a good mind to have you recalled. Declared persona non grata."

Throttled by emotion, Wincarnis took off one of her shoes and started banging the table with it. "You three are part of a plot got up by the right wing press." By this time she was screaming at the top of her voice. "Filth, that's all you are, right wing scum."

This was altogether too much for the Australian. He had grown up in the out-back where men were men and women lay on their backs and thought of knitting patterns.

"No bloody Sheila talks like that to me," he bawled, instilling utter silence amongst his audience. No one had ever spoken like that to Wincarnis and got away with it. He walked around the table and grabbed the Prime Minister by the lapels of his coat.

"Listen to me yer gutless bloody runt. It's about time you took that mouthy bitch in hand, it is you that is supposed to be running this show, not her. Who wears the trousers around here anyway? If you'll accept my advice son, you'll march her upstairs and take your belt to her, what she needs is a bloody good lamping."

"That's right Fred," urged the Kiwi. "You tell the bitch." He turned to the Prime Minister. "I'd advise you to listen to Fred. You go and give her a fucking good hiding and keep your frigging hands off our Queen."

"Cos," declared Aussie Fred. "If you don't I'll tell you exactly what is going to happen."

"Now let's not be hasty Mr. High Commissioner." Condo when in extremis had a talent for grasping at the bleeding obvious. "You would not want to say something you might come to regret afterwards would you now?" This was too much for Wincarnis, who was ready to start off again, and would have if Macmurdo had not delivered a kick to her shin hard enough to expunge the air from her lungs. He feared to antagonise her, but feared even more the repercussions of her shooting off her mouth any more than she already had, and as neither her husband nor Condo possessed the guts to do the necessary, it had been left to him.

"Now don't interrupt me son. You lot bugger about with our Queen and we'll send all your bloody migrants back to you. Australia's got hundreds of thousands of whinging bloody Poms, so busy complaining about everything, you start to wonder if they ever have a chance to draw breath. Well, if you don't toe the line, then you can have the bastards back, we'll hire a couple of super tankers and ship them back to Blighty. Imagine the effect that will have on your precious N.H.S." Condo and Mac could, only too well.

The Prime Minister had already gone into intellectual remission, triggered by terror of what Wincarnis would do by way of retaliation for her humiliation.

"Right then lads," continued Aussie Fred. "We're finished here, time for the rubbedy and a pigs ear. As for you." He jabbed his index finger at the Prime Minister. "The Queen's given you notice to quit the premises, so, pack your ports and git." Come on you two, we're wasting good drinking time The three ornaments of the Corps Diplomatique departed with no further ado. It was then that Wincarnis started, she continued for the rest of the day, at the end of which every pane of glass in the room was shattered, Alf and Mac were the proud possessor of a black eye apiece, and Condo was observed to be wearing a truss for over a week.

5.

The Queen was settling in nicely at Charlottetown, the capital of Prince Edward Island. The State Premier had been turfed out of Government House, oh so politely of course, and the Queen had moved her family into the Victorian mansion, where they continued to bitch and moan about everything, not to their mother naturally. The matriarch had been a little tetchy of late, and none of her tribe was going to risk the consequences of upsetting her equilibrium any further, except of course for Princess Anne, who could not keep her gob shut even if it were to be fitted with a zip.

The Royal Collection had also arrived on the North American Continent. A tidy chunk of the riches were put on display in Ottawa, but the bulk, containing the choicest artefacts went to New York. The Queen had bought the Fifth Avenue premises of a department store, which had gone bust, not that Her Maj anticipated going into the retail trade in a big way selling tat embroidered with the Royal Cipher, oh no. The premises were refurbished as a setting for the art works, and the public were admitted at the going rate of twenty bucks a pop. New York went wild, as did the rest of the country, it instantly became a must see for the residents of North America and anyone else who happened to be visiting the big Golden Delicious. People were visiting at an annual rate of six million, at twenty a time, that worked out at one hundred and twenty million smackeroos per annum. So pleased was Her Majesty at the success of the venture, she decreed the family could share a bottle of cooking sherry every Friday evening. A rare extravagance indeed.

The showing of the art collection was not the only deal Her Majesty had organised, there was one of far deeper significance in train. The family had been intrigued by the appearance of a strange New Yorker at Government House, he stayed overnight, but no-one had been allowed to see him except Sir Ralph Settles, and not even Princess Anne, by threatening to correct an oversight of nature by castrating him if he would not spill the beans, could get anything out of the man.

The Queen's children were all faffing about, trying to solve the mystery, when Prince Harry, always the practical one, decided to put them out of their misery by obtaining answers to the conundrum by the simple expedient of caressing the key hole with his ear. In possession of the requisite info, he returned to the family and put them out of their misery.

"She's not!" gulped Prince Charles.

"Well I'll be buggered!" Prince Andrew.

"You've got to give it to the old girl, she's way ahead of the pack." Princess Anne.

Later that day, Sir Ralph put through a call to London.

"Sir Percy my dear chap. How are you? Bearing up under the strain of national celebrity?"

"Coping Sir Ralph, needs must when the devil scrutinises the expense account chits, and no-one scrutinises like Conrad y'know."

"We do. We do. This is an open line, so I will be discrete, so, if I say to-morrow, you will know enough."

"I will indeed, take it as read."

"By the way, I was chatting to Her Majesty this morning and she is frightfully pleased with all you have done for her. I do believe she mumbled something about a peerage, if you get my drift." Percy got his drift all right, it was all he could do to restrain himself from shouting yippee down the line. He did manage a more dignified response.

"Do give my deepest respects to the dear Queen."

"I will, and good-bye Sir Percy." Sir Ralph gently replaced the receiver, there was only one way to shut Perce Tcherkoff up, that was quickly and before he'd had a chance to start.

The following morning in London, bowels were turning to porridge all over Westminster, and none more so than in Downing Street. The Telegraph was at it again, banner headlines, front page given over to one story, QUEEN SIGNS TWENTY FIVE MILLION DOLLAR CONTRACT FOR MEMOIRES. The first paragraph said all that needed to be said, the remainder of the paper was devoted to rubbing salt into the wound.

'Yesterday in Canada the Queen signed a deal for a twenty five million dollar advance against her memoirs with New York publishers Screwem and Shaftem. The two-volume work, largely compiled from M15 and M16 files, is to be called, My Prime Ministers And I. The memoirs will be serialised in the Telegraph in six months time.'

CHAPTER X.

The penny had finally dropped, the implications of the Queen's decision to commit her memories to paper finally sunk in. If it was true, and there was no obvious reason to believe otherwise, that Her Majesty had looted the files of the security services for background material, then the repercussions would not be confined within the gates of Downing Street, or to a few doddering ex Prime Ministers still succeeding in avoiding the ministrations of the grim reaper. The fall out from all of this would be wider, much wider. They were swapping Viagra for Valium all over Westminster, panic had superseded bluster as the most popular affectation.

Number Ten was not immune to the frisson passing through the closets of the Establishment. Whatever the rest of the mob was suffering from, Downing Street was on a double dose. Of course, Alfred Sawse was too dumb to do anything daft, a grim fact from which the public had been carefully shielded, they had been encouraged to believe the Prime Minister to be incredibly smart, a peacemaker, an international warrior fighting on behalf of the oppressed of the world. If the truth about the man came out they would feel duped, they would feel angry, what was worse, they would vote for someone else, especially if they found out that it was Wincarnis who thought she ran the Government, but Macmurdo and Condo who actually did, and that Alfred Sawse was only there to make the tea.

If that was not bad enough from the Government's point of view, there were much greater threats queuing up to chuck it under the chin and lead it by the hand to the political knackers yard. Macmurdo had called a Cabinet meeting, the real Cabinet, he had wanted to do this for some days, but had to wait until Wincarnis was away on an official visit to Prestatyn. Folk did not actually want her in North Wales as they had enough gabby females of their own in that neck of the woods, but Macmurdo had bribed the council into inviting her with the promise of a fact-finding visit to the Seychelles. It had not been decided what facts it was they were to study, but it would take two weeks to study them all the same. Expensive, but worth it to get Wincarnis out of the way, the woman had always been troublesome, but now she was becoming positively lethal in her meddling. If he, Mac was not careful, her antics would result in them all fleeing down Whitehall, suitcases under their arms, tickets to Rio in their hands and the mob on their heels.

The Cabinet was in session, the real cabinet that is, Condo, Mac and Alfred. The reason for this gathering was secret intelligence from the

Treasury, very hush hush. Mac had a spy in the Chancellors office, his secretary to be precise, who imparted her intelligence in return for regular bonking sessions with Macmurdo, who she fondly thought was in love with her, and would make an honest woman of her when circumstances permitted. A more prosaic explanation of the situation was that she had a face like a monkey's bum, she thought personal hygiene meant wiping her nose on her sleeve after sneezing, and Macmurdo, given some choice in the matter would sooner have stuck his dick in the mangle than screw her, but needs must when the information flowed, and what she had passed to him the other day was worth every excruciating second he'd had to spend in the Cleveland Street clap clinic on account of her ministrations.

The boffins at the Treasury like to think it is they who have the brains in the civil service, why not? There are folks amongst us who are convinced they are handsome specimens of humanity, despite the periodic evidence of the bathroom mirror. Nevertheless, there are time when the laws of random chance dictate they should get things right, and this was one of those times. Basically, the Treasury panjandrums had come up with irrefutable evidence that the economy, known to insiders as the Zeus of the electoral cycle, was about to go AWOL. This, like dodgy M.P.s and sex scandals happens to all governments, and how they handle them depends on how long they are able to avoid being garrotted at the polls. The news given to the Chancellor was just about as bad as it could get. Being a canny individual he kept the information to himself, planning to use it to his own advantage, for if he could pull the rug out from under Alfred Sawse, the Premiership was his for the taking, a situation he felt should have happened years ago. Macmurdo was well aware of this, he knew, without having to wrestle with the equation, that should the Chancellor get his ambitious mitts on the top prize, then everyone associated with Alfred Sawse would be out the door before one could formulate the instruction to bugger off.

The Magi of Government were gathered around the table in Macmurdo's office. Normally there would have been copious supplies of herbal tea, but as Wincarnis was safely out of the way, a large bottle of expensive Scotch Whiskey did duty as a lubricant for the larynx. Alfred was more nervous than usual.

"What do you think she'll say in the memoirs?" asked the Prime Minister, clearly hoping the answer would be nothing.

"Depends on what she's got," hedged Macmurdo, determined not to stick the boot in before he had got what he wanted out of the Prime Minister.

"She's got everything, take it from me." Condo was not in the mood to spare feelings, he felt he had been sidelined by Mac and the Prime Minister of late, and he was more than prepared to harvest the schadenfreude. "There's nothing the Queen does not know, and she'll use it. She has nothing to lose and everything to gain. The Aussies and Canadians will egg her on of course, but she will not need any encouragement from them. Let's be blunt. Let's be very blunt, we made no secret of what we thought of her, we undermined her at every opportunity. Face it Alfie, you only consented to speak at the Jubilee after the private polls told you there'd be an electoral backlash if you didn't. Well, now it's pay back time and she is going to stick the boot in, when she has finished with you, Alfie boy, you'll need hospitalisation." Condo leant back in his chair, extreme satisfaction producing an electrical charge in his gonads. The look on the faces of the other two, confirmed the accuracy of his assessments.

"What if I sent her a birthday present?" squeaked Alfred. "That might soften her up."

"It's not her birthday for months," intoned Condo, determined to wring the last dregs of hope from the Prime Ministers breast. "And if it was, and if you did, she would probably send it back. The only pressie the Queen wants from you Alfie, is your bonce on a pole, which she can stick over the door to Government House."

"He's right Alf. She is going to dump all over us, and there is nothing we can do about it." Mac took a slurp of whiskey. The Prime Minister thumped the table with his fist, petulance triumphing over fear.

"If we can't do anything, then what the hell are we doing here?"

"Oh. That's another matter altogether," stated Mac, eager to get the proceeding back on the track he had outlined for them. "There is a little matter of the economy."

"For our benefit Mac, darling," drawled Condo, trying his damndest to be offensive. "Try evacuating the bowels of your mind, purge yourself of its contents."

"The economy's fine, the Chancellor told me it was the other day." The Prime Minister beamed at his two companions, his face aglow with the light of the terminally witless.

"He's been pulling yer plonker again Alfie." Condo winced at Mac's coarseness, but his ears pricked up all the same. Those antennae essential for survival in the political jungle were transmitting." Something tells me this may be important Alfie. What is it Mac?"

"We have eighteen months max. Then the economic shit will hit the public fan, believe me it will bring the house down."

"But the Chancellor promised everything would be alright," pleaded the prime minister.

"You don't want to take anything he says too seriously," declared Condo. "He has one ambition in life and that is to get rid of you, and if he can bring the roof down on you in the process, the so much the better, it would add to the enjoyment of the event."

"Condo's right Alf. The egomaniacal sonofabitch has loused up good and proper, and he's fixed it so that you carry the can."

"What's the gen then Mac?" asked Condo, the Prime Minister was too frightened to participate any further.

"The whole bloody things out of control, we can do one of two things, borrow up to the hilt."

"The interest rate goes through the roof, houses get repossessed, then we get hung out to dry at the next election!"

"Got it in one. The alternative is to tax to hell and back to cover the deficit."

"And we get hung out to dry at the next election. Anything else?"

"Not much, but the health service is about to fulfil it's destiny and implode. Oh yes, while I remember, the pensions industry is about to go bust. Apart from that, all is fine and dandy."

"Do you think it would help if I turned Catholic?" asked the Prime Minister plaintively. His two henchmen did not think it worth answering him. They had their own skins to think about.

"How long have we got Mac?" asked Condo.

"Can't delay the election for more than twelve months. That's the cut off date. Delay any longer and it will be too late."

Something must be done," mumbled the Prime Minister, wondering how it all went wrong, and what Wincarnis would say when she found out.

"We'll keep this from Wincarnis for the time being," soothed Condo. "No sense in making matters worse than they already are."

With that the meeting broke up. Mac and Condo retired to the Chairmen, Alfred would have liked to have joined them but Wincarnis had told him the gas cooker needed cleaning.

2.

It is in the nature of things that opposition parties sit around dreaming of power while waiting for Governments to lose it. Her Majesty's loyal opposition had come to the conclusion that the present administration was poised to make the crucial transition from amiable cack handedness to the point where voters could not wait to get shot of them. The only fly in this particular jar of ointment, was that while the electorate considered the Government to be awful, they considered the opposition to be useless, a state of play which Binkie Wetherspoon, leader of the opposition was only too painfully aware.

The opposition was led by Binkie Wetherspoon, who had one slight disadvantage, nothing of major consequence which a good perruquier could not sort out. Yes, the man was bald as a coot. Binkie, the Southampton slap head, as he was known on the football terraces, which he frequented in order to access a little working class credibility. Why he should have gone to such trouble is one of the mysteries of modern political life, and in this he was not alone. Politicians of all parties, stretched mendacity to extraordinary lengths in their efforts to give the appearance of being working class, while the population at large was busting a gut to sign up to the middle class. On such confusions are our national life constructed.

The Shadow Cabinet were having their weekly meeting, where they pretended to concoct a strategy while hoping that none in the media would be so unsporting as to remind folk they did not have one, a modus vivendi which paid homage to disappointment on an extravagant scale. The topic due for mastication at today's confab, was the abdication and the consequences of what followed on.

That the populace was seething with anger at the current situation, was apparent to those who dwelt in the oxygen tent that was Westminster, in common with the Government, the opposition were not entirely sure as to what action should be taken, but, they did appreciate that the political tailors would have to be brought in, and put to work in turning a few coats.

Binkie was in something of a quandary, by attempting to offend nobody, he had achieved the distinction of offending practically everybody, and by seeking to shine in the eyes of the urban intellectuals by striking attitudes they would approve of, succeeded only in alienating those in the wider world who might otherwise have considered voting for him. Nowhere was this state of affaires more luridly highlighted than in the opposition's attitude to the Monarchy. In their metropolitan myopia, they failed to appreciate the distaste Mr. and Mrs. Average felt for the constant undermining of Elizabeth II, they sat back, saying not a word in defence of the crown, and when the backlash arrived, they were as surprised as the Government, and equally perplexed as to how they were to march recent events in the direction of electoral advantage.

"Where's the Party Sec.?" asked Binkie, looking down the table.

"You sacked him yesterday. Remember?" This was Sebastian di Roma, the token dago in the Shadow Cabinet, who was too good looking, too clever and infinitely too popular with the voters ever to be voted to the leadership by his colleagues.

"So I did. I must be getting absent minded."

"Or hoping that we were," continued Sebastian, who had nothing to loose by indulging in a little boldness, unlike the others he did not need to be in the Shadow Cabinet to boost his ego, he could get a job on the telly any day of the week, and be paid a fortune for his efforts into the bargain. "If you continue to sack people because the tabloids say they can do the job better than you, there will be no-one left in the Party." This was confirmed by too many titters of agreement for Binkie's comfort.

"Let's not quarrel girls," urged Frank Conway, the Shadow Chancellor, who could always be relied on to kiss the leaders bum, resulting in him being universally known as chocolate lips. "We must rally round Binkie."

"Thank you Frank, as always you are the voice of reason, what would we do without you?" Sebastian jumped in before Binkie could continue.

"Old Maggie said every Government should have a willy, but is it absolutely necessary that we have a resident prick?" He looked pointedly at Frank, who failed to recognise either the barb or it's intended target. Those around the table, erupted into laughter before withdrawing into communal silence, the leader had made it perfectly clear on many occasions that they were not to laugh at any of Sebastian's jokes. Binkie decided he had better take charge before Seb managed to hijack the proceedings to the benefit of to morrow's headlines.

"The voters have to see us as loyal to the throne."

"That will be difficult considering that for the past few years we've been trying to convince Hampstead that we are not." Added Sebastian eager to apply the semantic equivalent of the thumb screws to the discussion.

"Nevertheless," continued Binkie. "That's the only option open to us. Carpe diem!" Binkie did not actually understand the meaning of the words carpe diem, but he ritually peppered his private pronouncements with Latin tags in order to fool the inhabitants of Islington, who had been to public school and pretended they had not, into hinting he had, and was of them."

"How?" Sebastian could be succinct when circumstances warranted.

"We'll send a delegation to the Queen in Canada assuring her of our continued loyalty." Binkie was speaking ex cathedra, and expected to be accorded the appropriate reverence, which is what he took the silence following his pronouncement for. Not even Sebastian could be bothered to laugh.

3.

Original thought, like honesty is not something regularly encountered with any regularity in the loins of the political class, which is why the Deputy Prime Minister of the United Kingdom and the Shadow Chancellor of the Exchequer were sharing an aircraft to

Canada. The shares in the plane were not equal however. The Deputy Prime Minister had commandeered the entire fist class section of a British Airways Airbus to transport himself and a tin of Quality Street across the pond, while Frank Conway had to make do with a seat in steerage, jammed between a petrified first time flier, who thought the only way to ensure the safety of himself and his fellow passengers was to read aloud from the book of Genesis, and a female of indeterminate age who spent a fortune on ethnic clothes and chewed garlic cloves in the fond misapprehension that the activity proved her international credentials.. By the time the flight to Montreal had ended, the Deputy Prime Minister was paralitically drunk, and threatened to have the stewardesses fired unless they allowed him to screw them on the cabin floor, while Frank had come within an ace of committing both murder and blasphemy.

Deputy Bert, and Frank, were on their way to pay their respect to the Queen. Their respective leaders, in the teeth of contrary advice from their advisors, had each dispatched an emissary to the former Monarch, who the public still persisted in regarding as their legitimate head of state. Both leaders felt that an endorsement by Her Majesty would be to their electoral advantage, which would have been the case. The ruling pygmies of British politics were too shallow to be able to accept that Her Majesty might not wish to play ball, as indeed their advisors had cautioned.

The two delegates did not arrive on Prince Edward Island in tandem. Frank had no difficulty in boarding the internal flight to Charlottetown, but for Bert, things were slightly different. On arrival at Montreal, the Deputy Prime Minister, suffused with self importance, had demanded the use of the V.I.P. suite while he awaited the flight. Told that he would have to wait in the transit lounge with everyone else, he threw a tantrum. This type of behaviour normally got him whatever it was that he wanted, not so this time. The Canadian authorities were unimpressed by Bert's standing in the World and disdainful of his state of sobriety and they reacted when told they were nothing but a bunch of colonial toss pots, by slinging him in the drunk tank for thirty six and a half hours, the time it took for the British representatives in the province of Quebec to come up with the fine levied on him.

Frank Conway took a taxi direct from Charlotte town airport to Government House in Victoria Park, assuming that Her Majesty would be waiting for him. A cock up at party headquarters back in London, ensured that Her Majesty was in total ignorance of the impending visit, not that it would have made the slightest difference to her had she known about it. Frank paid off the taxi and martched up to the front door of the mansion. He rang the bell. The door was opened by Andrews, the head footman, who was suffering from an almighty hangover, which had blighted the normal sweetness of his temper.

"Yes," he barked.

"I'm the shadow Chancellor. I have come to see Her Majesty."

"Got an appointment?"

"Of course I've got an appointment. Do I look as if I'm the sort of person whom would turn up to see Her Majesty without an appointment?"

"Yes. Now fuck off." With that the faithful retainer slammed the door in the petitioner's face. Not to be deterred by the eccentricity of the Queen's domestics, Frank made his way round to the back of the building. The back door happened to be open, he walked in to find Princess Anne giving the cook an earful on account of his inability to produce a decent plate of porridge, she looked quizzically at Frank, not recognising him at first.

"If you're the man who's come to do the drains then you're late."

"No. No, your Royal Highness. I'm Frank Conway, the Shadow Chancellor."

"Oh yes, so you are. What the devil are you doing out here? Don't tell me you have resigned to spend more time with our Royal Family."

"No mam."

"Well? What is it then?"

"I've an appointment with Her Majesty. London made it."

"In a pigs ear you have. And London's done nothing of the kind, this is the first we've heard of it. Well you had better wait here, I'll see if the Queen will receive you, although if she's got any sense she won't." The Princess disappeared out of the kitchen, she found her mother in the back parlour, re-arranging the knick-knacks in a vitrine of great taste, which was exactly what it's contents lacked.

"Ma, you'll never guess who's just fetched up on the doorstep."

"Of course I won't but I'll put a fiver each way on whoever it is being a pain in the neck for me."

"Spot on. It's none other than old mother Conway."

"What! Old chocolate lips Conway? That's all I frigging need. I traipsed half way round the world to get away from those sods. Can't they take the hint? What's the bloody old woman want anyway?" Her Majesty in irritation was a magnificent sight.

"Didn't say, except that London is supposed to have fixed it up. Shall I tell him to clear off?"

"No. My curiosity is up and running now. Wheel him in, but no tea and bickies, there is a caff round the corner he can use afterwards if he wants."

The Princess did as bid, she returned a few minutes later with Frank, who entered the room courtesy of an unregal shove in the back.

"Old mother Conway ma." The subject of her observation went a florid shade of pink.

"Your Majesty," he stuttered, forgetting to bow, an oversight which doomed his mission before it had begun. Royalty was most pernickety over such matters.

"Well! What do you want? I'm busy, so be quick about it."

"I bring loyal greetings from the Shadow Cabinet Your Majesty."

"Is that all? Christ! Even the Magi managed to rustle up some gold frankincense and myrrh amongst them."

"The Shadow Cabinet have asked me to assure your Majesty of their continuing support and loyalty. We are all adherents of the house of Windsor."

"Are they be buggered." Her Majesty had spent a lifetime respecting the subtle nuances of the British Constitution, frequently against her better judgment. Such constraints were no longer operative and Her Majesty had every intention of choosing short shrift from the menu now available to her. "And where was all that loyalty when I needed a bit of it over the last few years? When I was being nit-picked as if I was the star attraction at a louse lovers convention. Answer me that. Go on then."

"But your Majesty." Frank was not permitted to advance any further with his protestations, answers might have been demanded but they would in no way be tolerated.

"Don't you dare interrupt me you little squirt. You sanctimonious two faced duplicitous bastards were quite happy to stand by and watch me being pilloried in the press when your focus groups in Broadcasting House told you it was the politically smart thing to do. Well now I have gone, and you lot are already making a pig's ear of things, and the public have cottoned to the fact. You are all in the shit up to your eyeballs and now you want me to pull you out of it. Well, my answer is no bloody way. Now get out of my sight before I say something I may regret when it is leaked to the papers."

Princess Anne, grinning hugely at her mother's bravura performance, grabbed Frank by his collar and yanked him out of the room and through the front door. Assuming his diplomatic efforts had reached a terminal stage in their development, Frank shuffled off to find some accommodation before returning to London.

4.

Having been duly sprung from the jug at Montreal airport, Bert Colchester finally achieved his destination a day behind Frank Conway. He checked into a hotel, where he had a blinding row with the receptionist, who refused to give credence to his spectacular eminence in the affairs of the International Community, and demanded payment up front. Faced with the alternative of sleeping on a park bench, Bert was forced to ante up the dosh. That settled, our man toddled off to Government house.

After the intrusion of the previous day, Her Majesty had ordered a notice pinned to the front door, an instruction uncompromising in its ferocity, No Hawkers, Bible Bashers or British Politicians. Now, your average party, having read that, and found himself in one of those categories, would have taken the proffered hint, and scarpered. Not so our Bert, the fellow had been to school, rumour favoured one Thursday afternoon in nineteen forty seven, but could develop no affinity with reading writing and doing sums, therefore the notice on the front door had been unable to impinge upon his consciousness to a degree that might have affected his actions.

Finding the door bell out of order, and nobody bothering to answer the front door, Bert saw an open window. With considerable difficulty, due to his girth, he was a fat son of a bitch, clutching the five pound tin of Quality Street he had brought with him from London, he managed to squeeze himself into the mansion. His egress into the building was made even more undignified by his losing his balance at the crucial moment, and going arse over tea kettle onto the drawing room floor. As his nose banged onto the parquet, his teeth flew out and the tin of chocs burst open, sowing it's contents over a considerable area of the room. Hurriedly, Bert set about re-filling the tin, which, against the advice of Macmurdo and Condo, the Prime Minister had insisted on sending as a birthday present for the Queen. Bert was thus engaged, head down on the drawing room floor, arse in the air, when the Queen walked in on the scene.

"Who the devil are you, and what are you doing here, you vulgar little man?" This was not quite the welcome Bert had envisaged. He attempted to introduce himself, but the absence of his National Health grinders had a debilitating effect on his diction which could not be described as sound under the most propitious of circumstances. "What was that you said? I can't understand a word you are saying." The Queen yelled for her daughter. "Anne come here there is an intruder." Time had not the chance to adjust the crease in it's crutch before the Princess arrived, rolling pin in hand.

"Don't worry ma. I'll clobber the bastard whoever he is. Come 'ere you little runt." Fortunately for his cranial integrity, Bert discovered his teeth before the Princess had the chance to match the contours of his noggin to her weapon.

"It's me Queen. It's me." squeaked the terrified man. "Don't hit me please." He looked up imploringly into the eyes of offended majesty.

"Bert Colchester," exclaimed the Queen. "As I live and die, and why couldn't you have had the decency to have done so years ago? What are you doing here? Can't you read man? There is a notice on the door, no British politicians. Comprendez? And what the hell are you doing in my drawing room?" Bert struggled to retrieve the last of the chocolates from the floor, stuffing them back in the tin. He held it, minus the lid, up to the Queen. Now, in order to do this, he had to stand up, a deduction which should not embarrass the intelligence, unfortunately he had forgotten to do up his flies and neglected to put on any underpants. This sartorial and physical faux pas did not go unnoticed by the queen.

"Cover yourself up man."

"I can't mam. I left me 'at in the 'otel"

"Not your head you fool," spat the Princess. "Your crutch. You've left your flies undone. Cover your cock up you dirty old sod, do you think the Queen wants to see that at this time of the morning. Not that it is worth looking at.

I've seen better examples on the corpses in Cairo Museum."

Frantically, Bert clutched at his flies; an action which guaranteed the sweets retraced their safari across the floor.

"What are those?" asked the Queen, pointing at the scattered confectionary.

"Quality Street your Majesty."

"I can see that you clown. What are they doing here? And you for that matter?"

"They are a birthday present from the Government mam."

"A birthday present!" The royal mouth was starting to froth a bit. "My birthday is not for another nine months. All I got from the Government for the last one was a card that came a week late, and I only got that because a poll said the people would not like it if the Government didn't send me one. It's a bloody insult that's what it is. You lot must think I'm simple."

"Hey! Look ma," said Princess Anne, pointing at the scattered offerings. "The green triangles are missing."

"Oh shit," mouthed Bert to himself. "Bloody Wincarnis again. That woman can't keep her paws off anything."

"That does it," snapped the Queen, thoroughly miffed at the filching of the green triangles. "They are my favourites." She pointed at the chocolates. "Pick them up and take them back to Alfred Sawse and tell him to stick them where the monkey stuffed its nuts." A less intelligent entity would have given up there and then, but as Bert was unencumbered by cerebral handicaps of any variety, he soldiered on to his destruction.

"The Prime Minister was hoping you'd do a party political for us your Majesty." Princess Anne had the good sense to get out of the room before her mother resorted to violence. Bert beamed expectantly at the Sovereign.

'Would you now? First I get old mother Conway pleading on behalf of that bald headed prat Weatherspoon, and now I get you trying to sign me up for a dollop of Sawse."

"Wincarnis sends her love as well," lied Bert, the Queen knew full well Wincarnis had done nothing of the sort.

"The only thing that rat faced bitch would send me is a bouquet of poison ivy. And don't try flannelling me, it's been attempted by men more expert in the science than you. Alfred Sawse and his wife, the queen of the castrating shears, have been plotting against me since the day they gained office. Well now I have gone and they can sort their own problems out, I am not going to do it for them. Besides, I have not enjoyed myself so much for years. Now hop it." Reasoning that he was unwelcome, Bert shuffled out from the Royal presence, clutching his tin of Quality Street. In the hall, he met the waiting Princess Anne, the sight of whom had the effect of administering a hypodermic of dignity to his backside.

"I'll have you know Princess Anne, the welcome I 'ave 'ad in this 'ere 'ouse 'as aborted my feelings."

"Is that so?" Solicitude oozed from between the royal lips. "Then here's something else for your feelings." With that she administered an expertly aimed right hook to Bert's jaw, which sent him sprawling across the floor to end up face down in a bowl containing the dog's dinner, bemusement was etched between his crow's feet.

"Whadya do that for?"

"So that you'll know what the electorate feel like you fat bastard. Andrews." Yelled the Princess, Come here" The pride of Treorchy scampered up to the Princess.

"Yes mam?"

"Turf that lump out and make sure he don't get back in again."

Bert and Frank returned to London on the same flight. An account of their mission, suitably annotated for publication in a family newspaper, had hit the streets, in the form of the Daily Telegraph, before they had landed. The report added greatly to the gaiety of the nation and Princess Anne was declared a national treasure.

CHAPTER XI.

Ivra Maninand inhabited that special corner of Heaven reserved for those whose delusions and self importance had never been penetrated by the penis of reality. For all of her life there had been someone on hand to reassure her that she was special, set apart from others. As the daughter of a former Foreign Secretary, she had been given a lifetimes membership of cloud cuckoo land, and had used her ticket to obtain up to the limit all it's available advantages. The job of Regent went to Ivra's head, she had always suffered from delusions of grandeur, but these had worsened with the advent of the menopause, and her appointment to the Regency was all it had taken to push her over the edge of that precipice where reality waved ta-ta to the deluded.

Ivra's behaviour had become insufferable, she treated the Buck House servants with appalling rudeness, insisting they turned and faced the wall whenever she approached them. She was unable to comprehend that civility was the hall mark of class and not a confirmation of its absence from the genes. Had Ivra's behaviour been screened from outsiders by the palace walls, all might still have been well, but they were neither high enough nor thick enough to prevent tales of Ivra's tantrums from trickling through to the mill pond of public contempt, and even if they had been, the cars would have put the public's back up.

Ivra and her motorcades had come closer to provoking the greatest uprising in London since Wat Tyler's rebellion. At first, Ivra and her thirty jam jars swanning about the town had merely caused irritation. People assumed the novelty would soon wear off, after which she would be content to stay at home and bollock the servants, not so, she had become addicted to the activity to the extent that at least twice a day she would take off from Buck House with thirty empty cars in tow, and not so much as a security guard amongst them as special branch had ascertained that while it was probable that one day one of her staff would throttle her, no self respecting terrorist could be bothered to do so.

All these journeys were quite meaningless as there was nowhere for her to go. The Queen would have been invited to all manner of functions around the capital, but no one wanted Ivra at their jollifications, the Queen would have been content with a bob of the head from her hosts, Ivra expected them to fall to their knees and remain there for the duration of her visit. One visit to the offices of Marks and Sparks and another to an exhibition of shitty nappies encased in perspex at the Tate Modern, and that was enough for le tout Londres. Ivra was off the A list and on the 'Over my dead body' list, never to be invited again without giving a promise in writing to commit hara kiri before witnesses.

What really put peoples backs up was the knowledge that royalty would never have behaved in so cavalier and tasteless a fashion, besides, the British public have no toleration for those who give themselves airs and graces, which explains why you can live for twenty years in your average residential suburban street without exchanging so much as a word with the neighbours. The cabinet were not too concerned with all this, they were all cut from the same cloth, treating the voters with the same disdain the noblesse of Eighteenth Century France treated the peasantry. To them it was perfectly natural to gorge themselves at the publicly funded trough with all the tact and delicacy of a sow in labour, they were honest enough in private to admit that they would have behaved no different to Ivra had they been in her position. This complacency was noted by the electorate, it served to fuel their outrage at Ivra who seemed to be kerb crawling for unpopularity with her insistence of trying to out queen the Queen, and her determination to surround herself with them, chief of whom was Condo Maites.

Condo had wasted no time in getting his feet under the moulded plastic tables of Buck House, the better to encourage Ivra in whatever follies chanced to engage her attentions, she might have got the job he wanted, but he had by no means given up on his ambitions. When time and fate positioned Ivra for a tumble, he would be on hand to make sure it was fatal, with a damn good shove.

Ivra returned from the bathroom and cheering could be heard through the open windows.

"Oh Condo,' she simpered. "The dear people are cheering me again. I can't think why."

"I can Ivra darling." And he could. Ivra had taken it into her head to introduce purple tinted water into her private loo, Condo had persuaded her to have the appliance to play God Save The Queen whenever the flush was pulled. Ivra was enthusiastic and allowed Condo to organise the installation, which he did with a modification or two. Whenever the lavatory was flushed, the Regents standard flying over the Palace was lit up with a spot light. Word had soon got about for the reason behind the phenomenon and crowds had taken to gathering outside the palace gates to witness the periodic indication of activity in the Regent's bowels, waiting for Ivra to crap had become as popular an activity as the changing of the guard had been under the previous regime.

"Now then Condo, off we go to the East End."

"Is this an official do Ivra?" he asked, knowing full well the answer.

"Not exactly. I thought I would drop in and surprise everyone. So much more exciting that way, and people won't have to go to all the trouble of redecorating on account of me."

"Not that they would in any case," thought Condo, taking care that Ivra had no inkling as to his assessment of the situation. "Probably run a mile if they knew you were about to blow in," he smiled in that special manner of his which made insincerity an act of carnal pleasure.

"Off we go then. The car's waiting and so is my public." Ivra was dressed in a pink chiffon ball gown, a tiara perched on her head drew attention to the fact that her roots needed doing, the diamonds of course were fake. It was still only ten in the morning.

The motorcade pulled up in a shabby side street in Whitechapel, besides an old school building which had been turned into a training centre, a vehicle by which those who knew how to manipulate the system, bilked the taxpayer of considerable amounts of money in exchange for doing nothing of any value or use to anyone. This particular example of the genre specialised in running things like courses in public speaking for people who were barely able to master the rudiments of the English language, but who turned up because if you signed the register you received two pencils, a rubber and a toffee apple. Ivra, alone except for Condo, who was careful to stand away from her, stood in the middle of the shabby foyer, an interior space which had received little attention since coronation day, Queen Victoria's.

"I am the Regent of England," announced Ivra in case anyone should mistake her for the ghost of Barbara Cartland. A little man in a shalwar kameez shuffled up to her and said something in a language she did not understand, she replied in English, a language he obviously did not understand either. Stalemate. The man scampered off, returning presently to award Ivra with a handful of pencils and a couple of toffee apples. Ivra and Condo ate their apples, fearful that not to have done so would have given offence to whomsoever it was who held the distinction of being their host. After standing around for half an hour, they decided to call it a day and return to the cars.

Condo had prepared the ground well, he had tipped the press off with guarantees of a good story, he was true to his word. The motorcade was in place, Ivra gave the waiting camera men a gracious wave of the hand, with a smile to match, which disappeared as the poor woman realised there were no drivers and the cars were all locked up. Ivra was stranded on an East End pavement all dolled up like a Christmas Fairy, wondering what the hell was going on. There was one fairy who could have told her, Condo Maites. Condo had arranged that the waiting drivers be solicited by one of the local daughters of frivolity, who conducted her business out of the Sally Army flats around the corner from the training centre. They were told that the lady was having a promotional day, and that there would be no charges whatsoever. The thirty drivers trooped off to the flats where they lined up outside the door to number forty two, awaiting their turn. As Condo had had the prescience to supply them with a Fortnum's hamper of India Pale

Ale and jam tarts, a merry atmosphere was soon gestated.

A rumour soon circulated amongst the rat pack, some of whom had pretensions to journalism, of the goings on round at the Sally. These were soon verified and photographed, the journos soon returned to give Ivra the third degree on the morals of her retinue. She, the poor woman, had no inkling of what they were talking about but egged on by Condo, Ivra made a run for it. Pursued by the press she took refuge in a Brick Lane curry house, where she ordered half a bottle of gin and a vindaloo. Not carrying any money, Ivra was unable to pay the bill, resulting in another sort of bill being called for, the type which came with a uniform. The entire episode was given front page treatment in the following day's papers. "Regent Nabbed For Diddling Naff Caff While Her Staff Were Boniking Whitechapel Tart" was one of the more restrained observations. Downing Street was not amused.

2.

If devolution had any effect on the tribes who inhabited the British Isles, other than to burden the shoulders of the long suffering tax payers with yet another regiment of wastrels, whose expenses knew not the boundaries of either reticence or shame, it was to let the genie of nationalism out of the bottle into which for centuries it had been contained. Once out and on the rampage, that spirit proceeded to masturbate over the fool who had so thoughtlessly pulled the cork from the bottle in the first instance. As the leather uppers of the state boot signalled their intentions to part company with the soles, the Celtic fringes thought it would be nothing if not neighbourly to help the process along by decobbling the United Kingdom.

To the land of John Knox, Ivra Maninand with her chiffon ball gowns and tasteless extravagances, was anathema, not at all the sober totem they required at the head of their state. Things had bumped along since the abdications, high and low in Scots society, took to grizzling and grumbling at the pass things had come to, topped off with the age old rational which ran along the lines of, what else could you expect of the damned English. Into this stalemate of antique provenance stepped Lachlan Macgregor Siciliano.

LMS as he was universally known as, was a prominent member of the Scottish National Party, a body he had not joined out of conviction, nor any interest in, or even a remote feeling of sympathy for their policies. He was not exactly sure what those policies were, nor did the man care. The only reason LMS had signed up was on account of his surname. Scottish names did not usually end in a vowel, a fact that did not go unnoticed in his case.

LMS thought that by becoming more Scottish then the Scots, and joining the Nats, then folk would desist from calling him a dago, which they did, well, to his face at least.

In common with his ilk, LMS liked nothing better than to be on the telly, it flattered his considerable ego, but more to the point, he would be ferried by taxi to the studios, where before and after the performance, stupendous amounts of food and booze would be laid on for those consenting to insult the viewing public with a demonstration of the paucity of their talents, usually nurtured at great public expense.

LMS swaggered into the green room, a long internal space with lots of comfy seats and a buffet of posh nibbles. He filled his plate with fried scampi and pork pies, grabbing a can, he positioned himself in the centre of the room, the better for all to appreciate him. Unfortunately, people were not in an appreciative mood, they were all too aware of their own importance to pay any heed to his.

The producer spent ten minutes with LMS rehearsing the spontaneous question and answer session they would have on screen, after which he was whisked off to the actual studio. Standing by the doors, waiting to enter the recording area, LMS and his fellow guest were regaled by the sight of six men running down the corridor stark bollock naked.

"Don't worry," drooled the assistant in charge of their welfare. "It's only the male strippers, they were on before you. Here we are folks, in we go." They were herded onto the sound stage, having first deposited their cigarettes on a table by the door. At a signal from the stage manager, the audience clapped and cheered, having no notion whatsoever for whom they were applauding. The interviewer was the sort of local celebrity who dressed like a thirties Hollywood star, and whose skin tone had to have come out of a bottle. He read the cue cards before asking the first question.

"Mr. Siciliano, or Lachlan, I may call you Lachlan, may I not?" LMS was about to reply with a no you fucking can't, but was given no opportunity to invade the conversation, as, in the interviewer's opinion guests should only be allowed to speak when it could not be avoided. "What is the Nat's position on the Middle East?" Here the presenter paused to smile at the camera, a fatal mistake as the gesture gave LMS the chance to enter the discussion, an equally fatal move on his part, as too much lager and not enough grub had an entirely predictable effect on his jerry built powers of deduction.

"What about Mid Lothian? Who cares about the damned place?"

"No, no, not Mid Lothian. The Middle East."

The presenter had known it would be a disaster to have this clown on the programme, but the producer had insisted on the grounds that LMS' presence made for good television.

"Never heard of the place. Near Aberdeen is it?"

"Not quite." Despite the frantic efforts of the producer, the audience made no attempt to curb their amusement. LMS, mistaking their amusement for approbation, not that he would have understood the technicalities of the term, even had it been explained to him, jumped up and ran to the front of the stage, grabbed the hem of his kilt and raised it to the level of his chin.

"Hey lassies, fancy this wi ye neeps and black pudding?" The spectators were awestruck, unable to comprehend why anybody in their right mind who had inherited such a paucity of assets, should have felt the need to have presented the world with so physical a demonstration of his poverty. Pandemonium erupted amongst the production staff. The floor manager completely lost his bottle and shrieked at the presenter.

"Get him off, we'll be pissing banned." LMS, whose hearing was as impaired as his wits, misheard the phrase and replied accordingly.

"Aye. That's right, Princess Anne. Annie for Regent of Scotland." That was all that was heard before they pulled the plug on the transmission, but, that was enough. It was too late to make the first editions of the mornings papers, but it swallowed up every subsequent edition and all the news broadcasts, and that is how History is invariably made, the outcome of a collision between a fool and a cock up.

The whole story of Princess Anne for Regent of Scotland would, in all probability have ended there and then, had it not been for two deciding factors. The first of these was the London intelligentsia, who could not have kept their traps shut if their jaws had been padlocked to their insteps. Hampstead and Islington joined hands to proclaim that the idea of a separate Regency for Scotland was an absurdity, quite unnecessary as monarchy was as good as dead, the only reason the country had a Regency was because there had been a delay in calling in the undertaker. Scotland quivered with indignation at these pronouncements and promptly put Princess

Anne for Regent at the top of the national agenda.

The second factor to shape events was the London Government, all members of which were ordered to the T.V. and radio stations by Wincarnis and ordered to assert with the utmost authority that a separate Scots regency was unconstitutional and in no way would it be considered. That was it. The clans rose to avenge Culloden, no more would Sassenach interference in the affairs of Caledonia be tolerated. In response to nationalist outrage, English television programmes were banned from Scots screens, an act that had to be rescinded as soon as it had been passed as nobody wanted to miss out on Coronation Street or Emmerdale Farm.

After sorting out what the populace could and could not watch on the box, the Scottish Parliament addressed the Regency question. Scotland had no representation in Canada, but they did have a tourist office in Halifax, Nova Scotia. The manager of this outpost of Celtic culture was dispatched to Prince Edward Island. The discussions were brief and to the point, Her Majesty having decided well in advance of the arrival of the representative, that her only daughter should accept the position.

Within two weeks of Lachian Macgreggor Siciliano, son of a dago ice-cream seller, advertising his meat and two veg on late night television, H.R.H. the Princess Anne, held her first official reception in the state rooms of the Palace of Holyrood House. She had also sent a change of address card to Wincarnis.

The Welsh were not too concerned about the Regency question, as long as the bingo halls remained in operation, the mass of the population reposed content with their lot. As for the ruling class west of Offa's dyke, as long as life stuck to the path pre ordained by God, then they saw no reason to summon the energy required to rock any boats, in it's essentials this boiled down to the people agreeing to vote unsuitable candidates onto the local councils and not complaining when they stuck their fingers in the till. The Taffia admired a tranquil life. Things would have continued in this vein had it not been for their Celtic cousins to the north, if the Scots could have their own regent, then why should they be stuck with old Ivra. National lethargy rapidly transformed itself into tribal affront.

Wales rapidly came to the conclusion that it was made a second class country by lacking its own head of state. Questions were asked in the assembly, and a man called Bonvilston Evans Prothero, wrote an article in the Glamorgan Gazette, demanding Prince William be made Regent of Wales. It was Scotland all over again, the principality erupted into a state of emotional incontinence, and before anyone knew what was afoot. Prince William was winging his way across the Atlantic to take up residence in Cardiff Castle.

The London establishment spluttered and blustered, but that was all they did, guts had never been their forte and after the arrival of Prince William, they were all sporting colostomy bags.

The Prime Minister was too frightened to tell Wincarnis what had happened, he scarpered off to the Mile End Road, where he holed up with Ikey Solomon, leaving Macmurdo to break the glad tidings on his behalf to his dearly beloved.

3.

The Prime Minister's sojourn with Ikey was not of prolonged duration, the poor man had hardly sat down to a breakfast of pork pies and Guinness, when Macmurdo barged into Ikey's back room where the Prime Minister sat, surrounded by pigs carcasses and assistants making the faggots for which the establishment was famous.

"Little wonder," thought Mac. "That he feels so at home here." Alfred did not need to ask the reason for the intrusion, ask not for whom Win calls, she calls for me. Mutely accepting his fate, Alfred allowed himself to be ushered into the official car and ferried back to Downing Street, wishing he had some of that narcotic the French aristos used to chew on the way to the guillotine to dull their senses.

The Prime Minister's reception by his missus was all he had expected it to be and worse. He returned to his office physically and morally demoralised, wishing he had never allowed Wincarnis to enter him for the political equivalent of the Grand National. To add insult to injury, she had confiscated his jigsaws as a punishment.

"Why blame me?" He whined "I did not abdicate, it's not my fault. I did not cause any of this."

"What was that Alfie?" The Prime Minister had not heard Condo enter the room. He sat down opposite his boss.

"All this constitutional crap Condo. It's not my fault is it?" Condo had the intelligence and honesty to recognise that it was the Government's fault, it was their deliberate actions which had triggered the series of seismic shocks to the unwritten constitution, which were now tearing the country apart in a manner not experienced since the civil wars of the Seventeenth Century. However, he was not stupid enough to share the fruits of his understanding with anyone, particularly with the leader.

"Cheer up now Alfie. It's always darkest before the dawn." The Prime Minister loved the banal, invariably mistaking it for prescience. "By the way, I've just put out a press release, it's about how I gave Wincarnis my recipe for peach jam."

"But she can't cook, doesn't even know how to boil an egg."

"I know that as well as you do, but it will make her look housewifely, help win the Women's Institute vote, very big on jam making the W.I., and it will give me a bit of cred with my constituents to be seen being friendly with a woman. You know how it is." The Prime Minister did, only too well, reactionary bastards' constituents, they thought P.C. a high falutin name for the public crapper.

"What am I going to do to get out of this mess Condo? It gets worse by the day. That fiasco of Ivra's in Whitechapel was the last straw. I thought they would quieten down with time, but that gormless bint stirs things up every time she pokes her nose out the door of Buck House. Help me Condo." He wailed.

"Don't panic Alf. All we have to do is hang on a bit, then all will be well."

"If the bloody public don't hang us first."

"All that lot need is a bit of a diversion."

"Oh no. Not that one again. Remember what happened last time you came up with a line like that. We all got eviction notices. Some members of the Government have been forced into buying their own homes for chrissakes."

"Ah, but listen. This is different. You yourself said that the problem is Ivra swanning about the town like Mary Queen of Scots done up in a Vivien Westwood Basque. We sort Ivra out, and ipso facto we sort the problem out at the same time. Got it?"

"Come off it Condo. Ivra give up the Regency? I don't think so, and we can't sack her, she's screwed too many back benchers. Think of the trouble they'd cause if she blackmailed them into supporting her."

"Not if there was the sort of scandal the great British public like to read about in their Sunday newspapers" The Prime Minister's interest was slowly forming an intellectual erection.

"What are you getting at?"

"What's Ivra's greatest talent?"

"She hasn't got any. That's why we had to sack her as minister for lesbian affairs and give her a peerage."

"Think Alfie boy. Think. Running off with other women's husbands, she's made a career of it. That's her one and only ability."

"So?"

"Randy Ivra's been with Billy-Bob for all of two years now, which for her is practically a record. Billy-Bob may be able to bonk for the Confederacy for all I know, but that does not alter the fact that she is due some other woman's husband by now. All we have to do is to ensure that the one she trots off with, so horrifies the voters that they go off like the Nagasaki bomb and then no-one will dare stand in our way when we give her the chop."

"Sounds good in principle, but does such a person exist apart from the Pope?"

"Oh yes he does Alfie, and we won't have to go to Rome to find him."

"Who is it? Come on Condo, you can trust me. I won't tell, honest."

"Only Wincarnis, which is like telling half of Whitehall before tea time." thought Condo. What he actually said was "You just leave it to mc to sort out. You know how you like a surprise, don't you?" He lapsed back into thought. "And this one will be a lulu."

CHAPTER XII.

Condo Maites prided himself on being all things to all men. The success of his ambitions could be attested to by an extraordinary number of the male sex, some of whom had actually been grateful for his ministrations while others were more career minded. There were occasions, not many to be sure, when as a tribute to rank expediency, Condo wrapped his natural inclinations in a burial shroud and pretended to like a woman. To this exclusive club he now added the name of Gertrude Gunter M.P. If Condo's plan to scupper Ivra was to succeed, he would have to have Mrs. Gunter on message, as the juvenile jargon went.

Gertrude Gunter, the peoples Gert, was a hairy arsed lesbian, who for some inexplicable reason, enjoyed great popularity with the great British Public, who had taken her to its collective bosom. As one of her fellow members of Parliament had remarked of this populist symbiosis, one tit deserves another, but then good taste and elegance of language had never been pre-requisite for entry into politics. Gert was of singular appearance, as short in stature as she was wide in girth, with a moustache Kaiser Bill would have given an arm and a leg for. The whole physical ensemble signed off with a gait which suggested the woman had shit herself and had not yet worked out how to confess to the misfortune without causing embarrassment. Although a lesbian, Gert swung both ways. Unfortunately for her husband Norbert, she did not swing his way very often, which could explain why he was referred to by those in the know as Norbertawanker. If Ivra could be manipulated into pinching the cherished husband of the peoples Gert, then there was bound to be uproar in the pubs and bingo halls of the nation. The ensuing public outrage would enable the Prime minister to get shot of Ivra.

"So you see Alfie, all those backbench pricks she's been bonking won't dare to stand up for her, she'll have to go."

"Oh Condo, that really was worth waiting for. You have come up trumps this time. But how can we get Ivra and Norbert together? Ivra thinks Gert is common."

"So does everyone. This is politics Alfie. Politics. We all have to shit in the same ruddy pot from time to time. Just leave it to me. I'll deliver the result you want. Trust me."

"I do Condo, with all my heart."

"False bastard hasn't got one," thought Condo. "All he's got is that bloody swingometre the Beeb used to trot out on election night." He turned up the charm before addressing his boss. "What we need in the Regency is someone with grace, dignity, education, who will glide with elegance through the ceremonies of state. You do know what I mean, don't you Alfie?"

"Of course I do dear boy. I know exactly what is on your mind. Leave it all to me. Just run along and plot the Ivra and Norbert scenario, do a Shakespeare on it for me."

Condo departed leaving the Prime Minister to plot a few machinations of his own. Once Ivra had been given the bums rush, he could replace the unpopular Regent with Gert, who might with a little luck, and one hell of a lot of spin, be able to wean the public from its reactionary monarchical sentiments, especially those perfidious ingrates the Scots and the Welsh. The Prime Minister was careful to keep his Gert for Regent scenario secret from Condo, this was to be the Premier's contribution to the gaiety of the nation. The Prime Minister was perfectly aware of Condo's intention to insert himself into the post of Regent. Condo for Regent was a non starter if ever there was one. Ivra was bad enough, but Condo's boy friend, 'Shepherds Pie', mincing over the national stage was more than flesh and blood outside of Old Compton Street would vote for. Condo as Regent would mean Alfred Sawse for the dole queue, and the Prime Minister had no intentions of helping to facilitate that outcome.

2.

Over the sea and far away, on Prince Edward Island, the Royal family was settling in nicely, and the local economy was doing very nicely too as a result of their taking up residence in Charlottetown, where the tills of the local traders were rattling like teeth in the mouth of a palsied geriatric.

This upsurge in the economy was not due to the Queen blowing money on the locals, Her Maj. Would not have known how to blow money even had she been given a pair of bellows for Christmas. Her Majesty had made it plain from day one that she expected generous discounts on all her purchases, and if she did not get them, the goods would be sent back. They soon learnt. No, the economy was enriched by the flood of socialites from south of the border, the cream of North American society was flocking to Prince Edward Island. Anyone who had a room to rent had it made, property values made a mockery of Isaac Newton's laws of gravity. As for Martha's Vineyard, which had so recently been the posing patch for the socially aspirant millionaires, forget it, today you could not have given the place away. Maisy Wilson, who had recently taken in washing as a way to make ends meet and pay for the occasional six pack, was now taking in Vanderbilts and Rockefellers. So successful was this enterprise that soon she could afford to buy vast quantities of silk drawers from the mail order catalogue.

The exhibition of the Royal collections was a smash hit, it had ignited an enthusiasm for all things royal on the American Continent, a side effect of which was the Queen developing an interest in commercial entrepreneurship, or, in layman's language, how to turn a fast buck. There had been several family councils on the subject, none of which had avoided ending in acrimony, the younger members of the family feeling that such enterprises as were being suggested were too vulgar for words. Her Majesty, finally loosing patience with her brood, pointed out that they would find it infinitely more vulgar to have to go out and work for a living as she was not prepared to subsidise them for now and ever more. 'Queen Elizabeth's Pantry,' an exclusive line of groceries, was the outcome of the deliberations.

The Queen gave a regular series of garden parties at Government House, tickets were available at the gates, and American millionaires were particularly welcome, in fact they were practically the only ones who could afford them. A cup of Rosie with Her Majesty did not come cheap, nor did any one expect it to, except members of the Canadian Parliament and the American Congress, who were admitted free of charge. The elite of the Americas were bowled over by being on cucumber sandwich terms with the Queen, who played the situation like the pro she was.

"So nice of you to come. What do you do?" The Queen smiled at the party of gentlemen standing in front of her as if she was actually interested in hearing their answers.

"Samuel Q. Driberg mam. Chairman of the Senate Foreign Relation Committee."

"Really? How very interesting. And what are you working on at the moment?"

"The Tasmanian Question your Majesty."

"Oh yes. I know all about that." The Senator was surprised.

"I thought our debates were supposed to be secret."

"So they are, but I do have my sources you know."

The Tasmanian Question had started as a rumour on the internet, to the effect that Cuba was going to invade it and set up a marxist republic in the Southern hemisphere. The rumour had rapidly gained credence amongst the gullible, who were instrumental in having the electronic fable accepted as established fact, with the result that large swathes of the Worlds population were convinced that America was proposing to invade Tasmania and save democracy for the world.

"The Prime Minister of England is standing by us."

"I would not be too sure of that Senator He has been telling your President that he supports him, while at the same time, the two faced sonofabitch, excuse my French won't you, has been running around Europe, telling anyone who will listen, which is practically everyone, that the President is a brain dead moron and that Europe should have nothing to do with his schemes, and that if he goes ahead with it, then Europe should use the situation to bring about the collapse of the dollar." The Senator was visibly shocked.

"Is that really so, Mam?"

"It is indeed. As I said, I have my sources, and they are impeccable. The English Premier is planning a visit to Washington next week, as I understand it."

"That's so, your Majesty."

"In light of what I have just told you, and if I was in your place, I would not be too enthusiastic to welcome such a man to my capital."

"You're dead right, Mam. Dead right I say. Soon as I get back to Washington I'm going to put an end to that visit. Full stop."

"And this is your wife, Senator?" asked the Queen, indicating the lady at the Senator's side. She assumed it was a wife as the woman had undergone extensive plastic surgery, and men always dumped their trollops before they reached that stage in life.

"Why no Your Majesty. This is my sister-in-law, Miz Myrtle Quinzey Crabtree the third, the Chicago prophylactic heiress." The Queen extended her hand in greeting.

"How fitting." The audience was clearly at an end, there remained but one ritual to complete. "You have not visited the shop yet." This was not a question. The Queen insisted on an up to the minute report on who spent what and when in the shop at Government House. Nobody got away. "Harry, be a good boy and show the Senator and Mrs. Crabtree to the shop." Off they went, leaving the Queen in a high state of satisfaction. As Queen of American society, she held far greater sway over British policy than she had as Queen of England.

The shop was situated in what had been the butlers pantry, Edward and Sophie had been put in charge, she because she could count the change and knew how to smile at people, and he because nobody could think of anywhere else to put him. They were both dressed in straw hats and plastic aprons with the Royal arms embossed on them. The Senator was intrigued by one of the offerings.

"Gee Myrtle. What's this?" His sister in law inspected what it was he held in his hand.

"I don't rightly know Sam. Never heard of such a thing before. Piccalilli? Nope." She turned to Prince Edward. "Say sonny. What is this?" She held up the jar.

"A jar." The Prince had recently been given a home study book on charm, but had yet to get around to reading it. Sophie leapt into the breach. There would be hell to pay with her mother-in-law if she and Edward failed to make their sales target.

"That's Piccalilli, sort of vegetables in a mustard sauce. An absolute give away at one hundred and fifty U.S. a jar. It's all made here under Her Majesty's direct supervision you know." They did not know, nor was it, the stuff was made up by an outfit in Moosejaw Saskatchewan.

"Hear that Sam. Preserves made by the Queen herself. Well, we just got to have some of these to take back with us." Eventually they left with three carrier bags full, and Sophie had met her financial targets, both parties satisfied with the deal.

3.

The Regents of Scotland and Wales were settling into their jobs nicely. Both had a perfect instinct as to what would please their respective populations, and encouraged by the national Parliaments, were putting the wind up the London Government with alarming regularity, alarming that is for London's elite, everyone else in the country, including the English, thought it great fun.

Prince William was first off the mark, signing into law a local edict halving the amount of fuel duty levied in Wales. This act was totally without legal foundation, but nobody in Wales gave a damn about that and London was too terrified to make any moves to restore the original levels of duty. The result of this was a massive infusion of cash into Wales, as the English flocked across the border to fill up. Soon commercial tankers were crossing the border to be primed, and before anyone knew it, half the crude oil landed on the British mainland was coming in via Welsh ports and the Chancellor of the Exchequer was damn near suicidal.

Admiring the instincts of the Welsh, the Scots decided to embark on the same route, in their case with whiskey and cigarettes. As in the Welsh case, the borders were choked with folk in search of cheap booze and fags. These were the problems Alfred Sawse had to wrestle with, and he was not very good at the activity. Ivra was becoming more unpopular by the day. The opinion polls were so bad he refused to read them, and Wincarnis was becoming unbearable, blaming him every time she did something to make the situation worse, which was roughly twice a day.

For the Prime Minister, the delights of republicanism were becoming a mite shop soiled. Republicanism was a position he originally took as a method of persuading his party to vote him into the leadership, once there his wife made him write it into the political catechism, an act he was happy to undertake for the sake of a quiet life. As had others before him, Alfred found to his cost and ultimate discomfort that a quiet life could carry onerous penalties for those who took the coward's shilling, the interest on which was becoming due. Were it not for fear of his wife, he would have swallowed his pride, jettisoned his party's principles and publicly called on the Queen to return as head of state, thereby saving his political bacon. Even while trying to sooth his fears with such imaginings, he knew it was a non starter, as Condo had said when the dream had been confided to him, rather than acquiesce in bringing about such an eventuality, Wincarnis would do a Samson and bring the roof down on the lot of them.

The Prime Minister had one remaining hope of salvation, that was to shoehorn Gertie into the Regency and hope that her general popularity would dampen down the public anger, but this solution had its perils, foremost of which was Condo. Condo was making no bones over the fact that he wanted the Regency as a pay off for getting rid of Ivra, oblivious to the uproar this would generate. There was no way the Prime Minister could grant his friend's wish, yet at the same time, he could not afford to offend him. The matter would require careful and devious handling.

The second obstacle to the Prime Minister's plans was Wincarnis, who did not like Gert any more than she liked Ivra. Wincarnis was one of those women who hated other females, instinctively classing them as competition. Alfred would have to keep Wincarnis in ignorance of his plans until it was too late for her to do anything about them. There would be ructions if he managed to pull it off, but then he could always blame it on Macmurdo, she'd swallow that with no difficulty at all.

CHAPTER XIII.

Wincarnis Sawse, wife to the dear leader, who God save him was becoming less dear to all and sundry by the day, had been given many names by all sorts of people. Most of these were unofficial, whispered behind discrete hands, and all, excepting those sanctioned by the vicar at her Christening, excessively uncomplimentary to the point of blasphemy, the most widely disseminated of these informal appellations being the Macclesfield mouth. The woman's actual name, Wincarnis, was the subject of considerable speculation as to why her parents should have named her after a tonic wine sold in chemist's shops to fortify old codgers. There were numerous theories put foreword as a solution to the mystery of her curious moniker, the most popular doing the rounds at the current time, averred that her ma and pa had thought Port and lemon too common a name for their little princess and Sherry too middle class, they were artistic folk who made a great song and dance about being working class, while busting a gut to ensure they lived neither near to or like the great unwashed, arty folk are like that.

A clash between Ivra and Wincarnis was guaranteed the day the Regency was announced, without putting too fine a point on it, Wincarnis hated her rival's guts. The Prime Ministers wife had been given a strict nonconformist upbringing, and her parents, despite their artistic pretensions, had gone to great lengths to ensure their little treasure developed a mind as narrow as a gnat's back passage. It was therefore inevitable that she would be outraged by Ivra's sexual levity. That apart, there was the simple question of good old fashioned jealousy. Wincarnis was riddled with it. Wincarnis had always, since her husband had attained the Premiership, a period long before the first abdication, thought of herself as, and insisted on being addressed as, First Lady. Naturally, there was no man in the Government with the necessary testicular equipment to tell her different. As was Ivra to do later, Wincarnis acquired some airs and graces which solicited caricature, considering herself to be the greatest lady in the land, she had resolutely refused to curtsy to the real queen, considering the gesture beneath her, and she was damned if she was going to throttle her principles and do so to that raddled old slapper currently dossing at Buck House.

Ivra, on the other hand, felt very much the same about Wincarnis, she had been born into the metropolitan political elite, wrapped in the party banner for her christening, made a peeress in her own right. To Ivra, the Prime

Minister's wife was nothing more than "Northern tripe done up as Ciabatta," as she told every dinner party she was invited to, until over the years it became her signature phrase. It can come as no surprise that the two ladies, if that term be not an oxymoron, were heading for a phenomenal bust up, particularly over Wincarnis' habit of commandeering what was still known as the royal train, whenever she could be absolutely certain that Ivra wanted to use it. Wincarnis was en route to her daily inspection of the Downing Street complex, a self imposed task she refused to delegate, when she bumped into Condo on the main staircase.

"Morning Win. Lovely day for it isn't it?" His voice combined molasses with arsenic, the lethal combination he used when setting someone up for a nasty experience.

"Lovely day for what?"

"Why, Ivra's visit to Wales of course, I thought you knew all about it." Knowing full well she did not, nor did anyone else except for Condo, who had been told about the event by Ivra in the strictest confidence.

"What! That's impossible, the Welsh would sooner give up eating chips than invite Ivra."

"Oh, they did not invite her, in fact they don't even know she is coming. One of her little impromptu's if you know what I mean?"

"I do."

"Exactly, London is sick of them, you can't even so much as visit your local library without running the risk of Ivra paying one of her so called state visits. It's embarrassing for people. They don't like it Win, you know that don't you?"

"I do indeed. There's one good thing about this though."

"Yes?"

"The streets of London will be free of that preposterous motorcade of hers. For one day at least the traffic will be left to congest of it's own accord. The Welsh can put up with her clogging up their streets for the day."

"Oh no. You're wrong there Win lovey. She's taking the train."

"She wouldn't dare, not after last time."

"She has. It's all booked and waiting at Paddington for her Regencyship."

"I'm going to put a stop to this once and for all, I'm not having it I tell you."

"Can I do anything to help?" Condo could be the ultimate in solicitude when moving in for the kill.

"Yes you can. Phone the station, re-book the train in my name."

"Where shall I say you are going?"

"I haven't a clue, I'll think of where I am going when I get there. The main thing is to stop that promiscuous cow using the train."

"Well you get along then and I'll do the necessary, just leave it to me." Which of course she did. Wincarnis scurried off in search of the Prime Minister's limousine, it was parked outside the front door. The Premier was settling himself into the back seat when his wife came hurtling out of the house.

"Get out Alfred. Get out of that car this instant, I need it at once."

"But Wincarnis I'm on my way to Heathrow to meet the President of France."

"Can't help that I need it myself ".

"But Win, you promised I could meet the President."

"Don't argue Alfred. This is important." Wasting no further time on the corroding art of semantics, she yanked open the back door of the car, and pulled her husband out onto the pavement. "You'll have to take the tube." With that she slammed the door shut. "Paddington." She snapped at the driver, not even considering the employment of a please or a thank you. Alfred Sawse stood at the curb side, staring after his car and its driver as it disappeared into Whitehall. If he legged it he might make the Piccadilly line and Heathrow.

Wincarnis' car swept onto the platform at Paddington. To her fury, Ivra was already there, being greeted by the station master, with as little respect as he could get away with and still keep his job. A small crowd of rubber neckers stranded by a cancelled train had gathered to watch the proceedings, and to assuage their frustrations with public transport by making improper gestures with their fingers at the regent.

At the sight of the Prime Minister's wife, a gasp of amazement went up from the crowd. To a man they thought it had been worth being stranded to have been able to have witnessed such a vision of a traditional domestic goddess. When Wincarnis had set off on her tour of inspection, she had expected, on completion of her task, to return to her room and prepare for the day ahead. In her eagerness to put one over on Ivra, she had not even thought about her appearance. It was only as she fronted up to the sniggering Regent that she realised that her hair was in curlers and she was wearing a shapeless flannelette nightie the colour of surgical stockings.

Condo had tipped off the press, who were waiting to record the impending storm for the annals of the nation. There was a particularly strong representation from the Daily Truth, the editor of which had deeply displeased Wincarnis; she felt he did not treat her with the deference she considered to be her due. Wincarnis had by now reached the "Off with his head" stage of her career. Anyone who crossed her was for the chop, she constantly badgered Bondi Patterson to remove the offending editor, but Bondi had no intentions of allowing himself to be dictated to. The editor had got wind of Wincarnis' campaign, and decided on one of his own, with Condo's help this was to be the first stage, and Wincarnis would make the front pages of the next edition of the truth.

"Wincarnis darling," purred Ivra, just loud enough for everyone within a hundred yard radius to hear. "What an interesting outfit. What is it exactly, a fashion statement or a novel method of birth control?" Subtlety in any form was wasted on Wincarnis.

"You're not having this train, it's mine."

"Now now dear. This is the royal train and I am the Regent, and I am about to use it on an official journey."

"No you're not. I'm using it."

"And where are you going exactly?"

"That's nothing to do with you. It's none of your business where I'm going."

"I'm sorry dear, much as I'd like to stay here and chat, I have a schedule to keep." Ivra turned on her heal and made to enter the train, Wincarnis had the same urgent ambition. An unseemly tussle between the two women developed, finally, one tripped up and fell into the train and the other fell on top of her, the station master seized the opportunity to be rid of both of them, slammed shut the door, blew his whistle, and before Ivra could land one more punch on Wincarnis, they were off.

Condo had warned a friend in the Welsh assembly about Ivra's intended visit and the friend, in turn had alerted a loyal chum on the railways, who duly engineered a diversion. Instead of entering the Severn Tunnel, the Royal Train headed north. Such was the intensity of the acrimonious exchange of views between the two passengers, that they were passing through Shrewsbury before they realised that something was not quite what it should be.

The entire scheme had been carefully planned in advance. The drivers had been given strict instruction and the communication cord nobbled, it was many hours later that the regal caravanserai bearing the still bickering political divas, pulled into Carlisle station. Condo had used the time well, with Wincarnis safely quarantined, he had safely re-instated Gertie into a Government position, which after Ivra and Wincarnis slugging it out on the platform at Paddington, was the main item on the evening news bulletins.

2.

The Daily Telegraph continued to be the newspaper of choice for those holding a particular interest in the nether regions of the body politic, there was even talk of its circulation overtaking that of the Truth, an extra bonus to the readership in the guise of a slanging match between the rival proprietors, who looked on their sales figures as a form of penile extension. The Telegraph did not disappoint its readers, it contented them with a regular drip of insights from the royal writing desk. The Queen's memoirs were coming along a treat, and the lady made sure her favourite Grub Street rag had advance notice of the best bits. As she had all the back up evidence to hand, none of those favoured by a mention, dared to implement the favoured political reaction of false outrage too impertinently, or risk embarrassing revelations by using the rolling pin of mendacity to clobber the truth in the form of a libel suit, and to trouser a few grand into the bargain. When it came to fighting dirty, Her Majesty could teach the politicos a thing or two, and they did not in the least appreciate the lessons so freely given. 'How They Stitched Up Maggie,' was one such headline, which gave a detailed account, including names, of the machinations by which the former Prime Minister had been deposed, causing the Tory Party to fall apart, not that it had far to fall in the first place.

The Tory disintegration was the genesis of much comfort for the Government, that is until the next headline. 'Sawse Gives Contract to Nepalese Company Registered in Cayman Islands.' This story wiped any residual grins off the collective chops of the administration, it told of how in return for a bung to Party funds, an offshore company, with no British connections had been given the contract to build a new embassy in Buenos Aires, the greater scandal was that the old building had only been completed six month earlier.

All the members of Parliament, who were not in therapy before the abdication, were certainly queuing up for it by now. Nobody could be sure who was next up for exposure, and as they all had something to hide which could either cost them their careers or their liberty. The nervous tensions in and around Westminster had not existed in so concentrated a form since Mary Tudor stopped burning folk for heresy. One or two M.P.s whose nerves were not up to taking the strain had gone so far as to take extended leave in Rio, where they were making frantic efforts to make local girls pregnant, thereby making themselves ineligible for deportation should they be indicted on home territory, a tropical lucky dip so to speak.

3.

The Queen, thrilled by her success with the glitterati of the North American continent, decided to consolidate her position with the purchase of a base in the United States, her chosen location being Virginia, whose good citizens felt that the revolution had done absolutely nothing for the social tone of the neighbourhood and that a gentleman had not been sighted anywhere near the ranks of the Yankee Government since General Lee had resigned to lead the armies of the South.

Her Majesty had taken a lease on a colonial mansion not far from Washington, it was in the shape of an H, the crossbar of which formed a large ball room, ideal for entertaining all those Senators and Members of Congress. The Queen had taken to popping down to the American Capital on a regular basis, to wine and dine the influential. The President of the U.S.A. was becoming distinctly edgy over the presence of the Queen, her influence and opinions were becoming an established fact in the capital, her advice eagerly solicited by the legislators, who would frequently ask themselves "What would the Queen think?" Before passing any controversial legislation into law. The American public had also come to appreciate the Queen's advice, they were coming round to the opinion that George III might not have been quite so bad after all.

The one person who was not thrilled by the current situation was President William Gort, who was outraged by Queen Elizabeth overtaking him in the opinion polls, a situation he regarded almost as a declaration of war.

The director of the C.I.A had been summoned to the Oval office, he knew the reason in advance, he was to engineer the restoration of the queen to the throne of England before she totally took over the

States. The President was completing a phone call.

"Well that's mighty nice of you Prime Minister. Speak to you soon now. Bye." He replaced the receiver in the cradle and turned to the Director. "Gee Sam, that Limey Prime Minister's a dumb sonofabitch, just been telling me what they been talking about during the Cabinet meeting. Ah already know what they said, we got the place bugged for Chrissakes, and here he is repeating it all over again."

"But he does not know the place is bugged Mr. President"

"Well I'll be Danged. Think I ought to tell him Sam?"

"Hell no Mr. President. It's a secret."

"Oh right. Now then Sam, you and your boys gotta get the Queen off my back. She's six points ahead in the polls and that's not decent."

"What do you want me to do Sir?"

"How the hell should I know, you're the Director of the C.I.A. not me. Get a revolution goin' or sumpin."

"A revolution?"

"Yeah! Great idea Sam. Get to work on that wife of Sawse's. An uppity bitch if ever I met one. From what I hear, the Brits think she is a pushy cow and long overdue her comeuppance.

He brought her to visit once and all she could do was talk about the Marx brothers."

"I think you mean Karl Marx Mr. President."

"Probably. Wasn't that the one who played the piano and was always chasing after Margaret Dumont?" The Director decided to give up while he still had a chance of winning and staying sane at the same time, he made a rapid exit; wondering who in his organisation could be bludgeoned into coming up with a scheme to overthrow the Government of the country's closest ally, and who could plausibly carry the can when the whole cockamamie scheme went pear shaped. Whatever was done, it would have to involve a scandal, the British were a most censorious race of people, they may have exported plenty of Puritans to the New World, but the kept the best of the bunch for home consumption.

CHAPTER XIV.

Condo Maites, the Machiavelli of modern British politics, for whom the term devious would have fallen short of the reality by a considerable distance, had not been wasting his time in sitting on his whoopee cushion, dreaming of a glorious future. Dreams had to be worked for, and Condo had been on overtime for days past, this time, he was determined he would not miss out on the Regency.

First stage in the plan had been the re-instatement into government of the people's Gert against the wishes of the Prime Minister, who without Wincarnis to supply a short term lease on a yard of backbone, had finally given in to Condo's demands for her to return to the fold and keep company with the rest of the flock. This had been no easy task. Gert had committed the cardinal sin, a bell, book and candle job, the woman had the effrontery to become popular, not only popular, as if that was not bad enough, but more popular than the Prime Minister. She was also hopeless at her job, but that was an easily forgivable transgression, almost a guarantee of promotion in this Government, but popularity, oh no, the next re shuffle and she'd be out again.

In light of what had gone before, the reluctance of the Prime Minister to re-admit the dame to the magic circle around the Cabinet table was perfectly natural, but, there was another, more down to earth reason for the man's distaste for her, which caused him to grit his teeth. Gert was far too common a soul for the comfort of the prime Minister's upper middle class susceptibilities. Gert made a career out of being as common as muck, for her it was a political mission statement, calculated to Garner votes, she was the sort of woman who thought nothing whatsoever about picking her nose and farting while being interviewed on Newsnight.

Condo had made his calculations with the greatest of precision, with Gert and Norbert back on the Government circuit, it would be impossible for Ivra to ignore them, they would be together at many official functions, from that point there would be no impediment to Condo orchestrating a suitable scenario between Norbert and Ivra. A bit of sex, a bit of financial skullduggery and hey presto! Ivra would be made ambassador to Outer Mongolia and Condo would be able to hand the lease to Buck House to his beloved Shepherd's Pie, and if that did not put a stop to the screaming queen's tantrums, then nothing would.

The opening gambit in the campaign to be shot of Ivra, involved the manipulation of Billy-Bob Thorpe, the Regent's partner, the latest in a long line of fat arsed thickos filched from other women. The object was to discredit Billy-Bob and to get Ivra's hunting instincts primed for fresh game. Condo had a wide range of acquaintances, amongst who was Dosser Bates, so called because every time he fell out with his boy friend, he ended up sleeping in a cardboard box behind the Army and Navy Store in Victoria. Dosser was experiencing one of his al-fresco periods when Condo picked him up at the hand outs at Lincoln's Inn Fields.

"Condo! What are you doing here? They made you resign again?"

"No. Get in." He opened the door of the taxi.

"But I haven't had me grub yet. It's chicken curry to night, and if you let the bastards give you a sermon then say you've found Jesus, they give you a bar of chocolate."

"I'll give you a feed, now get in you red headed bastard." Dosser jumped into the back of the taxi, he gave his friend a cheesy grin, he had all his own teeth, unfortunately, they looked like National Health dentures.

"We're eating at your place?"

"No, we're just going there to get you cleaned up, you can have some of my clothes, then we're off to the Aspidistra."

"Ere, what have I got to do to justify the cost of a meal in that joint?"

"Nothing you have not done before and charged for."

"I've reformed since them days."

"Yeah. And I've turned straight. Don't worry, it'll be a doddle. This is what you've got to do." Condo then explained what it was that would be required of Dosser.

"Is that all?"

"Yep. And a fifty quid bonus if all goes to plan."

"Well! I'll be buggered."

"Don't worry, you won't be." An hour later they were sitting at a discrete table in the Aspidistra, where they were joined by Billy-Bob, who was encouraged to drink more than he wanted to the point where he did not give a damn. When Billy-Bob's wits had been inundated by the cheapest booze on the list, Condo suggested a walk to sober up a bit, he received the enthusiastic endorsement of Dosser.

"You want to be able to walk a straight line when you get back to the missus, don't you?" That was the clincher.

"Right there Doss. Ivra's a bit picky since becoming Regent. Where are we going?" Such are the ways by which lambs and innocents are slaughtered."

"Hampstead." Announced Condo, "It's quite the mode to be up here at this time of night. Everyone's doing it. It'll be a nice drive." Condo settled the bill, while Dosser indulged his sensory urges by having a flaming row with the waiter over the size of the portions and then they were off to the Heath. Condo parked the car in the Groves. "I'm feeling a bit tired as a matter of fact, you go off with Dosser. I'll wait here." As soon as they were out of sight, Condo was on his mobile, coordinating what from his point of view was to be the highlight of the evening.

Dosser and Billy-Bob crossed the open area and entered the woods. Abruptly, with, an unconscionable lack of consideration, the light departed.

"Christ," thought Dosser. "One of these days I'm going to break my neck in this damn place. It's like being down a bloody mine, they ought to hand out canaries instead of fucking condoms." He pawed the air in the vague direction of Billy-Bob. "You OK Billy? Watch your step, it's pretty steep around here."

"Fine Dosser." And these were his final words before going arse over tea kettle down the embankment.

"Christ Bill," yelled Dosser, imagining with no superfluous embellishment what it was that Condo would do to him if he loused up on this one. "Where are you?" His concern was rewarded with a groan somewhere to the left of him. Dosser did not find Billy-Bob, he fell over him, giving the poor fellow a boot in the teeth as he did so.

"I hurt myself. Shit Dosser, this ain't no night out in Seattle."

"Let's have a look at you. I've done a first aid course." Dosser ran his fingers over Billy-Bob's torso, making a swift diversion for a quick feel between the legs, enough to conclude that it was true what they said about the dick from Texas. "Ivra is a lucky girl isn't she?"

"Eh?"

"Never mind, no bones broken. Off we go. Come on." He hauled Billy-Bob to his feet. They set off down the path, their eyes learning to accommodate what little moon light the trees would permit to percolate down to ground level. They strolled along various paths, shadowy figures gazing at them as they passed by. Occasionally, strange sounds, resembling a diffused stereo system, indicated forms of life had taken root behind the bushes, disturbing the uniform silence, for although there was plenty of life, as represented by Homo Sapiens Sapiens, it seemed it was a life disinclined to speak its name at any pitch audible to the human ear.

"Hey Dosser. How come no-one's doing any talking? They's just looking at each other like they was window shopping."

"It's the etiquette of the Heath Bill. Sort of a local custom if you know what I mean." Billy-Bob nodded his head, living as he did with Ivra in Buck House, he knew all about etiquette, he practically had it administered as a suppository before breakfast each morning. "Not the done thing to make a noise." At that point the hush was violated by the sound of someone having their bare arse walloped to within a stroke of orgasm.

"Listen to that Dosser. They're breaking the rules making all that noise. Think we ought to go in there and explain the etiquette?"

"No, no, they'll come down to earth soon enough, take it from me." Condo was saved from making prolonged efforts of prevarication by the appearance of two cute lads in tee shirts and shorts carrying a large wicker basket between them, the sort Miss Marple would have used to go shopping.

"Evening girls," said one of the lads. "Here you are now." He fished into the basket and handed Dosser and Billy-Bob a couple of condoms apiece. "Nightie night, shag tight."

"What the hell was that?" The encounter was beyond the purlieus of Billy-Bob's cultural experiences. The poor fellow was quite shocked. "They called us girls."

"It's the light Bill. Can't see a damn thing, could just as easily have thought us to be a couple of Martians."

"Ah guess so." He was so gullible bless him. "But what they giving us these Johnnies for? That's mighty fishy if you ask me."

"Haven't you heard Bill? The Pope made an announcement that birth control is now ok, so the Government declared this to be national condom week. There's teams of people all over London handing out rubbers." "Well now, I call that right neighbourly seeing the damn country isn't even Catholic."

"That's the Brits for you Billy-Bob boy." They had now reached a particularly remote region of the Heath, Dosser suggested they stop and soak up the atmosphere, Billy assumed this was but an extension of the ritual and etiquette required of the locus. A man jumped out in front of them; apart from a diamond earring he was stark bollock naked.

"Don't panic Bill," advised Dosser. "It's quite normal hereabouts." The man gave Dosser a big grin, the sort that would have given Gorgonzola a bad name, before turning his attentions to Billy-Bob.

"It's my doctor you see," said the man as if the entire world was au fait with his particular condition. "He said my cock will make medical history. End up in the papers like as not."

He pointed at his member which was erect and covered with gold spangles Not knowing what to say, Billy-Bob opted for the option of saying nothing. "Take a closer look," urged the man.

"Not to-night pal. I'll take a rain check if it's the same to you." Dosser whispered in Billy-Bob's ears.

"Go on Bill. You have to. Etiquette and all that, he'll be terribly offended if you don't take an interest. Trust me." And like the dork he was, Billy-bob did. He inclined his neck an inch or two. "No, not like that, get right up close. Kneel down, that's right. Now take a real close look. Attaboy Billy-Bob."

The Texan was kneeling on the ground, his face half an inch from the gilt spattered cock, when the darkness was momentarily banished by the explosion of a flash gun, then several others went off in quick succession.

"What in God's name was that?" Doubt came within an ace of piercing the armour of Billy-Bob's intelligence. "What's all them people doin'?"

"Oh. Don't worry." Dosser had learnt the script to perfection. "This place is a favourite for Swedish tourists. They are just taking holiday snaps, and that one there is a photographer from "Outdoor Health" magazine."

"That's right guy," acknowledged the staff photographer from the Daily Truth, before sauntering off.

"We'd best be getting back Bill, and I am proud of you. You let those tourists take your photo, I bet that made their holiday for them.

Billy-Bob Thorpe, you're a great human being, you know that?"

"Gee Dosser. I don't know what to say." And God himself never said a truer word.

Back at the car, Condo received a call on his mobile confirming that all had gone to plan. When that little lot hit the headlines, Ivra would be well on her way to the divorce courts, and he, Condo Maites, on his way to the regency.

2.

The commerce of diplomacy, as traded between nations, is housed in many different divisions, the importance of which changes with the currently prevailing fads and fashions, but the premier of those divisions does not change, as immutably fixed in the firmament as the North Star, it goes under the name of the state visit. This is a peculiar institution, it consists of one head of state visiting another with a platoon of officials in tow, the whole shebang costing an inordinate amount of money. The respective parties make a great show of adoring one another, and the two countries involved, swear undying friendship for one another. The proceedings gallop along for about three or four days and end in mutual expressions of sadness at parting etc., after which everyone goes back to the infinitely more satisfying enterprise of hating each others guts.

Ivra had one last great ambition to fulfill, a state visit. The only problem with this was that nobody would have her, and she had proved such a disaster at her job that the Government was in no circumstances prepared to risk diplomatic ructions by insisting that somebody put her up for a few days and throw in a motorcade and a banquet or two. Not one to take adversity in the missionary position, Ivra had advertised on the internet for someone to invite her on a state visit. Predictably there were no takers, well, not among the established polities of the planet.

The Hutt River Province was situated in Western Australia, although a little clarification would not go amiss at this particular point in the narrative. Firstly, the place was not a province at all, it was a farm. Back in the Seventies, its' owners had found agriculture a vexing proposition, simply put the joint was going broke and nowhere else, when the cavalry, in the form of some bare faced cheek, came charging to the rescue. The owners declared unilateral independence from Australia. They transformed themselves from Len and Shirl Casey, into Prince Leonard and Princess Shirley, and went into the business of flogging stamps, passports and knighthoods at competitive prices to all comers.

The Government of Western Australia, in common with similar entities the World over, lacked both common sense and a sense of humour, it kicked up a hullabaloo of the kind which inevitably generated the sort of publicity money could not buy, ergo, the Hutt River Province was up and running, and paying a handsome dividend to its owners. The enterprise had graduated summa cum laude, now it was about to achieve it's greatest accolade, a visit from the Regent of England.

Ivra had left for Western Australia the day after Billy-Bob's walk in the Black Forest of North London, he was not to accompany his wife to her triumph in the antipodes. Condo had made certain of that, they were told that they could not both be out of the country at the same time for reasons of state, the flattery to their egos ensured unquestioning compliance. For her official escort, Ivra was awarded Norbert, ostensibly to convey the personal greetings of the Prime Minister to Prince Leonard and Princess Shirley, who of course were no more royal than Ivra, they'd get on like a house on fire, and if they did not, then so much the better.

The trip did not go quite to plan, but then these things never do. The Chancellor had refused to sanction any extra spending for the visit and the regal party were thus forced, from reasons of economy, to travel steerage, not the most comfortable condition in which to spend nineteen hours of non-stop flying. On arrival in the West Australian capital of Perth, there were no red carpets or brass bands to greet them, they were subjected to a humiliating customs search, during the course of which, Ivra was threatened with arrest for using foul and abusive language and Norbert had six bottles of Scotch and a sex instruction manual confiscated. Having negotiated the customs inspection to the dissatisfaction of all concerned, they could have been forgiven for feeling their troubles were behind them, but the arm of Condo Maites was long and exceedingly thorough. Ivra and Norbert were somewhere over the Indian ocean when the news of Billy-Bob's adventures on Hampstead Heath broke. Condo had been exact in his timing of the release, by the time Ivra landed at Perth, her dearly beloved was front page news on three continents. The British press was in its element, relishing the hypocrisy they habitually wrapped themselves in when denouncing sexual hanky panky amongst the celebrated. On such occasions the press were wont to describe themselves as family newspapers before making fissile contact with the salacious details, as would a dog make contact with a lamp post. Such self description of familial status could only be recognised as valid if one included Caligula, Messalina and Eskimo Nell amongst one's relations. The Daily Truth as usual set the tone with a picture of Billy-Bob considering the evidence, with the caption, 'Watcha Cock.'

Ivra ignored the questions shrieked at her by the press pack, shocked into silence at the sight of front page pictures of her spouse being held up for her inspection, the so called Swedish tourists had been meticulous in their attention to detail.

"I'll murder him. So help me God I'll bloody murder the fornicating bastard." They were well out of the airport precincts before Ivra was able to articulate her rage to her satisfaction. Her hosts were too embarrassed by the situation to comment. Norbert attempted a little diplomacy.

"Well, it could have been worse luv. At least he wasn't with another woman."

"Jesus Norbert. I could have put up with a woman, but to be ditched for a bloke with hairy legs and a dick that looked as if it had been polished up with Brasso. I'll divorce him. Just wait until I get back."

"But what about the scandal of a divorce?"

"After what he's been photographed doing, a scandal is the last of my problems. That sanctimonious bitch Wincarnis, she'll have a field day with this she will" Norbert was inclined to agree with her on that last point.

When they finally arrived at the Hutt River Province, Ivra and Norbert were exhausted, it was late at night and all they wanted was a bath and a comfortable bed, which of course was exactly what they did not get. All the accommodation was taken by paying guests, the State Visitors, were given two tents separated by a portable thunder box. Norbert had to share his tent with the two Downing Street minders Condo had selected for the task.

Despite the lateness of the hour and the bedraggled state of the Pommie luminaries, Princess Shirley insisted they go ahead with the first of the state banquets. A total of twelve people, the men of the party dressed in their very best shorts and vests, sat down at the kitchen table to dine off tinned stewing steak, tinned potatoes and fresh frozen garden peas with Chicko Rolls on the side, this should have been followed by Lamingtons, an Aussie delicacy, but as someone had forgotten to take them out of the freezer, the dignified assembly had to make do with mugs of stewed tea and some pretty abominable speeches. Only after the formalities had been completed to the satisfaction of the host and their neighbours, were the official couple allowed to retire to their tents, closely watched by the paying guests who naturally had not been permitted to observe the toffs at the trough.

Ivra had by now calmed down, and was suffering the onset of anticlimax, which in her case took a rampant ungovernable desire for sex, the only candidate to hand was Norbert. Ivra had her doubts concerning his capabilities, as she, in concert with everyone else in Government circles knew that it was a long time since Gert had let him get his leg over and he would probably need a few practice runs before getting it right.

"Nightie night Ivra." He turned to go to his tent, but Ivra was quicker than he, she grabbed him firmly by the arm.

"Not so fast laddie. You want a bit of bod?" It was not so much a question, rather an informing him of her needs. "Come on now, don't dawdle." She propelled him into her tent. The poor man was utterly bemused. "Don't stand about. Get your kit off, let's see what you've got." The poor man was far too frightened to argue, he did as bid. Shortly he stood before Ivra, clad only in his socks, sandals and a particularly unbecoming pair of Y fronts.

Ivra, unfortunately, was having a bit of trouble, the unaccustomed heat coupled with the long haul flight, had caused her body to swell, a more experienced traveller would have warned her not to undertake such a journey wearing a corset, which in any case was two sizes too small. The result was that she was unable to remove the offending garment by normal means.

"Help me for Christ's sake Norbert."

"How?"

"Get a scissors."

"Where?"

"How the fuck do I know. Use your bloody initiative. Go and look for a pair. Go on man, get on with it." Norbert was torn between fear of Ivra and fear of being seen blundering about in his undies. Fear of Ivra decided his course of action. He blundered off to his tent, where one of the aides, after ferreting about in Prince Leonard's back yard, came up with a pair of garden shears.

Norbert returned to free Ivra from her body armour, and here things might have ended in the time honoured fashion, had it not been for Willy Alsop. Willie was one of those children, who, while possibly loved by their parents, engendered in the rest of humanity the conviction the race of men would have been better served had the brat been drowned at birth. As Norbert was opening Ivra up like a tin of pilchards, Willie slipped a Carpet snake under the canvass of her tent. Now, a Carpet snake is not venomous, but Ivra and Norbert did not know that. They shrieked, they hollered, they screamed in terror, before dashing out of the tent into the back yard, where they continued their panic inspired cacophony without interruption. The lights came on, folk gathered to appreciate the spectacle of Ivra half in, half out of her corset, rolling on the ground having a good old fashioned dose of hysterics instead of the thorough rogering she had planned for. Norbert, having discovered the reason for the snake's appearance, grabbed Willy and started giving him a bloody good hiding. The lad's father, quite unreasonably took exception to this line of action, and laid one on Norbert. What followed was recorded by a reporter from the West Australian, who, unaccountably, had been waiting in the wings for such an eventuality. Norbert and Willy's dad were still beating the bejesus out of each other when Duncan, one of the Downing Street mafia was on his mobile to Condo back in London, reporting that all was going to plan.

3.

The State Visit by Ivra to the Hutt River, received saturation coverage, as a topic of conversation, the British public had had nothing comparable to get their teeth into since George III had gone bananas, which was just where the Government was going. Naturally, they got the blame for the entire shambles. There emerged a national consensus that Ivra should be tarred and feathered in Trafalgar Square. As far as the people were concerned, no punishment could be considered so extreme that it could not be visited upon the shameless trollop. As for the people's Gert, that poor woman had been unjustly humiliated by the feckless Norbert. The people, in their sentimental wisdom, elevated her to sainthood, in their eyes she could do no wrong.

Gert adored her new status, she revelled in it, ignoring no opportunity to ram it down

Wincarnis' throat. Wincarnis, true to form, made the Prime Minister's life hell with her demands that Gert be fired, terrified as he was by his wife, he was even more terrified by the thought of what the people would do to him if he did as bid by his marital harridan. Desperate, the man practiced the arts of prevarication with an intensity that was an affront to moral probity.

Saint Gert had no intention of rushing off to the divorce courts, her present state of martyrdom was too valuable to risk being negated by a decree nisi. No, she would calmly await Norbert's return from Australia. She would meet him with dignity at Heathrow, quietly grieving for the benefit of the press. After the public greetings, she would take him back to their home, and listen quietly to whatever explanations he would have managed to dream up, and when she had done all that, and only then, she'd give the witless bastard a bloody good hammering.

As for Ivra, Gert had not quite decided what she would do, although she had given the possibilities considerable attention; but whatever it was she would ultimately settle on, it would constitute a very public and embarrassing put down.

CHAPTER XV.

The C.I.A. had been assiduous in its plotting of nefarious deeds, as had Condo Maites, although not in tandem with each other. The American agency had come up with a scheme to discredit the Prime Minister's wife, and with her the Government which she unofficially headed. Naturally, Wincarnis allowed her old man to pretend in public that he was the gaffer, even she realised the convention should be observed now and again for form's sake. No one was fooled by that little ploy, the cat had been let out of the bag on too many occasions for the public to be fooled into thinking that was where it habitually resided in contentment. Least of all were the readers of the Daily Telegraph, Percy Tcherkoff, had a direct line to the doings of the first family, via the C.I.A and one Violet Parsons.

Vi was a charwoman at Chequers, the Prime Minister's country house, not that she was called such, politically correct observance decreed she be designated charperson, one more fly in the ointment of her discontent. Vi considered the Prime Minister to be a traitor to his class, a cardinal sin in her codex of what was and what was not permissible in a well ordered society. The redoubtable char had been born and bred a Conservative, and strongly disapproved of the nobs going socialist, and in her particular edition of the encyclopaedia of life, Alfred Sawse was marching to the wrong drum and in a contrary direction to that in which he should have been going. Now, as for Wincarnis, in Vi's eyes, she was a different kettle of fish altogether, getting above her station in life was how she phrased it. Wincarnis, despite some third rate elocution lessons, still sounded as common as muck, which, incidentally was how she treated the domestic staff in general and Vi in particular, who made no attempt to disguise her contempt for the self styled first lady. This situation had not gone unnoticed by the London Station Chief of the C.I.A.

If Vi had any weakness whatsoever it was for fortune telling. She was a sucker for a deck of the Tarot, or the tea leaves. It was the easiest thing in the world for the C.I.A. to effect a meeting between Madam Demetrios, in reality, an operative of the company, and Mrs. Violet Parsons. One of Vi's neighbours worked on the Telegraph, with careful orchestration and the co-operation of Sir Percy, Madam D. would feed Vi with info about the Sawse's, ostensibly received from the spirits, Vi would then be pumped by the neighbour, and Percy would publish it the next day in the Telegraph, and all concerned would have clean hands.

After a few trial runs, which went off to the satisfaction of all parties concerned, the C.I.A inaugurated its first major campaign against Wincarnis. This involved leaking to the public the fact that the first lady had not breast fed her latest baby. Now, that was not as trivial as at first might seem to be the case. Egged on by some of the wilder elements of the medical profession, desperate to see their mugs on the telly and a few terminally gormless sociology professors, the Government had initiated a campaign to coerce the women of the land into breast feeding their offspring.

Like all such initiatives called into being at the behest of the great and the good, it's perpetrators, once they had the bit between their teeth, were determined, come what may, that the populace should fall into line, irrespective of what their individual attitudes may have been, and do exactly what they had been told to do. These arbiters of the national welfare held no brief for personal licence, for them, such a concept was a direct challenge to their right to decide what was best for everyone else, and that those folk had a moral duty to do precisely as they were told.

Wincarnis was firmly behind the policy, so eager was she for its implementation, she turned it into a personal crusade, demanding that women do the deed wherever they fancied, causing legislation to be enacted making it illegal for shopkeepers to prevent breast feeding on what was essentially their private property. The fact that the majority of the punters in MacDonald's might object to women whipping their tits out and thereby putting them off their hamburgers, not to mention the outrage to public decency, was of no consideration to these fanatics. Doctors and social workers of all description were ordered to bully the women of the country into compliance. All this was backed up with a pernicious campaign of television advertising, plugging the notion that any woman failing to give suck was a bad mother who deserved to have her children taken away from her.

In the fullness of time, the irritation with all of this would have petered out, slaughtered by the next great issue to take up residence in the limited accommodation of the public mind, but this was not to be. A particularly Bolshie journalist from the Daily Mail had the temerity to ask Wincarnis if she had given the tit to her latest.

The first couple were outraged at the impertinence of this intrusion into their private lives, which they scrupulously kept private, except when their doings would make for a good photo call. Alfred and Wincarnis suddenly went all regal on the nation at the asking of this perfectly legitimate question, that is, they refused point blank to answer it. This refusal only served to add a bucketful of turps to the bonfire of public debate, an outcome anyone other than a politician could have predicted. The issue refused to do the decent thing and overdose on journalistic exuberance. The more close lipped the first couple became, the greater the demand for answers. Ministers were even banned from giving interviews, a first for that Government.

The public need not have worried, just when the Government thought things could get no worse, Vi Parsons, via the Telegraph, let the Nation into communion with Downing Street's secret matter, and she did not need the prompting of Madam Demetrios to do so, as she was witness to the secularly padlocked world of Alfred and Wincarnis. With a whisper to her neighbour, Vi let the nation know that the latest infant to be whelped by the first couple had been weaned on Cow and Gate milk powder. The women of the land rose up in fury, there were parades and demonstrations, a few more bricks than usual, experienced the trajectory which propelled them over the garden wall of number ten. Why? the women of the Nation demanded, were they being forced to suffer sore dugs in the cause of some feminist Valhalla, when the Macclesfield mouth gets off scot free.

2.

The C.I.A was delighted the way its campaign against Wincarnis was laying golden eggs. The President was impressed and had sent a personal message of congratulations to the London Station Chief along with an injunction to keep up the good work, an unnecessary spur as the agency was already planning the second prong of its attack.

Wincarnis, Alfred, Condo and Mac were in the gallery at Lancaster house, standing in front of a huge montage of a country town, there was a sign post reading:
LLANFAIRPWLLGWYNGYLLGOGERYCHWYRN DROBWLLLLANTYSILIOGOGOGOCH.

To the left and right of them stood two step ladders, Condo was perched on one, Mac on the other, each holding a watering can. At a signal from Condo a video camera was started. Wincarnis and Alf smiled gamely at the camera while huddling under an umbrella as Mac and Condo emptied the contents of the watering cans over them, thus simulating the climate of North Wales. The footage of this incident would be relayed on the news bulletins three days hence, giving the impression the first couple were enjoying a humble holiday no different to those enjoyed by what they had long since considered to be their subjects. The vision thus created would bear no relationship to their actual holiday which would be spent on a luxury yacht cadged from a Jordanian Millionaire.

"How much longer do I have to put up with this?" snapped Wincarnis, who thought it beneath her dignity to have to pander to the envious instinct, of the mob.

"Nearly there Wincarnis love. One more can should do it." Predicted Condo, determined to string out her discomfort for as long as feasible. An aide passed him up a refill, unfortunately, he overbalanced giving Wincarnis a thorough drenching in the process.

"You fool Condo. I'm soaked to the skin."

"Clumsy sod Condo. Look what you've done to poor old Win." This was Mac, he was always happiest when his rival dropped a bollock.

"Yes. Just look at me. Don't stand there Alfred. Do something."

After all those years of marriage, the woman had still not measured the limitations of her spouse.

"Yes dear." And that was all the poor dab could manage under the pressure of the circumstances.

"I've got a meeting in forty five minutes and here I am looking like a drowned rat." Her audience thought her summary of her appearance so comprehensively apt, they collectively thought it best not to comment. The grizzly silence was broken by a call to Wincarnis' mobile phone, which rang out to the tune of 'Who wants to be a millionaire'. She answered the call. "What now? Yes, of course I can. No trouble whatsoever." She was almost as good a liar as Macmurdo. Wincarnis turned to her husband. "The meeting has been brought forward, I've got to go at once." Not waiting for any reply, nor thinking one necessary, she swept out of the room, water still dripping from the hem of her designer denim skirt, leaving behind her a relief which was palpable.

The nature of the CIA's attack on the first couple utilised their greed, like all of their kind, while volubly affecting to despise money, they made damn sure there was plenty of the offending substance available for their personal consumption. They were swimming in the stuff, and Wincarnis made sure their supply was regularly replenished, to guard against evaporation, caused by those occasions when they found it unavoidable to use their own wealth as opposed to enjoying the benefits of other people's.

Wincarnis had her own accounting firm, and very posh it was too, lots of lush Government contracts coming her way. It was well known in the business world that a short cut to Government favours was to use Wincarnis' firm. One day, out of the blue, the firm received an enquiry from the representative of the Cocos Keeling Islands, wherever they may be, nobody in the office was entirely sure of the location.

In common with her staff, Wincarnis herself was none too sound when it came to understanding the mechanics of geography, she invariably relied on the Foreign Office to tell her what ethnic glad rags to wear when on an overseas tour. But if the lady was none too sound on geography, then she knew all about governments. Governments were governments wherever on the globe they were situated, and governments had dosh, and, if they were short of a few readies, as most of the less professionally run entities were, then they could always print a bit more, or, if that did not work, the situation could be rectified by a dip into the foreign aid budget, a favoured ploy in the third world, whose rulers could not understand how they who governed the prosperous West, could be so gullible as to give it to them in the first place. A meeting with the Island's representative, Colonel Jervis, was requested and eagerly acceded to. The venue for the meeting did at first glance appear a little strange, but Wincarnis was used to the vagaries of foreign potentates, it was to take place at the Two Chairmen of all places, just around the corner from Downing Street, where the first family still lived pending eviction proceedings in the High Court. Queen

Elizabeth II had not forgotten them, not by a long chalk.

Five minutes late and still sopping wet from the soaking Condo had inadvertently administered, Wincarnis blundered into the Chairmen. She had never been in a pub before, she did not approve of them, but, this was business and the client had insisted. The Colonel came over to greet Wincarnis, the man oozed a phoney discount store sort of charm which someone like Wincarnis was bound to fall for. She did, he led her over to a corner table.

"Dear, dear lady. I may call you Wincarnis mayn't I, such a sweet name." If he had worn a bow tie which twirled and lit up at the press of a button, it would not have seemed out of place on such a character. Wincarnis simpered. "You will join me in a modest tincture won't you?"

"I'm teetotal." She almost bit her tongue off on sight of the pained expression this elicited on the dial of the Colonel.

"Now I'm sure you don't mean that. Just a glass of red wine to oil the path of the social niceties. Do say you will."

"Wincarnis was not about to make the same mistake twice over. This was business, and if a transfusion of the demon liquid was necessary to clinch the deal, then so be it.

From Wincarnis' viewpoint, all went swimmingly, with promises of profit almost beyond belief, enough gravy on offer to fill a channel tunnel freight train. Wincarnis was almost ovulating with excitement. A bit more haggling, more for form's sake than fiscal necessity, and the deal was struck in principle. That settled, the duo commenced the ritual socialising which always followed such dealings. It was the afterbirth of successful commerce, always accompanied by something alcoholic, in this case, a bottle or two of Merlot. For Wincarnis, unaccustomed as she was to any form of hooch, the indiscretions started after the first glass. To be fair, there would probably not have been any indiscretions had it not been for the efforts of the Colonel, who knew exactly what he wanted and where to go for it.

"The Royal Family! Don't mention that lot to me Colonel. Stuck up lot, and as for that Princess Anne, common, dead common, effing and blinding all over the place. Mind you, I did for them. Soon as the election was in the bag, I told Alfred to get rid of them."

"You mean it was you that got rid of them?"

"The whole shower. It was me who gave them the shove." Alcohol had delivered Wincarnis into fantasy land. Prompted by the wine, and bursting with a desire to show off, she answered every question put to her, never once thinking to query what lay behind such probing. Now that she had started, it proved impossible to shut her up, not that the Colonel would have wanted to.

"How did you find the President on your trip to Paris?"

"Bloody French fool. Typical. Stank of garlic the whole time at the state banquet, and as for the other, well, I hardly know how to put it into words."

"Oh, please do Wincarnis, please do." Wincarnis looked at him apprehensively, searching for a verbal formulation which would adequately encompass the experience, the words, when they came, came in a rush, and far louder than she had anticipated.

"He tried to feel me up under the table." Such was the timbre of her voice, she could have been heard the other end of Queen Anne's Gate. The entire pub was riveted by the spectacle taking place around the corner table at the back of the room.

"You really don't get on with Gertie Gunter do you?"

"Of course I don't. The people's Gert my arse, she's as common as a fart in a cow shed, if she changed her knickers as often as she did her wigs, then it might just be possible to get near her without passing out. It is not the odour of sanctity that surrounds that bitch I can assure you."

And so it went on, in vino veritas. You name it, Wincarnis said what she thought of it. The Colonel was utterly entranced.

3.

It should not be necessary to say this, but for those a few bob short of a quid, and a bit slow on the uptake, there was no such country as the Cocos Islands, no such country, but there is such a place, a few turds of land poking themselves above the surface of the Pacific. If you are flying to Perth, the pilot will announce at the due moment, that you are flying over them, but don't bother looking out of the window as they are too small to be seen. They are to be precise, a territory of Australia. The Colonel representing the Islands turned out to be a reporter for the Daily Truth. The whole episode was a classic Fleet Street sting, an act of revenge on the part of the editor, targeted on Wincarnis for trying to get him fired from his job, he had a little help from the CIA, not that he realised there was a transatlantic input into his triumph.

Naturally, the resulting article in the Truth caused ructions in Downing Street and other quarters sensitive and dependent on the survival of Alfred Sawse as Prime Minister. The Premier's principal personal assistant, the universally reviled Macmurdo Dunlossie, spun into overdrive.

"Now Prime Minister," intoned Mac. "I don't want to get personal or to hurt your feelings, but, that fucking cow is going to get us all hung before the world is much older or we have a chance to be. Did the silly bitch give that interview?"

"I think so Mac. She doesn't really remember, she was too pissed, but Marge from the typing pool was there and heard her sounding off.'

"So she did say it."

"Yes." The Prime Minister hung his head in shame, wanting to agree with Mac's assessment but terrified his wife might be listening at the key hole.

"We'll deny it of course. Then we'll sling a few writs around. You go, out and talk to the press. You tell them the whole thing is a complete fabrication. While you're doing that, I'll get on to the lawyers. We are going to sue the arse off the Truth, teach the bastards right for printing it for once."

And so the prime Minister stood at a lectern in the middle of Downing Street before the assembled press corps. He denounced the iniquities of the Truth, manufacturing such lies and an outright fabrication about his poor wife, who's only fault was to have married a politician. There was not a dry eye in the house, despite the fact that all those present knew it was a load of balls. In the meantime, Macmurdo busied himself with the issuance of legal writs.

Six hours to the minute after the Prime Minister's bravura performance, News At Ten broadcast a video filmed at the Two Chairmen, with Wincarnis in the staring role, she was three quarters into a bottle of Merlot, her accent slipping faster than a whores drawers when the fleets in port, offering the World a detailed account of a section of Ivra Maninand's anatomy that even within the confines of a gynaecological text book, would have been considered salacious. Her hair had gone all frizzy after her soaking by Condo, and the effect of unaccustomed alcohol had caused her to sweat profusely. As an aide to ventilation she had loosened the buttons on her blouse, exposing a black brassier, through the lace filigree of which, could be glimpsed wads of newspaper.

"It's true. God's honest truth it is. Reconstructive surgery? Forget it, No man would dare to go up there without a miner's lamp and a ball of string to find his way back."

Watching the broadcast, Macmurdo thought that perhaps he should hang himself there and then rather than wait for the inevitable to happen.

CHAPTER XVI.

The Prime Minister of what so short a time ago had been the United Kingdom, stunned beyond the horizons of what little reason he had originally possessed, sat alone in his study in Downing Street as his universe slowly disintegrated around him, as all those within his personal ambit committed acts of political genocide on their comrades and soul mates as a means to delay the inevitable, and preserve their skins. Condo and Mac were inexplicably absent, and Wincarnis had shut herself in the wardrobe and refused to come out. The man was entirely alone, no one to turn to, no one to tell him what to do, therefore he did that of which he was so manifestly capable, he smiled at nothing and told himself the world loved him.

Since the first of the abdications, British politics had become a concentration camp, abandon hope all ye who enter in. Keeper of the gates to this Auschwitz of the establishment was Bondi Paterson, Antipodean proprietor of much of the British press. Many years previously, Bondi had marked Alfred down as an electoral winner, he took the Brit under his wing, and threw the weight of his newspapers behind the rising star. Bondi's instincts had proved accurate, Alfred won his election. They became great friends, Bondi describing himself as throwing up in the same bucket as the Prime Minister, so close was their relationship. But, then the tide began to turn as the Government began to pocket the dividends it's arrogance had helped accrue. Friendship with the Government began to be seen as a liability no commercial enterprise could tolerate and survive. Bondi decided it was time to change horses. There was one other significant reason Bondi changed his coat, the President of the United States of America leant heavily on him to do so.

For Bondi, there was a quid pro quo for his unqualified support for the Premier, he had been allowed to buy far more of the media than he could afford or was good for the health of the British. More importantly from Bondi's perspective, he had been encouraged to trash any British institution which took his fancy. He was particularly encouraged to take pot shots at the Monarchy. The Prime Minister and his polytechnic pals hated the history, achievements and traditions of Great Britain. They particularly hated the Monarchy, which they accurately identified as the embodiment of all the traditions of the British. Bondi too had a chip on his shoulder, it was anti British and the size of the pyramid of Mycerinus, the arrangement with Alfred Sawse had suited him very well up until now.

Even had Bondi been inclined to row against the tide, and he still thought the Government might just have a stick thin chance of pulling through in the long term, he would not have dared to do so, forces more omnipotent than he had decided his course. Having made up his mind that it was time the Queen went home, the President had also come to the conclusion it was Bondi's duty to help in all ways he could, to assist the dear lady on her way. It was his duty as a new American that is, if he wanted to remain an American. Bondi did it because it was so tax efficient to be a yank, even a newly minted one. As a result of Presidential pressure, war would be declared on the Government by the Paterson titles. Bondi telephoned the editor of the Truth to inform him of the changes in editorial policy.

"That you Boyze? Mr. Patterson here. Got something to say to you." Boyze, assuming he was about to be fired for setting up the sting on Wincarnis, thought it prudent to stick his oar in first by telling Bondi exactly what he thought of the man, but had never before dared to.

"I suppose you're going to fire me for setting up the witch of Westminster, well, you can stick your job you bald headed boss-eyed Aussie wanker. I wouldn't work for you any longer even if I was the last cunt alive in Fleet Street and you had the last tampax on the planet You can find someone else to prop up those intellectual gobshites masquerading as a Government cos I've had it. The Australian Prime Minister told you to fuck off out of it and now I'm doing the same. So, what do you say to that blue?" Felix Boyze let loose a sigh of relief, he had waited a long time to get that off his chest, and had never thought he would have either the guts or the opportunity to do so

"Actually Boyze, the reason I'm ringing you." Bondi delivered his words with a slow magisterial dignity. "Was to tell you to change editorial policy. As far as Sawse and his pals are concerned, the gloves are off, it's open season on the bastards."

"You're kidding!"

"I never kid when it comes to business. Oh, and I want a campaign started calling for the return of the Queen. And as for the Euro, that's a big no, the bloody county's enough of a theme park without the embarrassment of introducing monopoly money as the medium of exchange."

"Yes, Mr. Patterson. I'll get on to it at once. And I do apologise for my hasty remarks I don't know what came over me, I really do not."

"I do, you had an attack of guts that's what, you just did not recognise it for what it was. But I'm keeping you from your work, you've a lot to do haven't you?"

"Yes, Mr. Patterson. Tomorrows headlines will be a declaration of war on the Government."

"That's the ticket. You get on with it. Then when you have done all that I have told you to do, I am going to fire you, you knockneed Pommie runt." With that out in the open, Bondi slammed the receiver down, he would have fired Boyze there and then if it had not been that such an action might have delayed the opening of the campaign and brought the President's wrath down upon his head. The President was not a patient man.

And so it came to pass, with Biblical implacability and trumpet blasts of righteousness, the Truth turned against the Government with a comprehensive viciousness which left it gasping for breath. Politicians, who are so adept at stabbing other people in the back, are invariably outraged when such behaviour is deployed against them. As things turned out, the Wincarnis sting, far from being a one off, proved to be the opening salvo in a far wider war.

Poor Alfred Sawse, he could not understand what was happening to him. When now his staff addressed him as Dear Leader, he detected in their voice something which had been lacking before, it was openly expressed and derisive. He did so adore to be loved, that is all he wanted actually, to be friends with everyone, but now no-one seemed to be his friend, not even Bondi, who he had considered to be his best pal. The Prime Minister was completely at a loss as to why Bondi had so savagely and comprehensively turned against him, the man would not even take his telephone calls any more.

2.

The sex lives of Ivra and Billy-Bob had not done a runner from the pages of the press to be succeeded in the public consciousness by the latest fads and fellatios of the lords of

Westminster. No, it was merely taking a breather while its authors polished up the next act of the drama, prior to it's publication. Needless to say, the mercury in the relationship between Ivra and her Texan had dropped an inch or two since his postprandial traipse across Hampstead Heath. Billy-Bob was still perplexed by lvra's attitude to him, as he was incapable of understanding what it was he had done wrong. As for Ivra, she had made up her mind that Billy- Bob had to go, she would hang on to him until she was ready to install his replacement. Ivra was uncertain whose husband to pick next, in Australia she had taken the measure of Norbert, but at just five and a half inches, felt he as not quite up to it. The matter would require careful consideration, in the meantime there were other things to inveigle her attention.

Ivra was a tough old bird, contemptuous of the opinions of others, but even she could see that she was no longer skating on thin ice, but was now down to water, she was possibly the only individual in the entire country not determined to see her out of Buck House. The Government, terrified as to its own immediate prospects, had made its feelings abundantly clear towards the Regent, and as for the dear demos, Lord love the little darlings, they had plastered the environs of the Palace with placards bearing endearing legends along the lines of "Ditch the bitch" and "Bring back the real Queen." Ivra had tried to get the placards removed by various means, including boxing the ears of London's Mayor, to no avail. The authorities were well aware that if the placards came down then the whole shebang was likely to go up in smoke.

Into this unappetising bowl of porridge, Condo Maites stuck his delicately manicured finger, well not quite, adhering to the form book he got someone else to do it for him. Dosser Bates, who was once more coerced by Condo into assisting the public weal, by the simple but devastatingly effective threat of having his dole cut off if he didn't. Dosser played ball as instructed, by cosying up to Billy-Bob at one of Condo's parties.

"Nice to see you again Bill boy, haven't seen you since the Heath. Hope you did not get into any trouble over those pictures in the papers?"

"Well, Ivra has been kinda peculiar lately and talking about change."

"Probably talking about the menopause. We all know what women are like at Ivra's time of life." Dosser knew nothing about women at any stage of their lives, but Billy-Bob was not to know that. Condo sauntered over to the duo.

"Hi there guys. Good to see you are such good friends. Are you hungry?"

"Condo, ahm plumb starving to death. What you got to eat?" Since lvra had taken to applying the Greek sanction to him, Billy-Bob was forced to substitute food for sex, he was ravenous.

"Pity, SP's got a strop on and the catty queen refused to do any shopping. Not a bit to eat in the place. Hey! Dosser, why don't you take Billy-Bob out for a burger, then come back after."

"Great idea Condo. Love to." Condo handed Dosser a fistful of fivers before waving them off.

Dosser took Billy-Bob to a hamburger joint round the corner from Condo's. Being in a posh part of town it was a bit more upmarket than the usual establishment, that is, the urinals were unblocked and cleaned once a week.

Dosser was particularly attentive to Billy-Bob's needs, feeding him 'till he wanted no more', which being a reedy sod, was a considerable amount. At no time was Billy-Bob allowed to collect his own grub from the counter. Dosser was the perfect host, carrying out his duties with aplomb and charm. Billy-Bob did not even notice that Dosser had spiked his food with generous amounts of sodium chloride, causing him to drink far more then he would otherwise have done.

Dosser suggested a stroll and a jog in the park before returning to Condo's. Billy-Bob, trusting and simple as he was, and not withstanding the consequences of his previous outing with Dosser, agreed. By the time they reached the park, the amount of fizzy drink Billy-Bob had consumed, was having it's predictable effect.

"Ahm busting for a leak Doss."

"Don't worry Billy. Down here, that's right down those steps, it's the Hyde Park Cottage."

"Cottage?"

"Yes. London slang for a public piss house." Billy-Bob rushed to the trough, pulling out his member just in time to avoid embarrassment. He sighed in relief as three quid's worth of Diet

Coke hit the porcelain. The figure next to him sidled a little closer.

"Hey mate, you able to split a fiver for me? You know how Bolshie them fucking bus drivers can be." Billy-Bob was fortunate in enjoying a negligible experience of buses and their drivers, but was always amenable to giving one of his fellow men a helping hand. They exchanged the coins for money, at the exact moment of the transaction, a flash gun went off, thereby awarding posterity with another free sample of Billy-Bob's talent for walking into disaster with his flies wide open.

"Dosser, some jerk off just took a photo of me taking a piss, whydah he do that for?"

"God knows. They're a queer bloody lot down here in London. Come on, let's get back, Condo'll think we've been kidnapped."

Dosser gave Condo a nod as he and Billy-Bob entered the flat, Condo's eyes lit up with pleasure, he did so like it when things went right He went into his study from where he could make a private phone call.

"That you Norm? Good. Got something for Sat's edition. This one I should charge you for, not give away, listen to this. There is a pic on the way to you this very minute, Billy-Bob Thorpe exchanging money with a rent boy in the Hyde Park Cottage." There was a gasp from the other end of the line. "I thought you'd like that. Ta ta'. He returned to his guests contented by the thoughts of all the faeces which would be hitting the air conditioning come Saturday.

On Saturday the balloon went up, passing as it did so, a bewildered Billy-Bob migrating in the opposite direction. Billy-Bob's brief encounter in the Hyde Park bog had been splashed all over the front pages of the principal organs of the gay press. By lunch time the event had made the television news and by Sunday had made a takeover bid for Fleet Street. The effect all this had on the marital standing of Billy-Bob Thorpe esquire was terminal. Billy-Bob was incapable of understanding what had transpired, while Ivra understood only too well.

"That's it." She screamed. "That's fucking it."

"Now honey pie, it ain't at all ladylike you using words like that."

"What would you know about a fucking lady? Chasing around the town after anything in trousers. It's that fucking Maites at the bottom of it. He's turned you, the fucking poofter. It's him that's done it. That fucking Wincarnis, I bet that cow's got a finger in all this somehow, her and that fucking Maites." The private secretary was listening outside the door, he felt terribly sorry for Ivra's father, the old boy had spent so much money on his daughter's education to insulate her from the pitfalls of a proletarian outlook, and when push came to shove, all she could utilise it for was to scream expletives.

"But Ivra honey, I just can't understand why you is so vexated. I ain't done nothing. Straight."

"Straight! You don't know what straight is you bent sonofabitch."

With those turbulent words, ended the eighth marriage if Ivra Maninand. Billy-Bob,

God bless the simple soul, was turfed out into the street there and then, his share of the marital assets restricted to the shirt on his back. Off with the old, on with the new might be rather commonplace, but, all the same, it was the motto Ivra lived by and she had no intention of altering her modus vivendi merely because she was a few bum tucks over the age of twenty one. A replacement for Billy-Bob had to be found, the nearest to hand was Norbert Gunter. Despite the disasters of corsets, tents and snakes, and his falling short of the yard stick by which she customarily measured her men, she had thoroughly put him through his paces during the state visit to the Hutt River, and, at a pinch, found him of a passable, if barely adequate standard. Norbert would be installed in Buck House as screw in residence.

Norbert was over the moon at Ivra's invitation. So excited was he that he did not bother asking the terms and conditions. Gert had left early for the office that particular morning. Half way through the committee meeting she was chairing, she had to adjourn the proceedings as she had left her briefing notes back home. On entering the house, she thought there were burglars from the sounds coming from upstairs, but realised that could not be so, as the place was covered by the security services. She crept up the stairs to find Norbert in the minute bedroom she allowed him to occupy, packing a suitcase. Norbert, totally unmanned screamed in tenor at her entrance.

"What do you think you're doing? You are supposed to be in work you useless runt. And what's that suitcase for? Don't think you are going on another ruddy jaunt cos the answer's no."

"I'm not going on no jaunt."

"Then what are doing? You don't pack a suitcase if you're only going to the lav." Norbert swallowed hard, he knew it had been a mistake to go back for his belongings, and if caught, would pay dearly for them.

"I'm moving in with Ivra." He blurted out before making a dive for the door. Gert was the quicker of the two, she got him on the landing with a rugby tackle.

"Are you by God! Well, if you are going to tickle the randy Regent's fancy we'll have to give a bit of attention to your appearance won't we?"

"Don't hit me Gertie. Don't hit me, please don't." The poor sap might just have asked for the introduction of snowballs into hell. It did not take Gert very long, but by the time she had finished with him, Norbert was black and blue all over, one particularly accurate boot in the nuts ensured the sorry specimen could be of no use to Ivra for at least two weeks.

3.

Billy-Bob was not the only one to have been exiled from the regal orbit, Condo had also been declared homo non grata by the Regent, who, for some time had suspected the true direction of his loyalties, and now felt that while having fairies at the bottom of the garden might be the acme of metropolitan chic, it was time to call a halt when they started plotting to take over one's Regency.

Condo, no fool by any standards, was perfectly aware that one day Ivra would rumble what it was he was about, he was therefore careful to take out insurance in the form of a couple of Palace employees, whose bribes were financed from the party funds set aside for market research. Billy-Bob had scarce left the Palace precincts before Condo was made aware of the situation.

Billy-Bob had exited the Palace in a daze, unable to comprehend the situation in which he now found himself, nor the reasons for it. Westminster Cathedral, erected in the nineteenth century to the glory of God and as an insult to aesthetic susceptibilities, was within spitting distance of Buck House, but it was the citadel of an entirely different world. Darkness had blessed the area, making the pile less obvious to the naked eye by the time Billy-Bob had chanced upon it. Tribal groupings ranging from the feckless to the leglessly pissed were huddled in groups around the piazza. Having no preference in these matters, he joined the first group to stray along his line of sight. By chance, one of the few people who had spoken to him of recent weeks, Dosser Bates, was amongst those he had joined.

"Christ Bill!" He was genuinely shocked. "What the hell are you doing here? Is it one of those T.V. things where a few celebs pretend to be homeless for the night, then go home to a fucking great breakfast?"

"She's kicked me out doss. I've got nowhere to go."

"What? She can't have."

"I ain't no ghost."

"But what for?"

"Ah don't know Doss, something about that jerk who took a photo of me taking a leak the other night. What fault of mine is it if some weirdo goes around photographing folk taking a piss? Ah didn't ask him to."

"Course it isn't Bill. Nothing to do with you. Bloody bitch."

"Here Bill, have a can." Dosser handed him a can of low cost, high alcohol cider, which was gratefully accepted.

"What in fuck my goin' to do Dosser?"

"Well you'd better come down to the Passage night shelter. We'll have another couple of cans then make tracks." Dosser was still fairly flush with the cash Condo had given him to help get Billy-Bob into this situation in the first place. They were into the second round of cans when Condo alighted on the soused tableau.

"Bill-Bob. My dear chappie. What in our dear Lord's back yard are you doing here? You look absolutely dreadful."

"Two faced shit," mumbled Dosser with a clarity of diction which ensured he could be heard by all within a radius of twenty feet. Condo bent down and whispered in his ear.

"Dole money sweet cheeks. Remember what your big sister Condo will do if you are a naughty boy, he'll have it stopped. Permanently. Comprendez? " Dosser did, understanding full well what it was that Condo would do to him if he stepped out of line.

"Condo ain't no shit Doss."

"Wasn't talking about Condo Bill. It was some bastard who just went round the corner, cunt threatened to grass me up to the DSS."

"Attaboy Dosser." There was genuine warmth in Condo's voice as there always was when he came out on top. "What are your plans for tonight Billy?"

"Dosser said he'd take me to the night passage. Whatever in hell that might be."

"Passage night shelter," corrected Dosser.

"Heavens above. We can't possibly have that," said Condo. The heathen bastard positively oozed Christian charity. "Not at all. You're coming home with me. You'll stay with SP and me until we've got you sorted out somehow."

"What about me Condo?" asked Dosser. In reply he received a smirk which was the equivalent of a benediction from the public hangman.

Billy-Bob settled into Condo's large apartment and was suitably thankful for the privilege, he actually preferred it to the abundant acreage of Buck House, and it had the added advantage that he did not have to hump old Ivra on demand. Billy-Bob rapidly came to the conclusion that Condo was a much maligned man, why, he mused to himself, if Condo was only a quarter of the things people accused him of being, then he would not have done as much for him in his adversity. Unlike piles, gullibility could not be eradicated by surgery.

The Texan Dork went so far as to make Condo his confidant, no detail of his life with Ivra was so intimate that it could not be transferred to the discretion of his friend and saviour, Condo Maites. The finest French vintages, intended for the more important diplomatic receptions, but filched by Condo for his private use, helped the indiscretions flow in torrents. Condo, who prided himself on his unshockability, found himself blushing at Billy-Bob's more forensic annotations to the history of his sex life with Ivra.

"Ya know how she liked taking it Condo?"

"I've led a sheltered life Billy." In that particular respect he most certainly had.

"Ah guess tha's so. Well, her favourite way of being fucked was doggie fashion, you know, on hands and knees from behind while wearing nothing but a string vest and a gas mask." That little nugget of information managed to rob even a man of Condo's verbal ability of a suitable riposte. "You think she was a mite kinky?"

"Some may come to that conclusion Billy-Bob. There is a dearth of charity in this world you know."

"An youse to good for this world Condo. I tell you man, you is a saint." Condo smiled modestly in reply. Within the hour, Condo was on the blower to Felix Boyze at the Truth with the latest tit-bit on the Regents conjugal whims. All Billy-Bob's indiscretions traversed this route. Condo had selected the Truth because his acute political antennae told him the Government was on the skids, the end may not as yet have been nigh, but it was certainly in the post, and by helping Felix in his campaign, he went a long way to securing himself a job when the gravy train hit the buffers of electoral vengeance. As for the Truth, well, no respectable journal ever let so distasteful a concept as integrity compromise its sources.

The subject of Ivra's sex life superseded the weather as the Nation's favoured topic of conversation, like Ivra, they could not get enough of it, what chance did cloud bursts over Manchester stand in competition with string vests and gas masks? So deep was the trust Billy-Bob felt for Condo, that he even divulged the details whereby he had been given a directorship of Ratner's in return for them being awarded the contract to supply the official jewellery to the Regent. Like all intelligences from that source it soon found its way onto the pages of the Truth, where Felix could be relied to put his particular slant on things. First sexual scandal, now financial skullduggery, the public was suffering from an embarrass des riches.

CHAPTER XVII.

Official London was en fete, or at least getting ready to be so. The first state visit of the Regency was threatening to descend upon the town with the sort of mercy Attila the Hun showed to Rome. The new establishment of Alfred Sawse's, chilled out Albion, whatever it was that ridiculous concept stood for, was busily employed in dusting down its glad rags in preparation for the festivities. As this establishment had never been persuaded to abandon the realms of student agitation, along with it's concomitant abasement of the sartorial, their understanding of what was meant by posh frocks, promised to be a history of C&A apparel. The schmatter had been out of date before it had left the store, not that the honoured guests would be likely to notice ought amiss. Anything that had not come out of a mail order catalogue was classed as posh by Prince Leonard of the Hutt River Province and his missus.

Prince Leonard and Princess Shirley had entered a competition run by a local dog food manufacturer, the first prize being a trip for two to Pommie Land. The faux royal pair had won. Naturally they informed their good friend the Regent of England of their impending arrival, expecting to be invited round to the Palace for a cup of tea and a sticky bun, which would have been adequate recompense for the hospitality they had afforded Ivra down under.

Now, just as no-one had wanted to receive Ivra on a state visit, nobody wanted to make one to her, it was impossible to persuade any legit head of state to risk his reputation by calling on the woman even the international press had dubbed 'gas mask Lil'. Then, just as she had given up hope, out of the blue arrived a postcard from Western Australia, Eubloodyreka, Ivra had got herself a state visit. After Ivra's cavortings had been extensively reported in the papers, the public were not unaware of the Hutt River and it's rulers, curiosity would ensure that at least some would line the route to gawp at, if not cheer these specimens of Antipodean royalty. They did, but there was nothing and no-one to see.

The prize Len and Shirl had won was a package holiday, the first stop after touch down at Heathrow was to be Durham, so, while Ivra was impatiently kicking her heels in one of the airport halls, awaiting the arrival of her guests, they were boarding the tour bus. They were half way to spaghetti junction before they were located. At a motorway service station they were transferred to an army jeep and returned to the capital, by which time the troops marshalled for the parade had been stood down and those few members of the public who had turned up to witness the proceedings, had progressed from being pissed off to getting pissed up, after which they had a nice little riot in Trafalgar Square, during the course of which the highlight was the sight of a large pig dressed up in a string vest and a gas mask. Members of the Metropolitan Police Force dispatched to quell the disturbance found the sight so funny, they joined in the riot instead.

Naturally, the focal point of the visit was to be the State Banquet, normally held, as such affairs always were, at Buckingham Palace, only that was now impossible. Unable to dislodge the Regent by legal means, not that such an undertaking was impossible, by no means was it so, but by initiating such an action, the Government would have to admit the appointment of Ivra was a mistake in the first place, and in the political version of the Nicene Creed, there was only one heresy carrying the sentence of burning at the stake, and that was admitting to being wrong, it was just not done, and Alfred Sawse and co were not going to be the first of their ilk to transgress.

As the Government were unable to openly ditch Ivra, they had to employ more subtle means to engineer her departure. The Chancellor, for the first time during his tenure of office, earned the approbation of the Prime Minister by using an obscure technicality to halt payment of the Civil List. Result, not only had the Buck House telephone been disconnected, but also, the power had been cut off by the Electricity Board for non payment. Banquet? The state they were in they could not have held a picnic. And still Ivra, the obstinate cow, refused to hang up her Ratner's simulated diamond tiara and admit defeat.

At the last minute, when all seemed lost, Ivra managed to secure the Banqueting House at Whitehall. Unfortunately, that coup proved only a delaying tactic for the relentless march of disaster. With perfect timing and brinkmanship, the catering staff went on strike, demanding the minimum wage, that's right folks, it was Wincarnis' brother's circus of third world cowboys who had been given the contract. As so many of his supporters were looking forward to a night of food and booze at Government expense, the Prime Minister was forced to grit his teeth and step in to save the day, so precarious had his support become that he could not afford to alienate anyone who might have a vote in his personal survival.

The only option open to the Prime Minister was to send out to the pizza parlour just down the road for one hundred and twenty three cheese feasts with garlic bread on the side. And that is how things stood at the start of the banquet, not quite, the booze. The intoxicants had been delivered before the strike, but had not been stashed away and therefore the south wall of the chamber was lined with cases of Algerian Burgundy. Now, as the guests had all arrived very early and the delivery of the pizzas very late, the inevitable came to pass, that is, the assembled guests, clocking the cases of booze, did not bother to wrestle with temptation, but got stuck in, and everyone got beastly drunk, including Gert and Ivra, who, sick and spewing, had to be led from the room in order that they could recover in private. All this mark you, before the arrival of the food.

Norbert was there as Ivra's consort, he was terribly impressed by the calorific offerings, he had not been used to such high falutin grub while living with Gert, whose notions of haute cuisine extended only to warming the beans before tipping them onto the plate. The proceedings were covered live by Channel Five, this was because none of the other broadcasters were remotely interested in reporting the event, decisions they were to regret before the evening made its bow to the progress of the calendar.

The great drawback to official events is that in return for free food and drink, one is compelled to listen to dreadful speeches made by worse individuals. On this particular occasion, the audience was to be pleasantly surprised. The speechifying was to be truncated by an exquisite entertainment worthy of an Irish wedding. Ivra rose to her welcoming address, although she was forced to hang on to the microphone in order to maintain a tolerable relationship with the vertical. Ivra, in an attempt to be suitably regal, had modeled her speech giving style on that of Queen Elizabeth in the early days of her reign, thus she inaugurated her address to the lower orders that night in the following manner.

"My husband and I." That was it, open day at the sewage farm, and a days production hit the fan at the same time.

"Which one?" howled the by now paralytic diners, sweating in their bri-nylon finery.

"I've only got one," bawled back Ivra, incensed by this display of lèse majesté.

"No you haven't. The fucker's still mine." This was the people's Gert. Norbert went white, the bruises had only just faded from the last pasting he had received from the flawed specimen of pulchritude, who in law, remained his legal spouse.

"Not that he's up to much. About four inches if I remember correctly."

Ivra was now past caring about what she said or who heard her say it.

"How would you know you mitch munching old dyke. The last time you had a man in your mouth he was made of chocolate and hanging from a Christmas tree."

"Thus spake the national turkey Gobble, gobble, gobble." What further would have been said remains concreted in the foundations of speculation, as Gert, in her unsteady state, stepped onto a plate into which some unfortunate had recently thrown up his contribution to the science of digestion. She went flying across the few feet separating her from the top table which overturned on impact taking Ivra with it. Ivra, thinking the upset to have been deliberate, set about Gert, who defended herself with a rigour the uncharitable would record as professional. The audience immediately formed a circle around the two battleaxes, egging them on and taking bets on the outcome. Prince Leonard and Princess Shirley were gobsmaked, the poor darlings had thought they were in for a night of culture, they might just as well have visited an outback pub on a Saturday night. The cameras got the lot. At Channel Five the managers were ecstatic, knowing that with the footage they had got, their careers were made.

2.

The morning after the banquet, the Prime Minister sat in his office alone, the door was locked and he would answer to nobody. Macmurdo had rushed to Downing Street with a full and totally biased account of the melee. He had not tarried in the residence after unburdening himself. Bad news was one thing, bad news and Wincarnis was in a dimension of it's own. He had witnessed too may performances to be able to tolerate another encore. Wincarnis had surpassed herself, and continued to do so throughout the night, blaming the Prime Minister for all the ills of the Government, ignoring the fact that the poor man only did what she told him to do.

Condo could hear the Premier moaning long before he reached the doors to the Prime Ministerial office, he asked for the papers, but the secretary informed him they had been cancelled. Condo tapped on the door.

"Piss off'. Sobbed a voice from the other side. "I'm not seeing anyone at all."

"Come on now Alfie, it's me, Condo."

"Go away."

"Open the door Alfie. Please. I can fix things for you. You know I can." After a short interval the door creaked open, and a tearful Prime Minister fell into Condo's arms.

"Help me Condo. Help me."

"Oh my God," thought Condo. "Look at it, the Protopopov of British politics. All the poor sap ever wanted was to be a local councillor, and he ended up as Prime Minister." In a corner of the room a television set was providing blanket coverage of Gert and Ivra knocking the stuffing out of each other. Condo grasped the opportunity to point out to the beloved leader a few facts of current political life. "You only have to look at it Alfie, I can easily imagine what the press will have to say about this lot, not to say what Joe Soap on the Clapham omnibus will be mouthing. It now has to be obvious to everyone that neither lady, if that be not a contradiction in terms, can be considered fit for the Regency. Not after that performance. The public won't wear it and what's more we are a laughing stock right around the world."

"I know Condo, but what can I do?"

"They've both got to go. The public just won't tolerate them any more." The Prime Minister was forced to agree, he did not want to, but after last night there could be no argument with Condo's logic, only with the man's altruism, and that had never really been in question. Condo loved Condo, and that was that.

The Prime Minister agreed with Condo's analysis, but understood only too well the consequences of handing Condo the keys to Buck House, the difficulties of reconciling rocks and hard places crossed his mind.

3.

Condo was well aware of the Prime Minister's reluctance to name him as successor to Ivra and the reasons for it, but he was incapable of understanding why it was inadvisable to flout public prejudice on such a matter. Condo had risen to the top via the political back stairs, he had never had to court the favour of the party drones to help him up the initial rungs of the ladder, and had therefore never had to tickle the underbelly of their beliefs with the payment of lip service in lieu of sincerity he wanted the Regency and he was damned if anyone was going to stand in the way of his getting it.

In the time honoured fashion of politicians since the days when they first learnt to tap out a falsehood on a tablet of stone, Condo planted a story in the Truth. The story stated as established fact that he, Condo Maites was to be appointed Regent. Once more the Government was forced into the bunkers to escape the fallout from the public's outrage. Deny it they did, but that was to no avail, the people had elected not to believe what Governments told them since Neville Chamberlain had returned from Munich and they were not about to reverse the habits of a lifetime to accommodate the shoddy bunch currently enjoying the trappings of office.

The public's reaction to the press reports was as nothing in comparison to that of Ivra, who was livid to the point of apoplexy. Throwing discretion and good taste to the winds, not that she had ever possessed more than a modicum of either, the woman issued a statement to the press stating unequivocally that she had no intention of standing down from office. If Ivra had left matters rest at that circumspect post house, no damage would have been done, but that would have been like praying for rain in the middle of a cyclone. Ivra went on to accuse Wincarnis of orchestrating an official vendetta against her, that came as a surprise to no-one, least of all to the public, who had accepted that as an established fact months ago. The real burst of shrapnel came with the revelation that Condo had planted the Regency storey. Ivra signed off with a vituperous flourish, stating that the closest Condo and his mates would get to Buckingham Palace would be the bushes in Hyde Park on a dark night.

Ivra's press release provoked a spate of infighting amongst the Government which was unprecedented in its intensity and personal viciousness, shocking even those who were accustomed to such internecine outbursts. To the public it came close to being the final straw before the camels back ended up in traction. The atmosphere in the country became tense and dangerous as people lost patience with a political class they had long held in abject contempt.

CHAPTER XVIII.

The Chancellor of the Exchequer, keeper of the public purse and all therein purloined via the tax system, from the much put upon folk of Blighty under threat of legal duress, was at the best of time, a charmless git, three stones over weight, four if one took the trouble to quantify his ego. This flatulent apparition, who normally operated backstage, now stepped into the arena to do his bit in assisting in the disintegration of the Government.

There are many descriptions which could be applied to the Chancellor, but if one is to dispense with circumlocution and adopt the call a spade a fucking shovel school of Freudian analysis, then one would have to label the man a Bible bashing tea-totaller, if one wanted to nit pick over the details, the man was a Primitive Methodist from the North of England, and they don't come more primitive than they do from that neck of the woods. In his capacity as chancellor, Humbert Repton had to attend a number of grand dinners, the grandest being at the Mansion House, home of London's Lord Mayor, definitely white tie and tails. In order to burnish his working class image, which he thrust down the throat of the chattering classes at every given opportunity, the Chancellor refused to dress appropriately for the occasion, he had turned up in an off the peg lounge suit, and even in this he felt himself to be ludicrously over dressed to suit his purposes, as the dungarees he normally wore to such events had failed to come back from the cleaners in time.

Repton's predilection for the eschewing of alcohol was well known, unfortunately for his reputation for sobriety, the CIA had decided to take a hand in his social development, and had arranged with one of the catering staff to spike his Tizer with something more spirited than faith in the Lord, their latest truth drug. The results of this action were catastrophic, both for the Chancellor and the nation. After that night, nothing would ever be the same again. Unlike most of his colleagues he was not used to narcotic stimulants of any kind, the small amount of the drug the Chancellor had ingested, made its effects apparent with startling rapidity, he answered all questions put to him during the course of the customary social chit chat with devastating honesty, including his opinion of the Mayor's wife's bust and how much she could get on an hourly basis if she turned professional, so obvious was the change in his condition that the Mayor ordered to waiters to take the Chancellor into a side room, but the man was having none of it, he had come to make a speech and that was exactly what he intended to do. Not the easiest proposition for a man in the condition in which he now found himself.

Repton had mislaid the two vital adjuncts vital to his making a creditable performance. The first was the use of his legs, he could hardly make his speech from under the table which was where he was heading, this was remedied by two waiters on either side, holding him up. As for his prepared text, that had mysteriously disappeared, so the Chancellor decided to speak extempore. What he had written and what he was to say, were two very different things, but in the state he was now in, he could never have judged the difference let alone corrected it.

"Ladies and gentlemen, there's been a great debate about the Euro, talk talk and more bloody talk. Well, some time ago I decided we needed a bit of action, and I took it. Of course, I did not tell the Prime Minister, that loon could not tell the difference between the laws of economics and a pimple on his dick." The Chancellor paused to belch, he always included a good belch in his speeches, very working class, authentic was his phrase. "As part of my plan for Eurofication, I have, over the last six months, liquidated all our gold and foreign currency reserves and put the whole lot into Euros. So, what do you think of that boys and girls?" The horrified silence with which this was received provided him with an adequate answer.

"Unfortunately, this morning, the Euro collapsed, you probably read about that in the papers. The Euro's down the pan and our national nest egg's gone with it. We're broke for Christ's sake. We're fucking broke." And with that he collapsed into tears of self pity. The audience had digested the hot pot, but were quite put off the apple tart and custard which was to have followed.

"You stupid God forsaken bastard," screamed the Mayor. That was the signal for the press corps to break ranks. They stampeded for the bank of telephones installed for their use, but as there were more reporters than telephone, a ruck ensued, three black eyes and a broken jaw were recorded before the first copy was filed.

In the halls of the European Commission, where incompetence and corruption were regarded as beacons of excellence, the worship of chaos became obligatory, they knew not what to do, and instead of trying to apply some, any remedy to the situation, devoted their energies to denying the persistent reports that the President of the European Central Bank had committed suicide by hanging himself from Blackfriars Bridge at the insistent urgings of the leaders of Germany, France and Italy. The rumours of course were accurate.

The Europeans had no option other than to apply to the International Monetary fund for a bail out. Asking ain't getting as they say. The I.M.F was controlled by the Americans, it was they and they alone who held the purse strings.

2.

The President of the United States was holding a meeting in the Oval Office with his chief advisors to discuss the European crisis. The National Security advisor held the floor.

"So Mr. President. Do we give the Europeans the loan, or let 'em sink?"

"What do they want a loan for?" asked the President who was engrossed in a rerun of the Lucy Show.

"The financial crisis, Mr. President. Their economy's down the tubes and it is not coming back."

"How will that effect the Congressional elections next month?"

"Not a bit Sir."

"Well, there's your answer Dixie. Those snotty nosed anti American European bastards have been telling anyone who'd care to listen, what it is they think of us for decades now. Not very nice thoughts either if I recollect correctly. Let the bastards sink, their comeuppance is long over due." With those words, the fate of Europe, England and Alfred Sawse was sealed.

No one should have been surprised by the reaction of the Americans, it did not require the talents of Mystic Meg to work out that the Yanks would put the kybosh on any bid to bail out the Europeans, as they did, and making no apologies for the pleasure they got from doing so.

Within two weeks of the Chancellors speech at the Mansion House, the European economy was well on the way to joining King Tut in its eternal rest, and not all the embalming fluids of mendacity could disguise that from the populace, who were not nearly so fiscally illiterate as their masters so fondly believed them to be.

Insulated from reality as he was, the Prime Minister still had an inkling that the voters did not love him as devotedly as he had been led to believe by his spin doctors, who were themselves, by now in need of a little surgery. Condo had his work cut out in preventing his master from changing his name and doing a bunk to Australia.

"All you need is a steady nerve Alfie. We'll come through this given a little time, and its years until the next election." We'll tough it out, get rid of Ivra, then in a few years the voters will have forgotten all about it." Condo's ability to kindle faith in his porkies was never more apparent than at that moment.

"Is that a promise Condo?" His eyes lit up, resembling those of a man who had been told he could have the last remaining berth on the Titanic for only a twenty percent premium.

"I keep telling you, don't worry. Look at these results just in from the latest focus group. Approval rating, up. Most admired Prime Minister in history, definite to win the next election. And so on, etbollockingcetera." The Prime Minister beamed at these glad tidings, although he would not have been so jovial had he known that Condo and Mac had spent all morning concocting the results. Condo left his boss suitably anaesthetised, he went in search of Mac, with whom he had concluded an armistice. They both had one thing only on their minds, and that was how to save their skins. They concluded there was no way for the Premier to avoid being strung up, perhaps not metaphorically either. If there was a chance of Alf and Wincarnis ending up like old Musso and his Clara, then Condo and Mac, founders of the opportunist party had no intentions of hanging around for the festivities.

3.

There is nothing the British press like better than kicking a man when he is down, and in the case of the press versus the Government it was as if all their expenses had been authorised without quibble, question or snide remark from their editors. Remorselessly they hammered the administration into the ground, only to dig it up so that they could have the pleasure of repeating the process all over again.

Scandal followed scandal in a stately progress through the pages of the national press. The fons et origo of these judicious leaks was Canada. The Queen was receiving a stream of inside information from a variety of sources on both sides of the pond. In some cases it was not high minded concern which kept the springs of indiscretion flowing to Prince Edward Island, but a need to insure for the future. There was, doing the rounds, an uncharitable whisper to the effect that that both Condo and Mac had bought themselves a little insurance.

It was only a matter of time before the press revealed that the Government was virtually run by Wincarnis, not as that came as a surprise to anyone who possessed the mental acuity to enable them to count up to ten without digital aide memoire. "So what" said the people, who possessed a mortifying refusal to be impressed by the bleeding obvious. The news that Wincarnis was using her husband's position to further her business career, likewise failed to impress for the same reasons, people had suspected it all along. Mind you, the revelations did not go down too well in the private apartments of Downing Street, where honest criticism was still regarded as a capital offence.

The Prime Minister was huddled in a corner of the sofa, wishing that his wife would either shut up or contract laryngitis.

"It's no good you sitting there sucking your thumb and wishing you were in the Chairmen. Oh yes, I know you've been sneaking over there on the quiet. You have got to do something about all these attacks on me in the press. I will not stand for it any longer Do try and be a man Alfred. I'm your wife, defend me." Which was rather rich as Wincarnis had didactically prevented her husband from being a man for most of their married life, in their household. Testosterone was something which had to be apologised for on an almost daily basis. Such was his state of depression he was incapable of responding to her tirade.

"And," she continued the flow of her narrative uninterrupted by rational analysis. "All those stories about me using Downing Street to drum up business. Put a stop to it Alfred. I am warning you, shut them up. And what's more I want that Felix Boyze fired." Alfred wondered if his wife inhabited the same solar system as the rest of them, she must be the only one in the upper echelons of power who had not grasped the fact that Bondi Patterson had switched horses, and the Truth stable was betting against them. "I will not tolerate such things being written about me. I'm the first lady." Perhaps it was desperation, perhaps he did not care any more, or maybe it was that he wanted to discover if there was more between his legs than a written apology for masculinity in general, either way, the Premier managed a reply to his legally wed termagant.

"Why shouldn't they print it? It's the truth."

"I don't care if it's the truth. What does that matter? They have no business printing things which I find offensive. And they'll regret doing so. Mark my words." The Prime Minister was not obliged to do any such thing as the telephone chose to interrupt the flow of dialogue. Alfred picked up the receiver. It was Mac on the other end of the line. The Premier listened intently, he went white. Just as he thought, once again that things could not possibly get any worse, fate had stepped in to underline his naivety. He thanked Mac, then quietly replaced the receiver.

"That was Mac."

"I told him we were not to be disturbed. I'll dock him a weeks pay for this."

"Oh shut up," yelled the Prime Minister approaching the outer edges of hysteria.

"What did you say?" Wincarnis was too shocked to be outraged, never had her husband dared to speak to her like that before.

"The Telegraph's got the details of Lloyd George."

"Impossible."

"So it might be but they have got them all the same. It's going to be tomorrow's lead. That's it, we're done for now."

Lloyd George was the Foreign Office cat, the best mouser in Whitehall, and famous with it, he used to get fan mail from the public by the sack full. But, alas and alack, Wincarnis did not like cats, considering them to be parasites. Poor old Lloyd George had been quietly put down by a Government vet. The press had asked questions at the time but had allowed itself to be fobbed off with a series of improbable stories, the most widely accepted being that he had been sent to Melbourne zoo to mate with a Koala Bear, but, now the cat was out of the coffin. The Prime Minister covered his face with his hands, he knew this was it, there was nothing the voters could not be persuaded to forget or forgive given sufficient time, but murdering Lloyd George? No, never. The Government would be out at the next election, no argument.

CHAPTER XIX.

The first family were not the only ones being put through the mangle by Fleet Street, they were only the most prominent of the victims. The Telegraph did a nice little job on Norbert.

Norbert and Ivra were to open the new catering concession on top of Mount Snowdon. Why they should want to do so, no one could understand at the time, and nor were they particularly interested in finding out. The Regent was no more welcome in Wales than she had previously been, but by now, the woman was held in such sickening contempt, none were prepared to pay her the compliment of protesting her presence in the Principality.

The visit was a disaster from the outset. Half way up the mountain, the train packed up, it ground to a halt and refused absolutely to partake in the honour of conveying the Regent to the summit. There was only one option open to lvra and Norbert, in whichever direction they opted to progress, they would have to hoof it. They opted to continue with the ascent.

It was a fine summers day in North Wales, which meant in practice that although it was coming down in stair rods, it was not cold enough to freeze one's unmentionables into sterility. Ivra of course, was ludicrously overdressed and her six inch heels were not the ideal footwear in which to engage in a jousting match with the mountain track.

"I knew we should not have come here. It was bound to be a disaster," moaned Ivra, having acquired considerable wisdom after the event. "Besides which, I can't abide the Welsh."

"Well, I don't suppose they are all that fond of you considering the trouble they went to, to prevent your last attempt at a visit." Norbert was becoming quite assertive since his liberation from Gert, he put this down to a diet of regular sex and not getting walloped every time he opened his mouth.

"Shit I've broken a heel. That's the last bloody straw, why does everything have to be uphill in this blasted country. We'll never get to the top at this rate."

"Well, if you'd shut your mouth and open your bloody legs, we might stand a chance of doing so this side of the second coming." They completed their bedraggled pilgrimage in silence.

They stumbled onto the summit of the mountain, anticipating a suitably obsequious reception, but the reality was not equal to their expectations by any yardstick one cared to use in the calculation of measurement.

"I'm the Regent of England," said Ivra in her grandest manner to the first of the natives they encountered, but succeeded only in conveying to her disinterested audience the fact that she was thoroughly pissed off with the hand fate had dealt her. "And who may you be my man?"

"Jones the box."

"Means nothing to me, absolutely nothing. I am the Regent."

"Never mind carriad, try putting a poultice on it."

"Really! These people. You try Norbert."

"We're here for the official opening."

"Bit late aren't you bach? Prince William did that the day before yesterday. Lovely it was and all. Beautiful."

"What!" Ivra may have been tempted to say a little more, she probably was, but her intentions were aborted by a dig in the ribs by Norbert, who had the sense to realise that this was not the time to start slagging off the exceedingly popular Prince.

"What is going on here then?"

"It's the Owain Glyndwr Society for the Propagation of Christian Knowledge, Farting and Sheep Shagging. Seeing as you are here, you might as well come in and have a cup of tea." As their options were severely circumscribed by their geographical limitations, Norbert and Ivra accepted the invitation, if only to get out of the rain. Just inside the door was a row of Wellington boots, an absolute essential for a successful sheep shag, they were as yet unused, through one of the windows could be seen a flock of sheep. His curiosity aroused, Norbert turned to Jones the box.

"What?" he enquired, trying to give the impression this was the most normal of questions to ask. "Has Christian knowledge got to do with sheep shagging?"

"Fuck all bach, but it sounds respectable like, don't it now?" Norbert accepted the logic of the statement with reluctance, but lacked the energy to pursue the matter. The central events were about to commence. In the large room, the competitors were being fed plates of sprouts and pickled onions. The contestants were judged on purity of pitch and stamina. The winner, by popular acclaim was Jones the box, an undertaker from Prestatyn, who, after consuming three plates full of sprouts and a large jar of pickled onions. Dropped his strides, bent over and farted through the first two verses of Bread of Heaven to the tune of Crimmond.

After that petomanic extravaganza, the sheep shagging commenced. This had a priapic effect on Norbert, he could not be induced to join in the bucolic pastime, so he availed himself of the next best thing, Ivra, who was more interested in food at that particular moment. Therefore they compromised and it was this that the photographer from the South Wales Echo caught on camera, a pictorial record of Ivra, bent over the kitchen counter, stuffing her face with bacon sandwiches, while Norbert screwed her from behind, he often wondered if her preference in sexual practices had anything to do with the fact that the first husband she had pinched had spent a considerable time in the

Navy. Norbert groaned in pleasure and his knees started to tremble.

"Ivra. Oh Ivra, how is it for you my darling?"

"Well they could have put a bit more mustard on the bacon." Delighted with his scoop, the photographer set off in his rented helicopter. The convention members also left at this time, the train having been repaired, only no-one thought to, or cared enough, to inform Norbert and Ivra of its departure and they were left stranded on the mountain. By the time the hapless pair managed to leave Wales, not only had the Echo's scoop gone around the world, but so had a damaging report in the Telegraph, detailing beyond all doubt or possibility of rebuttal, a deal whereby Bondi Paterson had loaned Norbert a considerable sum of money to buy the catering concession on Mount Snowdon. This, coming on top of the share buying scandal of Condo and Mac, caused yet another public uproar, but by now, the Government was beyond caring or coping, so traumatised were they by events, they had ceased even to be frightened of Wincarnis.

2.

Gert and Ivra continued with their war of attrition, a conflagration encouraged and fuelled by Condo, he knew the game was up as far as the Government was concerned. This only made him more desperate to get his hands on the Regency, if he only held the job for a day, he would still have been Regent, and a ruddy great pension went with the job and he had a strange premonition he was going to need one.

Condo may have been banned from the environs of Buckingham Palace, but he still had his spies in place, he therefore knew all that he needed to, he kept Gert informed of Ivra's movements. Ivra still insisted on her daily motorcades through the capital and visiting people who would, given the choice, have preferred to have had three limbs amputated than shaken hands with her. Gert arranged for Ivra to be shadowed at these shindigs by a troop of King's Cross hookers dressed in string vests and gas masks. The public had ceased to be amused at such carryings on, they no longer cared about the Regency and the undignified behaviour of Ivra, change was whistling through the gussets of the Nation. There was an unmistakable air of fin de regime, everyone without exception was marking time.

Condo had not been left unscathed by the tribulations the administration was undergoing, once more, scandal came a calling, and piddled all over the door mat. Money is the root of all scandal and this one had no intention of denying the laws of physics.

The party was broke, and had been for some time, as donors have an unhelpful partiality for winners. Condo had stumbled on a wheeze to rustle up a little extra for the coffers. A Finnish billionaire had lost his licence due to a drink driving conviction, which was rather unfair as it was generally considered a truism that Finns were seldom sober after they had been christened. Be that as it may, the individual hinted to Condo that he might be persuaded to part with a hundred grand donation in return for a British driving licence, a few days later, the transaction was completed to the satisfaction of all concerned. Before the planet had gained much in age, there was a queue of sozzled Scandinavians of ample financial proportions, lining up outside Condo's office for driving licences. The party finances improved considerably until the press got hold of the scam.

Condo sat uneasily on a rather uncomfortable chair in the Prime Minister's office. Across the room on an equally uncomfortable chair, sat the Prime Minister, behind him stood Wincarnis, the pair looked like a ventriloquist and her dummy. Which was exactly what they were.

"Terrible business this Condo, what with the press making a right dog's dinner of things." The Prime Minister always sounded his best when he had gone to the trouble of learning his lines thoroughly. Wincarnis said nothing, she stood behind her husband, her balled fists resting secularly on her hips and wearing an expression which would have done justice to Judge Jeffreys while presiding over the bloody assize.

"No more than you would expect from the press. That lot have no respect whatsoever. They think they can say anything about us and get away with it."

"True. So very true."

"Anyway, I denied everything and put out a statement to that effect and told the Finns to keep their traps shut."

"Excellent. Well, there's no point in going on about things is there?"

"None at all Prime Minister." Condo was always formal in the presence of Wincarnis.

"Best get on with things then. Win tells me you are seeing some party big wigs in Doncaster today."

"That's right. I'd better get a move on then hadn't I?"

"Yes. Oh, and Condo, always remember, you are still one of the family." Condo left the room, visibly warmed by the affection of the first couple. Condo had not reached the front door before Wincarnis was on the phone to Macmurdo.

"Mac. Draught out a letter of resignation for Condo, then put it out to the Press Association, Reuters, etc. Make sure it admits his sole responsibility for the cash for licences affair, the Prime Minister wants to be absolutely sure he carries the can. And when you've done that cancel his security pass and withdraw his car and driver." With that off her chest, Wincarnis replaced the receiver.

The political demise of Condo Maites did not receive undue attention in the press, it was overtaken by events of a greater portent to the national well being, besides it was hardly a novel occurrence, it had happened so many times before.

Every now and again, like a returning comet, some bug or virus commits an aggravated assault on the collective health of the Nation, thousands are laid low, a few pensioners die, doctors surgeries are overwhelmed and hypochondria, for a month or so, stalks the land before the normal state of affairs re-asserts its natural authority, in short, the traditional British method of coping with a crisis, muddling through. Only this time it did not work, the system of public health, unable to withstand the strain of yet another crisis for which it had not been designed, did what it had been destined to do since it's birth, and collapsed.

The cause of this event was a gastrointestinal virus originating in the Far East. There was an impressive terminology to describe the bug, but to Joe Soap on the Clapham omnibus it was galloping diarrhoea, and it did for the Government. It was a nation gripped in agony, a significant percentage of whom were voiding their bowels while lying neglected on a hospital trolley parked in a corridor for want of bed space, folk were saying this was the last straw, but they had said this so many times the national window box was full of the stuff, was there no end to peoples patience? Yes.

All this was an unbelievable trauma for the British public, who had been programmed from birth to believe that if their precious Health Service collapsed, then the fall of civilisation would not be far behind. This was a catastrophic assault on the national psyche, and it was the Government who was called upon to pay the price. The Government could not be blamed for the epidemic, although most people went ahead and did so anyway, but they could be blamed for the state of the medical services, and they were. Unable to cope with the emergency dozens of hospitals were forced to close their doors.

3.

Led by the Daily Truth, there was a clamour for a general election. The media demanded one, the people demanded one, the Government, after taking an inventory of its stock of intreptitude, replied "Bollocks." Not literally of course, but that was the implication behind their words. They were not completely daft, well, at least not all of them, they were perfectly aware of what it was that awaited them at the polls, and they had no intention of going there until legally obliged to do so, and there was no-one who could make them, or so they thought.

The Queen was visiting her Virginia residence, she stood in the airy drawing room, gazing at her reflection in a particularly fine George II mirror.

"Good morning Mr. President," she smiled, even though she was aware that she could be heard but not seen. "That mail order form I left for you last time I dropped by at the White House. I notice it has not been returned to me. Now I don't want to be disagreeable, after all, we are friends, but unless I get a substantial order for my home made piccalilli, damson chutney and sloe gin, then I will have no alternative." Here Her Majesty paused for effect. "Than to have this fucking place debugged. Oh, and I want to see the Director of the CIA here at four thirty this afternoon."

Punctually at four thirty, the Director of the CIA was shown into the Queen's drawing room, he accepted the offer of a seat.

"The President asked me to tell you that the order for the comestibles will be with you first thing in the morning."

"Excellent." Her Majesty poured some tea into two Dresden porcelain cups. "Milk and sugar Director?"

"Er, I don't like tea mam."

"I didn't ask you if you liked it, I asked you if you took milk and sugar. You do want milk and sugar don't you?"

"Yes mam."

"Good. Here, drink this. Now I've brought you here to discuss the plan to trigger the election in England."

"But your Majesty, that's top secret."

"Well of course it is secret. I would not be talking about it if it weren't."

"But how did you know mam? That information is restricted to the highest level."

"The Chairman of the intelligence committee, Senator Byegrove. I had him to dinner last night, he gave me all the details."

Inwardly the Director groaned, was there nothing the woman did not know? The President was right, she had to be got back across the Atlantic before she took the country over."

"We think it will be a success Your Majesty."

"And I think it is a complete pigs ear." The Queen then proceeded to tell the Director what was wrong with his plan and what he should do to make it workable. She then made him up to date on the foibles of a significant clutch of Members of Parliament, and more significantly, how this information could be used against them. The Director was awe struck, this woman was indeed dangerous.

"Now you know what to do Director."

"Yes, indeed I do mam."

"Then I will not detain you any longer. Oh, I expect you were given a mail order form for my pickles by the butler?"

"Yes mam."

"Good, then I can expect an order from you by the morning, along with that of the President." The Director groaned, one look at the price list assured him that even a modest order would eat up a goodly portion of his salary, there could be no alternative, he would have to take the kids out of private school, and put the wife back on the game.

"You can your Majesty."

"That's fine then. Good bye." They shook hands and the Director left with a hole in his wallet the size of the state of Rhode Island.

4.

It is a fact of public life along with flatulence and self regard, that there is nothing more your fine upstanding flamboyantly righteous Member of Parliament likes more than a junket at the expense of the taxpayer, the more expensive the better, the chiselling bastards love them. Now, it came to pass, not by any natural agency you understand, that an extraordinary number of Government M.P.s had received invitations to visit sundry sultry climes, all, coincidentally, at the same time.

Knowing well that the voters were waiting for them with the garrotte, they all without exception, accepted, on the principle that one should make hay while the sun still managed to shine, and grab as many freebies as it were possible to do in the time before the election.

The CIA had carefully plotted the moves, and when all the M.P.s and their secretaries, or in the odd case, their wives, were safely overseas and out of the way, a vote of confidence was called. This carillon of the democratic process was accompanied by an inexplicable breakdown in international communications and transport. The Government was unable to recall its legionaries in time, and lost the vote in the House of Commons. An election was called, it could not be avoided.

CHAPTER XX.

The election proceeded along predictable lines. On its side the Government made a complete hash of the event, not that it would have made any difference had they made a better fist of things. The electorate was voting them out and had made up its mind to do so long before the hustings were declared. The Government's campaign was a painful and ludicrous parody of those it had fought in better days, when all was centred on the presidential style of Alfred Sawse, but they knew no other way of fighting an election and were therefore forced to endure the derision their style elicited. Alfred and Wincarnis toured the country as much as they dared, he smiled at everyone while Wincarnis smiled at her husband and glared at everyone else, as a performance it was antagonism preserved in liquid nitrogen. The first couple resembled nothing so much as a pair of East European dictators about to be shot by the rebellious masses.

Binkie Wetherspoon, the Southampton slaphead did and said very little during the election, his advisors rightly feeling that anything he did say would cost them votes and that he should not be given any chance to snatch defeat out of the paws of victory, despite the talent he undoubtedly displayed in that direction. Binkie's aides kept him from contact with live voters, he campaigned to a television camera, making set piece performances where he assured voters that he hated muggers and loved gays. Unfortunately, the technician in charge of dubbing got things mixed up and Binkie was broadcast to the Nation assuring them he loved muggers and hated gays. His advisors were horrified, but as virtually no-one watched the broadcasts, no damage was done.

The people cast their votes. Overnight Binkie Wetherspoon was transformed into the Prime Minister of the land, it was a great relief, for the first time in years he could say what he meant and not what his advisors told him to. The first thing Binkie did on being catapulted into power was to fire Ivra. London erupted at the news, it was V.E. day all over again, for the people knew what that act portended.

The second act of the new administration was to order the ejection of Alfred and Wincarnis from Number Ten, easier said than done. The man who but few short hours previously had been deferred to by his acolytes as the leader, was so traumatised by being given the bum's rush by the electorate, he posed no trouble at all, he was incapable of putting up any kind of resistance. Quietly he was led out of the back door by two strapping young men in white coats who gently settled him into the back of an ambulance before driving off to an unnamed destination, somewhere in the country as they used to say in the war. Macmurdo Dunlossie had already legged it with the office tea money.

Now, as for Wincarnis, needless to say she was a different kettle of fish altogether. Her inclinations did not run to awarding the electorate the elementary courtesy of accepting their verdict and going quietly, or at all if she could avoid it. She had no intention of being turfed out of Number Ten just because the voters were too dumb to recognise what was good for them. Wincarnis ran through the building looking for somewhere to barricade herself in, she saw her husband being led away, but felt no sympathy for the man, she had written him off weeks ago, all that effort she had expended in making him Prime Minister, and what did he go and do? He blew it. Wincarnis was incapable of appreciating that she was largely responsible for his downfall. In the background she heard the voice of Sir Mordechai Davenant, head of the civil service, she knew he must be on her trail.

Sir Mordechai was certainly on the trail of Wincarnis, for years she had made his life a facsimile of hell exquisite in its precision, now, for him it was payback time and he was going to enjoy every moment.

"Yoo hoo. Mrs. Sawse, where are you?" cooed the deceptively benign civil servant. He knew he was close to his quarry by the quality of the silence. It was not natural.

Sir Mordechai and two henchmen from the Property Services Division tracked Wincarnis down in the kitchen, where in desperation she had chained herself to the gas cooker.

"Come on now, don't be a silly girl," said the knight with a sympathy that was meant to fool nobody. "Time to go walkies. Back to the real world."

"Fuck off, I'm not going nowhere." Wincarnis' religious scruples against the use of bad language had obviously withered away from not being watered of recent times.

"We're not going to be able to shift her without a pair of bolt cutters," said one of the henchmen after a judicial appraisal of the situation.

"Well she is not staying there whatever happens," stated Sir Mordechai.

"We could always disconnect the whole thing and carry it out with her still attached to it."

"Then do it."

"You can't. I absolutely forbid it." Wincarnis had yet to fully appreciate her position.

"Dear Mrs. Sawse, you, thank God, are not going to forbid anything around here any more. We are parting company at long last." With that he lit up a cigarette and inhaled deeply. "See what I mean? We are parting company at long last."

"That's it guv. It's free now. What do we do with her?" he indicated Wincarnis, still attached to the appliance by her metal umbilical.

"Shove her inside," decided Sir Mordechai. "We'll get most of her in with a bit of shoving." Ignoring her shrieks and protests, her tormentors stuffed Wincarnis into the industrial sized oven. They could not get all of her in, her legs were sticking out.

"That's it boys, now let's get her out of here."

"The back door sir?"

"Oh no. Not with the world's press outside the front door. We must see Mrs. Sawse off in style." Thus it was that the press corps was treated to the sight of Wincarnis partially stuffed into the guts of a gas oven being trundled out of Number Ten. A whoop of joy went up from the reporters, who all, at one time or another had been treated to the ferocity of Wincarnis' contempt.

"Lloyd George is avenged," yelled the man from the Telegraph.

"I'll get you, you bastards, every motherfucking one of you. I'll get you. And as for you Davenant, Sir Mordechai fucking Davenant, I'll cut your frigging balls off and stew them with apples and custard." Every word was recorded, not least because the curses were of originality no lady should have had any comprehension of, not only that, they were delivered in an accent that would have sent her elocution teacher running for the Prozac.

Still screaming curses, Wincarnis was last seen disappearing down Whitehall, she and her attendant gas cooker mounted on a front end loader hastily commandeered from a roadwork gang. Sir Mordechai Davenant was a contented man.

2.

After formulating his Government, the next item on the to do list for the new lot in Whitehall, was to invite the Queen to resume her position as head of the Realm. This was no quite so easy as might have been imagined. The invitation would have to be delivered in person by the new Prime Minister, such was the economic mess the country was in, that the Government could not afford any fuel for the R.A.F. transports, and the commercial airlines refused to extend any credit to the administration. America kindly stepped into the breach by letting the new Prime Minister hitch a lift on one of it's aircraft returning to Washington. Binkie was immeasurably grateful, and did not in the least mind having to make the coffee and sandwiches in return for the ride. The Queen happened to be visiting her Virginia estate at the time, she sent a car to Andrews Air force Base to collect the Prime Minister. Binkie was in a world of his own, in the space of a few days he had been transformed into the Premier, and now, here he was, about to bring the Queen home. Binkie had convinced himself that he was the new general Monk, certain in his bones there was peerage awaiting him at the end of the line.

Binkie bowed as the Queen entered the drawing room.

"Have they offered you tea or anything Mr. Weatherspoon?"

"No, Your Majesty," he replied, cosily anticipating a nice cup of Rosie.

"Good. Tea costs money and I see no reason to throw it around." Whatever it was that Binkie had been expecting by way of a regal welcome, this was not it. "Right. State your business Mr. Weatherspoon."

"I have come to invite Your Majesty to return to the throne."

"I see. Just like that." The Queen snapped her fingers dismissively. "So I just drop everything and take up where I left off."

"The people want you mam. They demand that they have their Queen back."

"I am well aware of the feelings of the people. It was not on account of the people that I abdicated." The sweat trickling down Binkie's neck had nothing to do with the Virginia climate. Things were not going as he had anticipated. "What is it exactly that I am expected to return to?"

"I don't understand Your Majesty."

"What constitutional arrangements would be in place?"

"Everything would go back to normal mam."

"Normal for whom? I have had a lifetime of standing silently by while you politicians trash my country. That is not normal Mr. Weatherspoon, that is torture. Over the past few years I have had to put up with Sawse and his republican tribunes actively undermining me. And as for you're lot, they did not raise a finger in my defence because you thought there were more votes in watching me be destroyed."

"But Your Majesty," Binkie was horrified, he had not traipsed halfway around the World for a dose of plain speaking.

"But nothing, Wetherspoon. You are here because you want me to pull your chestnuts out of the fire for you. Well the answer is no. Did you seriously think that I'd go back to being a door mat for the benefit of that gaggle of treacherous chancers in the House of Commons? Well the answer is no. I will not. As my daughter would say if she were here, go forth and multiply. Go on, hop it you gormless bald headed son of a bitch." Binkie staggered from the room, the elastic holding up his ambitions had just failed and they were now around his ankles.

The Queen gave a deep sigh of satisfaction, she had waited years for such a scene such as had just been enacted, her pleasure had not been dimmed by the waiting. Elizabeth II looked up at her Georgian mirror.

"Have a nice day Mr. President. By the way, I'd have Weatherspoon picked up and returned to London if I were you, otherwise he'll probably end up dossing on the White House doorstep. So embarrassing for you. Good bye."

The President was no less horrified by the outcome of Binkie's meeting with the Queen than Binkie was himself, he had even gone so far as to order a farewell dinner at the White House so confident was he of the Queen returning to London. The meeting had been relayed direct to him in the Oval Office, where he had listened to it in the company of the Director of the CIA.

"Ah told you ah wanted the Queen back where she belongs, that is in London, not Virginia, not Canada."

"We tried Mr. President. We did everything possible. I can't think of anything more we could have done."

"Well I can think of one thing to do and I am doing it right now."

"What's that Mr. President?" He swallowed hard, knowing what it was that was coming next.

"You're fired." With what dignity he could muster at such short notice, the Director rose and left the room. The President phoned the Deputy Director of the CIA. "Hal. I got some news for you. You are as of this moment Director. Yes, that's right. I just sacked the dumb bastard. Now you listen good, Hal, you got only one thing to do, and that is to make sure the Queen gets back on the other side of the pond. Pronto. I want her back where she belongs before I find myself listening to her delivering the State of the Union Address in my place. Which, the way she is going about things round here is more than likely." And that was that. On both sides of the Atlantic, everyone knew what had to be done, but unfortunately, no-one knew how to go about it.

3.

Back across the pond, on the benighted shores of blighty, pandemonium reigned unchallenged to the point where the Archbishop of Canterbury seriously considered making it a part of the catechism. The present lot had been put into Government to undertake certain tasks, but they showed no sign of doing so. Binkie Weatherspoon had returned, having worked his passage from Boston on a container vessel. His first Cabinet meting was fraught with emotion, not least because his deputy, Sebastian di Roma, had changed the locks on Number Ten and mounted a challenge for the leadership which had narrowly failed, but he intended to have another go the week after next.

"What did the Queen say then?" asked old mother Conway.

"Not very much," replied the Prime Minister.

"Well she must have said something," persisted Conway.

"She told me to go away." The Cabinet suspected the accuracy of his statement, especially as the papers had been full of what the Queen had actually said.

"We'll have to get this settled somehow," said the Chancellor, they'll go ape if we don't."

"They, who's they?" asked the Prime Minister.

"The voters of course, who else?"

"Oh them. Forget it. We tried, and she said no. That's it. Over." The Chancellor adopted a magisterial stance, which as the only member of the Cabinet who had ever held down a proper job of work in his life, he was fully entitled to do.

"Prime Minister, we were elected first and foremost by the people to bring back their Queen and I rather think that they might get a bit stroppy if we don't, then we will be in as big a pickle as Sawse and his crew were. We have to keep to our election pledges."

"This pedantic insistence on democracy is all well and good in its place," insisted the

Prime Minister. "But when the buggers expect to be taken notice of, that is taking things a bit too far. Besides, I ask again, what can we do?"

"You're the Prime Minister," said the Chancellor making a conscious effort not to be helpful and keeping one eye on the next leadership challenge.

"I have decided," announced the Prime Minister, with all the portentousness he could manage, which in itself was considerable. "To hold a conference on racism." The silence with which this was greeted, in no way intimidated the man. "And I am going to establish a commission to examine the Bible for homophobic references."

"They'll be dancing in the polling booths," said the most junior member of the Cabinet, whose name nobody could remember.

"I think," opined the Chancellor. "That we need a little more discussion on this. We are obviously not focussing on the main concerns of the electorate."

"Bugger the electorate. I've talked enough for one day. Meeting adjourned." With that, the Prime Minister got up and stalked out of the room. Upstairs, the Premier's hairdresser was waiting for him, Binkie was terribly conscious of his image. Unfortunately, Binkie had no Barnet to speak of, bald as a coot actually, therefore, with no hair to trim, the stylist whipped out a tin of Mansion Polish and had the duffer gleaming a treat in no time.

The crisis did not go away, despite the best efforts of the Government to pretend that it had, which did nothing to solve the problem and everything to ensure it got worse. Faced with this impasse, the Government did what politicians always did when faced with a problem of their own making, and which they had no idea how to resolve, they lied through their teeth to an extent that had they been private citizens, the reward for their action would have been a stretch inside.

The agreed Government line was that the Queen would not return to England because she had consented to stand for the office of Mayor of New York. Nobody with any sense, which encompassed most of those not engaged in professional politics and members of the theatrical brigade, was prepared to swallow such bilge. As a distraction, Binkie announced there was a challenge to his leadership, but as Sebastian di Roma was away making a television programme and therefore out of the running, and nobody else could be persuaded to do so, and agree in advance to lose, the plan was unable to earn any credibility, it soon followed the Queen for Mayor Storey into the obscurity it should never have left.

When all these ploys were seen to be not working, the administration did what all Governments did under similar circumstances, they hid in the closets of Whitehall, leaving the Civil Servants to clear up the mess as best they could, but as the Civil Servants preferred to work under direction and were disinclined to perform without any, nothing got done.

This state of affairs could not continue indefinitely, a few serious riots had broken out in Manchester and Liverpool. Politicians of all parties were petrified those sporadic outbursts might develop into something infinitely more threatening to their interests if something was not done soon.

CHAPTER XXI.

The country was in a morass, waiting for someone with a rope and a donkey to pull it out and give it a good rub down before setting it on the road to health and prosperity. There was a sense that something was going to happen, maybe good, maybe bad, only no-one was quite sure what. Binkie continued to bluster and have his bonce polished up once a week, which did nothing to re-assure people that they had a government which was able to distinguish one end of a milk bottle from another, but, out among the noisome huddled masses, one man was stirring.

Bonvilston Evans-Prothero, was a self made Welsh millionaire of the dot com variety, one of the few who had actually came up with an idea which made money rather than duping investors into kissing the stuff good bye, which was the usual case with such enterprises. Bonvilston's company sold chocolate sex aids on line, his frosted mint chocolate dildos were a sensation from Sidney to Swansea and all points in-between, one could not get on a bus without observing at least two brazen little trollops chomping on a chocolate dick. The man had three overriding characteristics, he was as bold as brass, he was as rich as Croesus and above all, and beyond imagination, he was as common as muck.

Bonvilston lived in a medium sized stone house on the edge of the common belonging to the small village of Cefn Cribwr in the county of Glamorgan. The village sat atop a mountainside overlooking the Bristol Channel, it was typical of such places, cold enough to freeze the hot water pipes in winter, while in summer, one was lucky to escape with nothing more serious then a dose of pneumonia, but the millionaire loved the place. Bonvilston lived in the house in which he had been born, he was fiercely protective of the edifice, determined that money should not be allowed to mar in any way the charms which had nurtured his boyhood. Therefore, the front garden was still given over to the growing of cabbages, the roof still leaked and the windows still rattled in the somnolent breezes, while he proudly showed visitors the bathroom his mother had installed to celebrate the Coronation, it was a corrugated iron lean-to tacked onto the outside wall of the kitchen.

That was the man who decided to save the Nation, he saw only too clearly that the only way to get the politicians to move in any direction was to employ the aide of a navigational boot to the backside, and he had a nice pair of sod busters ready for use. Bonvilston sat in his large office, overlooking the bay area of Cardiff, he looked out of the plate glass window, bitterly regretting the progress which had swept away the happy go lucky whores, replacing them with yuppies in off the peg suits talking a load of shite into mobile phones. He pressed the intercom and spoke to his secretary.

"Mafanwy carriad. Get me that Percy Jerkup at the Telegraph in London will you."

"Tcherkoff Mr. Evans-Prothero."

"What's the odds? Jerkup Jerkoff, the buggers probably a bloody wanker all the same. Anyway, get him on the line." The secretary did as instructed.

"To whom am I speaking?" Percy was trying extra hard to be pompous that morning.

"This is Bonvilston Evans-Prothero here. You know, Sex Dot Com. You probably seen our adverts, click click and lick a dick." Sir Percy had, a long time ago, and he still shuddered at the memory of the experience.

"How can I help you?" asked the great editor, determined he would do no such thing, but wishing to get rid of the vulgar little oik with reasonable dispatch.

"I'm going to put a stop to all this bloody nonsense in the country."

"Admirable sentiments sir. Just how do you intend going about so formidable an undertaking?"

"A referendum. What else?"

"The Government won't wear that Mr. Evans Prothero. If there is one thing they can't abide, it is doing anything, which even hints at taking account of the wishes of the public at large. They will never authorise a referendum."

"No, they won't, but I will."

"I don't understand."

"Simple Sir Percy, bach," instinctively lapsing into a welsh endearment. "I will organise and pay for out of my own pocket, a referendum to be supervised by the Electoral Reform Society. Now, will the Telegraph give me its backing?"

"We bloody well will sir, to the hilt. When can we meet?"

"I'll be on the next train out of Cardiff, be in Paddington for dinner"

"Righty ho. See you soon."

They did not meet quite as soon as they had anticipated, as when Bonvilston said dinner, he was thinking of twelve noon or thereabouts, while to Percy it suggested some time in the region of eight in the evening, therefore it was nine the following morning before they sat down together in Percy's office to plot the salvation of the Nation.

The referendum campaign was a stunning success. There was an upsurge in public confidence as people felt their views were at last to be taken notice of. The Government, to save its face, still maintained the fiction that the Queen was running for Mayor of New York, but so offensive had the replication of that lie become, that the Government was forced to drop it half way to voting day. In an early threat to thwart the referendum, the Government had refused to allow public buildings to be used as polling stations, on the grounds of health and safety, whatever it was that might mean. That obstacle was overcome by Tesco, who opened all their stores for twenty-four hours a day for three days, voting to be at the check out.

The Electoral Reform Society counted the votes. To the question 'Should the Queen return to the throne on her terms?' ninety two percent of those entitled to vote, did so, and of those who voted, eighty five percent said yes.

Bonvilston had the referendum results collated into the form of a petition, and, accompanied by a delegation from Abertillary Council, set off for Prince Edward Island.

With the Queen in residence, accommodation in Charlottetown was at a premium, the delegation managed to get a couple of rooms at Maisie Wilson's at a price which matched that of a room at the George Cinque in Paris. They set off for Government house in some style, Bonvilston leading the way, behind him, two of the delegates held up an enormous banner proclaiming Abertillary as the home of the Chocolate Dick, and Ianto Twp played a selection of hymns on the piano accordion. Charlottetown had glimpsed many notable sights of late, but none could match up to that one.

The delegation arrived at Government House during the course of one of the Queen's Thursday afternoon soirees. The place was packed out with a section of North America's best, who were bemused by a lack of organisation worthy of the best efforts of the British Government. Her Majesty should not have been held to be culpable for that state of affairs, only ninety five percent of the responsibility could reasonably have been laid at her feet. The royal staff had finally mutinied over the remuneration available to them. They had formed themselves into a union, with Sir

Ralph Settles as their shop steward. Their demand for higher wages was refused and Sir Ralph had led them out on strike.

Her Majesty had no intention of being intimidated by her rebellious staff, she set about organising things for her Thursday reception. Sophie was tricked out like a French maid, Edward and Andrew were deputed to act as butlers, and all the grandchildren were set to making the tea and sandwiches. The reception was held in the ballroom and a tasteful selection of jams and chutneys were laid out on top of the piano, along with order forms and a list of acceptable currencies, anything except the Pound Sterling and the Euro.

The front door was wide open when Bonvilston and his delegation arrived. With no one to give direction, they wandered about before ending up in the ballroom, making a noteworthy entrance as their banner knocked the chandelier for six.

"How do you do, Your Majesty? I'm Bonvilston Evans-Prothero." His voice was a high-pitched squeak, in total advarience to his considerable bulk.

"And this is the Abertillary Council," countered the Queen, demonstrating that she had done her homework. "Lovely town Abertillary." beamed Her Majesty, who, by that admission, confessed she had never been near the joint. "Let's go out into the garden shall we?" The Queen was not so much interested in displaying the horticultural delights of Government House, as she was intent on not having the place wrecked by a banner embroidered with a chocolate dick.

"Nice place you got here Your Majesty," observed Ianto Twp. "Cost much did it?"

"Only the last occupant his job, but it was worth it."

"Now talking about jobs Your Majesty," said Bonvilston with all the authority of a dot com millionaire. "How do you fancy having your old one back?"

"Well. That rather depends Mr Evans Prothero."

"We've brought a petition with us you know."

"Yes, I do know, and I am touched, oh, and talking about being touched, have you bought any of my pickles yet?"

"No. I haven't, come to think of it."

"Never mind, you can get some on the way out."

"Will you come home then mam?"

"I would love to, but not as things stand."

"But Your Majesty, the whole country wants you back, don't they boys?" He looked at his delegation for support, which was immediately forthcoming.

"That's right mam. Be a good girl now and come home with us," they chorused. The Queen beamed at them.

"Gentlemen, let me tell you why I will not go back as things stand." Her Majesty told them of her feelings over the constant drip of betrayals and the rank opportunism of the politicians of both parties, and how she had been sickened by all that being Britain's Queen had involved. Her Majesty also enumerated the conditions under which she would be prepared to return. "So you see boys, that's the way matters stand at the moment."

"Well mam, I don't think anyone would argue with that, would they boys?"

"No Bonvilston"

"But I will see Weatherspoon the minute I return, and I'll put what you have said, directly to him."

"I can ask no more. Now, I must attend to my other guests. No, don't get up gentlemen. Sophie, bring these gentlemen some sloe gin; on the house the first one, and don't forget to leave an order form with Mr. Evans-Prothero." The Queen swept off in the direction of the ballroom, calling as she went. "Edward, if you don't want a clip around the ear, then put a smile on your damn face."

After sampling the Queen's sloe gin, parsnip wine and carrot whiskey, the delegation found themselves back in their digs and decidedly worse for wear, except for Ianto Twp, who, mistaking a Canadian public trash can for a Parisian pisssoire, got himself arrested for indecent exposure. They were all disappointed at the outcome of their meeting, but sympathetic to the Queen's reasons for declining their request for her to return. They were also thrilled with the quantity of Royal Pickles Bonvilston had bought for them. As for Bonvilston, he had a feeling this would not be the end of the matter, he was determined it would not be.

2.

On arrival at Heathrow, Bonvilston was whisked off to meet with the Prime Minister. In a quandary at to what to do with the rest of the delegation, one of Binkie's bright young sparks, of whom he employed far too many for his continued electoral health, had the scintillating notion of packing them off for an afternoon at the Tate Modern. At the Tate, they were shown the latest acquisition, an absolute snip at a quarter of a million, the artist had necked three litres of Sainsbury's red ned, then thrown up over a second hand sofa, with an originality which defied the exercise of imagination, the resultant work of art had been christened "Morning After." Artistic London was in raptures and hailed the exhibit as a work of consummate genius. The boys from Abertillary thought the offering perfectly normal, they each of them possessed a sofa, which had looked the same after a night at the local workingmen's club.

The sight of this creative endeavour inspired Ianto Twp to go all artistic, he went into the restaurant, drank thirteen pints of Guinness, threw up on the table then asked for fifty quid on account.

"You're nicked," barked the attendant. All Ianto had earned for himself and his companions was a lifetime ban from the Tate and it's attendant institutions.

Over at Downing Street, things were not going well either. Binkie had not been at the front door to greet Bonvilston, he resented having been pushed into a corner by the results of the referendum, and his bruised ego would offer only the stark hand of animus to its author.

Bonvilston was shown into the Prime Minister's office, Binkie was wearing a ludicrously large Afro wig, he had decided that his lack of hair was responsible for his low standing in the polls, therefore he ordered a blond hair piece, but one of his bright young things, who despite the optimistic appellation, was pushing forty five, came up with the dramatic conclusion that blond hair was Euro-centric. Now Binkie, in common with most of the population, was not entirely sure what Euro-centric meant, but was content to accept the recommendation of the gormless twit from Central Office, and had ordered an Afro wig instead, which caused more than one commentator to remark that he looked like something cut from the back label of a jam jar.

"Golly." Said Bonvilston. "You do look a sight. What's that you've got on your head?"

"I'm wearing this as a gesture of solidarity with the non indigenous community." That is what he had been told to say by the back-room boys, he was proud of his ability to learn his lines, there was far more of Alfred Sawse in the man than he would ever realise.

"Well, it looks bloody daft to me, the country's going to hell in a hand cart and here you are farting about in a wig." Bonvilston's parents had tried to cultivate tact in their son, but had abandoned the effort when he had reached the age of four and a half. "And what's more, you were not voted into office so that you could practice being a pantomime version of Alfred Sawse."

Binkie glared at this affront to his amour propre, he had been in office only a short while, but that length of service had been long enough in duration to cement into the crevasses of his mind, the delusion that he was in possession of brains, ability and a divine dispensation to rule unchallenged, a trait known in the trade as Premiersclerosis. Binki had contracted the virus sooner into his term of office than most.

"I have no interest in your Cambrian outlook on life Mr, Evans-Prothero. I don't really know why you are here at all." Binkie would have said more, but was interrupted by one of his aides, who burst into the room followed by two men whose attire hinted that they had not been dressed by a Saville Row tailor.

"Oh Prime Minister. It's dreadful. Positively dreadful."

"Who are these damn people Piers? And what are they doing in here?"

"Sir, you'll never believe it."

"Give me a chance won't you."

"It's Wincarnis."

"What about her? She's gone with the Sirocco, and, what has she got to do with this bunch." Binkie made a contemptuous gesture in the direction of the men, who had started moving the Prime Minister's desk out of the room. "What the devil do you think you are doing?" demanded Binkie. "Put that down at once."

"That's the problem Prime Minister. Because of the economic disaster, Wincarnis hocked the contents of the house in order to pay the domestic bills. Well, we can't afford to keep up the payments, so they are repossessing the furniture. These are the bailiffs."

Binkie, shocked into the offside of silence, sank into the nearest available chair.

"Not there guv." Said one of the bailiffs before yanking Binkie out of his refuge.

"This is a pretty kettle of fish." Remarked Bonvilston. "Let's get on with things anyway, you'll be wanting to hear what the Queen had to say."

"No I don't, I want my fucking desk back." He began to scream, stamping his feet in counter point to the noise emanating from his throat. Bonvilston saw no point in extending the meeting into what would obviously have been its afterlife, he delivered a succinct summation of his meeting with the Queen, then left the room, thoroughly disgusted with Binkie's behaviour, and mentally giving thanks to his late mam, who would not let him enter politics, when, on making his first million, that irrational desire had briefly beckoned him in the direction of Westminster.

3.

Parliament has attempted many tasks over the years, but the eradication of mendacity from the ranks of its members has never been one of them. It was Prime Minister's question time, and in the press gallery they were organising a sweep. The winner would be the hack who accurately predicted the number of porkies which would be told over the course of the proceedings. Humbert Repton was looking forward to the session, his first as leader of the opposition. He was not really sad that his party had lost the general election, that event had inevitably led to the downfall of Alfred Sawse, and Humbert infinitely preferred to be top dog in opposition than to play second fiddle in Government to a score composed by Wincarnis. Humbert rose to ask the first question.

"Would the Prime Minister inform the House of the recent negotiations with Queen Elizabeth?"

"As you are all aware, earlier to-day, Mr. Bonvilston Evans-Prothero gave me a report on his meeting with the Queen in Canada. The Queen repeated to Mr. Evans-Prothero what she had said to me on a previous occasion, and that is that she has no intention of returning to this country, and that as far as she is concerned, the matter is closed." He sat down as Humbert rose to ask his supplementary.

"Did the Government do everything in its power to persuade the Queen to return, in accordance with the express wishes of the vast majority of the people of this country?" Humbert relished himself in the role of Queen's champion, seeing at least three points in the polls in it for him, and completely missing the irony that he had been one of the most rabid republicans of the previous Government.

"We could not have done more. Her Majesty's position on the matter is irrevocable."

That was all the press gallery was interested in hearing. To the fury of the Prime Minister and all other members who had intended to shine for the TV cameras, they all trooped off to file their copy before normal folk clocked off work and started clogging up the pubs.

There was a great sadness when the press duly reported the Queen's refusal to return home, people genuinely thought she would respond to the referendum, but, it was her decision and the people reluctantly accepted that she would not be coming home after all.

Bonvilston read the press reports despite the effect they were having on his blood pressure, although he made no claim to be suffering from any manifestations of surprise. What he saw written was what he had expected, and his plans had been laid accordingly. Binkie and his ministers were busy doing the rounds of the television studios, broadcasting their anguish at the Queen's decision to abandon the Nation, when Bonvilston Evans-Prothero called a press conference at Mrs. Pike's boarding house in Gower Street, he would have preferred the Ritz, but Mrs. Pike's was cheaper.

The press were a mite disgruntled at the refreshments on offer, they expected to have, and were invariably provided with, the finest drinks and canapes at such gatherings that somebody else's money could provide, all they got at Mrs Pike's was Co-op tea and bags of crisps past their sell by date. These dainty snacks were dispensed with an absolute lack of charisma by Mrs. Pike's divorced daughter,

Vera, who wore pebble spectacles, had buck teeth and shrouded herself in an aura of body odour which could not have been dispelled even by a bath in Chanel Number 5.

The gentlemen of the press and the dipso from the Times were determined to reward Bonvilston's parsimony with an extremely rough ride. The reporter from the Telegraph had some extremely pertinent questions to ask, but was in no condition to do so, he had brought with him a two litre pop bottle filled with Martini, and made the mistake of taunting his colleagues with that example of his prescience. They, taking umbridge at his alcoholic self sufficiency, promptly beat the stuffing out of him and pinched the grog, leaving the unfortunate man comatose behind the sofa where not even the fumes emanating from Vera's armpits could revive him.

Bonvilston entered and sat down at an oil cloth covered table, careful to avoid the deposits of egg yolk and red sauce, unaware of the animosity his generous soul had unleashed.

"Well, you tight arse Welsh git. Whadayagot to say for yourself?" This was the dipso from the times who had got the lion's share of the Martini.

"Who cares, let's duff the bastard up." That was the gentleman from the Truth, who could always be relied upon to add a touch of class to any proceedings. Bonvilston was shaken but not stirred.

"Now listen here you bunch of hooligans, if any of you know how to work a pencil, then shut your mouths and open your ears and listen." Silence, they were not accustomed to being spoken to in such a manner.

"Let's give the fat sod two minutes, then if it's not worth listening to, make him drink his own fucking tea." That was from the man from the Truth who unfailingly mistook journalism for literature and adjusted his conversation accordingly.

That had his fellow hacks yelling in approval. The man from the Mail had a far better idea.

"If it's no fucking good then make him fuck Vera." Vera's eyes lit up and a smile of eager anticipation scratched itself across her face, she had long since given up all hope of a damn good rogering. The silence of a coffin buried in concrete wrapped itself around the room. Bonvilston stood up, he looked confident, at this point, his audience could not understand why.

"You have all reported the Prime Minister's statement that the Queen refused to return. I can tell you now, that is a bare faced lie. The Queen did not refuse to return, she would like nothing better than to come back home, and Binkie Weatherspoon knows it because I told him." After that opening salvo, his audience would have given him all day to speak had he asked for it.

"You on the level Bonvilston?"

"Flat as a pancake boys. The Queen will not return only to have things go back to what they were. Standing silently by while being undermined by the politicians at every step of the way. These are the conditions she has set out for her return, and they must be passed into law. One. Foreign nationals will not be allowed to own British newspapers or television stations, that means Bondi Patterson would be divested of his papers. Two. Patronage would be permanently removed from the gift of the Prime Minister, thereby ensuring that people are honoured for their worth and achievement, not because they have bunged a few quid to a political party. Third, finally, and most importantly, her Majesty insists that members of Parliament can only serve for one fixed term of five years, that would go a long way to curbing the growth of this class of professional politicians who are dedicated to serving their egos, their wallets and nothing else." There was a short silence while his words were ingested by his audience with the mental equivalent of antacid tablets. First in was the man from the Mail.

"This is incredible Mr. Evans-Prothero, but at the end of the day, we only have your word for it."

"No. You do not." He looked around him, pleased at the effect his words were having. The pack was aroused and out for the kill. He produced two cardboard cartons. "There are two tapes for each of you. The first is a recording of the Queen, made in Canada, stating the conditions under which she would be prepared to return. The second is a secret recording of my meeting with the Prime Minister, where I told him of the Queen's statement. I also recorded his reactions. "That was it, the cat and everything else that could be imagined was out of the bag and having tasted freedom had no intention of returning to confinement.

CHAPTER XXII.

Bonvilston's revelation had blown the Government out of Whitehall and into reality in the time it took to broadcast the tape recording of the Queen outlining her conditions to Bonvilston. As far as the populace in general was concerned, this was the end of the line, they had had a belly full. The ruling elite, who for years had treated the country as a colony, and its inhabitants as recalcitrant natives, were about to harvest the rewards their diligence had earned for them. The uprising, which had threatened for months, finally materialised.

The individual people looked to for guidance was none other than Bonvilston, he became everyone's hero. No fool he, the man put his freshly minted authority to good use. Rioting was breaking out all over the country, Bonvilston realised these sporadic illustrations of impotent rage would soon peter out into a sullen resentment, which the Government would find easy enough to ignore, he put his organisational abilities to good use and the position was transformed.

Hundreds of thousands of people descended on London, where they converged on Parliament Square. Nothing on this scale had ever been witnessed in the history of organised protest. At all entrances to the square, Bonvilston had set up stalls selling his chocolate sex products, the Abertillary factory was working overtime to fulfill demand. The plan was simple, Parliament was completely surrounded and nobody could get in or out, the entire complex was sealed off from the outside world, and there were those who maintained it always had been.

True to the long established traditions of their caste, the incarcerated politicians secured their obduracy in a surgical truss of bluster and declared they would not be coerced into acting against the national interest, which, in translation meant against their own. There was not one amongst them who was not petrified at the prospect of only being allowed to serve for one term. The Parliamentarians could say what they wanted, but the people had had enough, this time they meant business, the politicos would remain bottled up until they agreed to legislate on the Queen's demands.

A carnival atmosphere descended on the square, with stars of the West End stage turning up to entertain the crowds free of charge. The first to enlist in this contemporary version of ENSA, was Dame Annunziatta Chump, the greatest living luminary of the London Theatre, who had been playing the juvenile lead for as long as anyone could remember, as one of the bitchier female hacks had described the Dame in her column, "Sweet sixteen at sixty six, and, unfortunately, still going strong."

Dame Annunziatta's current thespian enthusiasm, was for classical Greek drama in the original, spouting off in what to her audience was some heathen lingo which nobody could understand, and she continued to do so for an hour and a half, the lady would have continued for much longer if nature had not had the mercy to intervene, for her to scuttle off for a johnny riddle. They were a generous crowd, drenched in good humour. The Dame left to a round of enthusiastic applause, which owed more to the relief of the audience than an appreciation of the talent to which they had been so mercilessly exposed.

Various other actors and actresses strutted their stuff before the highlight of the entertainment programme, a brief appearance by Glitter Clit and the Tampons, a girl band who utilised a complete absence of talent to make a great deal of noise and an insidious amount of money, the crowd went wild.

Ianto Twp had come up from Wales. In no way had Ianto been discouraged by his experiences and expulsion from the Tate, au contraire, they had fired his enthusiasm for the artistic life to the extent that he had got a book on performance art from the library. Having thoroughly digested the subject overnight, he arrived in Parliament Square ready to take London by the creative short and curlies. After paying his respects to Bonvilston, Ianto took an overdose of Epsom salts, he called the resultant artistic outpouring "The

Spirit of Politics" then invited the public to come and inhale the aura of his artistic soul. There were some amongst the crowd who were either pretentious enough or daft enough to do so.

Apart from Bonvilston's chocolate dildos, the hamburger and hot dog sellers cleaned up as never before, one way or another, everyone there was satisfied. So profound was the universal enjoyment, there was serious talk of making it an annual event.

2.

The defiance of the politicians, could not of course last, the odds were too heavily stacked against them. The ranks of the besieging rebels contained folk such as engineers and their like who cut off the sources of power and water to the Palace of Westminster. Inside the Palace, mayhem was asserting its authority as essential supplies dwindled to infinity. Members could be observed trying to fish from the terrace, but that activity came to nothing, a team of rebels patrolled the Thames outside the building armed with sling shots and gob-stoppers, their aim was stupendous, they soon put paid the anglers.

Binkie and Humbert Repton came to blows over the last jar of pickled onions, an utterly pointless altercation, for as they were busily knocking seven bells out of each other, Gertie Gunter ran off with the onions. Up in House of Lords, Ivra, who was absolutely starving, pinned a notice on the doors of the chamber, stating that for the eminently modest fee of a jam butty, she could be shagged on the woolsack. The poor woman continued to go hungry, all who wanted to had been there years ago, and nobody was prepared to squander valuable nourishment on the sexual equivalent of a car boot sale.

The collapse when it came was rapid and decisive. Inside Parliament, they had been without food for two days, Binkie was all for holding out, his vanity unable to contemplate the ignominy of total surrender. The gridlock was broken by Sebastian di Roma, he lured Binkie into a broom cupboard, telling him it contained the entrance to a secret passage which came out in the kitchens of Macdonald's on Victoria Street, Sebastian locked the door, and that was the problem of Binkie sorted. The smell of frying onions from the hot dog vendors, and a relay of actors reading out the recipes from Delia Smith's cook books did the rest, led by Sebastian di Roma, who was practising for when he became Prime Minister, Parliament passed the legislation to meet the Queens demands. It was all over.

3.

President Gort was sitting in the Oval Office, his Secretary of the Treasury had given him an abacus, but the fellow was obviously having some difficulty with the instructions, he was in a high good humour despite his uncertainty with the contraption he had been given. The Queen was going home and America could go back to being a republic again, with him as its undisputed leader. He looked up as his secretary entered the room.

"Yes Hester?"

"The Queen's here Mr. President."

"What! Tell her I'm not here. Say I've gone to Patagonia for a month's vacation."

"Morning Mr. President." The Queen swept in, she sat down, facing the President across his desk. "Lovely day, isn't it? A cup of Earl Grey please Hester." Hester went off to get the tea, the President tried to gather his wits about him but could not recall where it was he had left them.

"Um. Er."

"Just one or two things to clear up before I go, you know how it is."

"What are you doing here? I thought you were going home."

"Oh, I couldn't leave without saying goodbye. I do so love our little chats, don't you?"

"Yes." If ever there was a chance the President would be struck down by lightening for telling fibs, that was it, but the Almighty stayed his hand and the Queen continued.

"I want to discuss the financial situation." She got out her knitting, it was a pullover for Prince Philip in goose turd green. "So soothing knitting, it helps me to concentrate."

"The financial situation?"

"That's right. As you know, well, who doesn't, the European economy has gone down the pan, and thanks to that asshole Repton." The President winced visibly, he did so wish the Queen would not cuss, it was so unladylike. "It's taken the British economy with it. Now I can understand your reluctance to let the Europeans stew, I'd have done exactly the same, but, we are different, special friends and all that, at least, that is what the British politicians say when they want to appear to be more important than they actually are, which is most of the time. You do agree with me don't you Mr. President." That was not a question.

"Yes mam." The President was too frightened to risk offering a contrary opinion and by so doing prolonging his agony.

"A line of credit is what we need to tide us over the crisis. Fifty billion would do nicely."

"Fifty Billion?" His eyes popped, and sweat broke out on his brow despite the best efforts of the air conditioning.

"That is what I like about you Mr. President. So quick on the uptake."

"But that is out of the question."

"Seen this morning's poll in the New York Times?" He had, the Queen was way ahead of him in the popularity stakes.

"Fifty billion."

"Nice tidy sum. I could not possibly go back with any less. Wouldn't even think of it." There was no point in arguing and the President knew it, if he wanted the Queen off his back, there was only one thing to do, cough up.

"I'll authorize the cheque. So you'll be off now then?"

"Good Lord no."

"No. I don't understand. When are you going?"

"Why, when the cheque has cleared of course. I know all about you politicians and your funny little ways. Oh, thank you Hester." The Queen accepted her cup of tea, continuing with her knitting while the President telephoned his instructions to the Treasury Department. "There's a good boy. Now while we're waiting for that to go through, tell me about your hernia, I've brought a special truss with me, should help you no end."

It was at that juncture the President fainted, the most closely guarded secret of his administration and she even knew that.

4.

The Queen returned in triumph to London, it was one of those days when the sun decided it would be fun to bankrupt the bookies by showing its face over the capital. Over two million people lined the route from Heathrow to Buckingham Palace. A public holiday had been declared and the population was delirious, all was well in the Anglo Saxon World, at least for the time being.

Unbeknown to any, there was a time bomb ticking away under Her Majesty. Around the world, leaders of nations had watched fascinated as events unfolded, and, from the President of the United States of America down, they had been terrified of the way she had manipulated events to her advantage, she could not, they determined, be allowed to get away with it, where would it all end? Once people got into their heads the ridiculous notion that they could demand and get the sort of Government they wanted, then before you knew where you were, it would be impossible for those in authority over them to impose the sort of Government which they knew people ought to have.

There was an overriding consensus amongst the great and powerful of the world that the Queen of England was an example which could not be tolerated, she would have to go, and the American President was determined that this time it would not be to Canada.

5.

The fate of the mighty is the antidote which softens the passing of time for the individual observer, a distraction from the brevity of the Biblical three score and ten and the likelihood that the medical profession will shorten it even further. For those whose doings have traversed these pages, nemesis was waiting with a salutary clip around the ear.

Alfred Sawse retired from politics to better utilise his mythical talents, he commenced his new life as a dish washer at the Two Chairmen, where he remains to this day, an ornament to the catering trade.

Wincarnis, whose business fell into decline after the Cocos Island incident, wrote a history of her family titled 'Bastards I have known', which were the only sort of relations she had, a tome which achieved a literary milestone by being remaindered long before the publication date. What was left of her savings she invested in a couple of caravans parked at Trecco Bay in South Wales, and she ended up as a kennel maid for the Liangeinor Hunt.

MacMurdo Dunlossie had hoped for a career in journalism, but alas, he had offended too many during his days of power for that to happen, the closest he got to the editor's desk was selling the Evening Standard from a pitch at Canary Wharf.

Condo Maites did not fare much better than his old sparing partner, the best Condo could manage was a job at a building society vetting the honesty of mortgage applicants. Who said there was no humour in banking?

Binkie Weatherspoon had hung on to office for a couple of months after the return of the Queen, but it could not last. He was toppled in a coup led by Sebastian di Roma. As a consolation prize, Binkie was shunted off as a Commissioner to Brussels, where he was able to use his influence to get lucrative jobs for his relations.

A grateful Queen rewarded Percy Tcherkoff with an hereditary peerage, not that it did him much good as his proprietor became insanely jealous of the honour done his employee and promptly sacked him.

As for Bonvilston Evans-Prothero, the hero of the readeption of Queen Elizabeth, he expected great rewards, and was about to receive them. An appreciative Sovereign had decided to make Bonvilston Duke of Llancarfan, the patents were drawn up, but alas, twas not to be. The night before the seals were to be affixed to Bonvilston's Patent of Nobility, the poor dear fellow was arrested, having been caught by two members of the Metropolitan Police Force, who discovered him behind the bushes in Bloomsbury Square, his trousers around his ankles, and blowing a rent boys trumpet.

Sic Transit.

www.ingramcontent.com/pod-product-compliance
Lightning Source LLC
Chambersburg PA
CBHW071301110426
42743CB00042B/1132